less meat, more plants

100+ Sustainable Recipes
to Nourish Your Body
and Protect Our Planet

ANNABELLE
RANDLES

FREMONT PRESS

LAS VEGAS

Pour Maman, Papa, Graham, Zac et Maya xx

First published in 2023 by Fremont Press

ISBN-13: 978-1-628604-94-8

Cover design by Elita San Juan and Justin-Aaron Velasco

Interior design and illustrations by Yordan Terziev and Boryana Yordanova

Printed in the USA

POD 0123

table of contents

introduction:
every meal makes a difference

It is easy to be unaware of how much our everyday food choices impact our health, the planet, and the welfare of animals. And the prospect of changing the way we eat, let alone going completely vegetarian or vegan overnight, can be daunting. It certainly felt impossible and unappealing to me at first. Why should I do it? How could I do it? Would I even enjoy it? These were some of the many questions that went through my head.

Adopting a plant-forward diet has been a life-changing experience for me. It's a diet that I have been able to stick to simply because it is not too restrictive. It has also given me a growing awareness of the links between food, health, ethics, and the environment and how I need to reconnect with the food I eat.

Understanding why I needed to adapt the way I ate was the key to making long-term sustainable changes that have become second nature. Feeling healthier and truly enjoying new foods that I never used to eat before have made the experience even more pleasurable. I am thrilled to be able to share with you what I have learned on my journey from committed carnivore to plant-based cuisine enthusiast, as well as some of my delicious plant-centric recipes.

You might decide to change the way you eat and reduce the amount of animal products in your diet for many different reasons. The path from where you start to where you end up is personal. This cookbook is not about demonizing meat, fish, or dairy, nor am I asking you to go completely plant-based—unless, of course, you want to. Instead, I hope this book will spark an interest in exploring the wonderful world of plant-forward cooking and shed some light on why it is a good idea to put plants at the center of your diet.

Wherever you are on your journey—whether you are just starting to cut back on meat (as well as fish, eggs, and dairy, although these tend to come later, if at all) or you are already a pescatarian or vegetarian and want to eat more plant-based food—this book will be relevant to you. Even if you are already following a vegan diet, I hope you will find some new ideas and inspiration here.

Many of us are lucky enough to have three meals a day, seven days a week. That's twenty-one opportunities to adjust the way we eat to benefit our health, support our planet, and promote animal welfare. Even small changes can make a difference, so dive in, have fun, and enjoy!

Annabelle xx

my journey...so far

So that you can understand my approach to cooking and how my diet has evolved, I'd like to tell you a little bit about my background.

a country upbringing

Born and bred in France, I grew up in a semi-rural village near Switzerland, nestled between Bourgogne and Alsace. I developed an interest in cooking at a very young age, while watching my mom cook. Sparing no effort, she always took pride and pleasure in preparing delectable meals that the whole family would enjoy together.

Even though she had a job that involved working long hours and sometimes night shifts, my mother made every single meal from scratch. She still does. Known to own all the latest kitchen gadgets, she would batch-cook, freeze, and preserve so we always had home-cooked meals. She let me experiment in the kitchen, sampling every single dish that I made and proudly presented to her, even the most unappetizing ones. She also learned to cook by watching her mom. My maternal grandmother was a gifted cook who, even in the midst of World War II rationing, endeavored always to have a meal on the table by being creative with whatever scraps she could find.

My dad is no stranger to the kitchen either, but he leaves the vegetable dishes to my mom and focuses on handling the meat or fish. An avid fisherman in his free time, he has always been keen on knowing where his food comes from (called "provenance" in French) and strives to buy higher-welfare animal products from local farmers. He detests farmed fish for its low welfare standards and poor taste and avoids it at all costs.

As the son of farmers, my maternal granddad was passionate about nature. He loved gardening and worked relentlessly to keep up our vegetable patch and fruit trees, while also being a keen forager and angler. He loved sauerkraut, which he made in the back garage. As a child, I found the smell of fermenting cabbage intriguing and would sneak behind him to check what was happening in those wooden barrels. Having raised farm animals, he knew better than to waste a single scrap of meat, and I also watched him prepare fromage de tête (headcheese), a cold-cut jelly terrine made from chunks of meat and odd bits taken from a pig's head. This delicacy of French charcuterie is, without a doubt, an acquired taste but has the merit of making use of edible parts that otherwise would be thrown away.

I cannot speak about my culinary heritage without introducing my late Sicilian great-aunt. In search of new opportunities, my great-grandparents emigrated from Sicily to Tunisia. My paternal granddad and his siblings were born there and, following Tunisia's independence, emigrated to Marseille in the South of France. I have fond memories of the meals my great-aunt prepared when we holidayed at her home: a cornucopia of Italian and North African dishes. A self-taught cook, she would wake up at dawn and make everything from scratch, from pasta, pizza, and hand-rolled couscous to elaborate pastries filled with honey, dried fruits, and nuts. Come market days, she was not to be messed with, giving a scolding to any fishmonger who tried to pass off a blurry-eyed fish for a morning catch. Every time we visited, holidays turned into feasts, and, in true Italian style, we only stood up from the table to shake the tablecloth before starting the next meal.

My mom's cooking, and therefore mine, was greatly influenced by our multifaceted family tree and the Franche-Comté region where we lived. From Alsatian choucroute (a dish made from sauerkraut, ham, sausages, and potatoes) and baeckeoffe (a casserole made with potatoes, mutton, beef, and pork) to beef bourguignon, veal or rabbit stew, couscous, and pasta dishes, meat and dairy were always on the menu, usually served with some of our homegrown vegetables. Fish appeared on our table only once a week, or maybe more if my granddad had a lucky catch. After my parents bought a holiday flat in the South of France, more and more Mediterranean dishes became everyday staples. Still, vegetarian food, let alone vegan food, was served only by accident, never on purpose.

I grew up with a bucolic view of farming. My French grandfather shared fond memories of growing up on a farm, raising pigs, rabbits, and poultry for meat as well as cows and goats for dairy. The village where I was raised had a dairy farm, and I remember watching the cows grazing in the fields surrounding our house. Fresh milk was delivered several times a week, and as soon as the metal milk containers were dropped at our front door, I rushed to take big creamy gulps. The milk was still warm and so irresistible that, much to my parents' annoyance, I often drank it all at once.

Living in France, I never thought much about how healthy, sustainable, or ethical my diet was. I assumed that the idyllic farming practices of the small family farms I grew up with were the norm. And while these traditional methods are hugely preferable to those of the now-dominant factory farming industry, heavy consumption of meat and dairy is problematic no matter how it is farmed.

learning to embrace plant-forward eating

Only many years later did I start to examine my food choices. My eco-husband (as I like to call him), Graham, was a big influence. We met in the 1990s when we were both living in New York. He was already a compulsive recycler and one of the first people I met to be genuinely concerned about climate change and the future of the planet. At the time, I was not paying much attention.

Graham loves food as much as I do, and over fifteen years ago, he started to question the environmental impact of our diet. This way of thinking was avant-garde at the time, and I found it odd. We already strived to source organic and local food, and that, for me, was good enough. But he was concerned that meat production was detrimental to the health of the planet and pointed out that we probably ate too much of it. The more he read, the more uncomfortable he became about eating meat, and he concluded that we should become vegetarian. I can't say I was thrilled by the suggestion, but he encouraged me to look into some of the issues around modern animal farming and its impacts on the environment and animal welfare. What I learned was unsettling, and slowly but surely, my attitude towards what I ate evolved.

Becoming parents further cemented our desire to live more sustainably and kindly. Changing our diet was a logical step in the right direction. One day, as we were enjoying a walk around the bucolic English countryside, our son, who was a toddler at the time, realized that the lambs grazing in the fields were also being served as food. A few weeks later, at Easter lunch, he refused to eat the piece of lamb he was given, declaring that he did not eat "babies." It was hard to argue his point, and none of us has eaten lamb since.

Still, for someone like me who had spent most of her life as a committed carnivore, the prospect of going vegetarian was daunting. I knew Graham was right, but I resisted change. When I discovered the flexitarian diet, however, eating in a more sustainable way instantly seemed much more achievable. I realized that it did not have to be all-or-nothing and that we could make a difference by going meat-free a few days a week.

The flexitarian (aka plant-forward) diet is a plant-based diet with the occasional addition of meat. Simply put, there are no rules. Some flexitarians have a meat-free meal once a week, while others rarely eat meat and other animal products such as fish or dairy. Ideally, most adults should aim for no more than two to three servings of meat a week, making sure to eat a balanced diet of protein-rich plant foods to meet their specific dietary needs. A serving of meat equates to about 3 ounces (85g) of cooked lean beef, pork, or poultry—easily visualized as about the size of a deck of playing cards. My personal preference is not to eat meat at all, but it might not be yours. Talk with your healthcare practitioner to determine what is best for you.

Graham and I started by cutting out meat once a week and built up from there. I bought a few cookbooks, borrowed a few more from our local library, and set off on a tour of world cuisines to find vegetarian and vegan inspiration. I was stunned to discover so many delicious recipes. We enjoyed this new way of eating so much that I began experimenting with my own recipes and decided to start a blog, which I named *The Flexitarian*, to share our experience with others. We were not only eating delicious food, but we started to feel healthier too. The more I educated myself, the more convinced I became that this was, for us, the way forward.

Travel has been another source of inspiration. Visiting new places has given me the opportunity to learn about new ingredients, dishes, flavor combinations, and cooking techniques. I never fail to come back from a trip with a few local spices and delicacies in my suitcase.

As an animal lover, I am ashamed to admit that empathy with other species was not the main driver for altering my diet. Yet the plight of animals packed into industrial-scale farms is real and abhorrent. Watching documentaries on intensive pig and dairy farming, as well as realizing that growing vast quantities of animal feed is one of the leading causes of deforestation and wildlife displacement, has convinced me that eating less meat and more plants is a better way to feed ourselves.

The way we eat as a family has evolved and in many ways is still evolving. I have lost my appetite for meat and do not eat it anymore. I never crave it and am even put off by it. However, I do have some fish and dairy from time to time. This is an ongoing personal dilemma that I need to reconcile with. Why can't I feel the same empathy towards fish or dairy cows that I do for other farmed animals? Why is it so hard for me to give up cheese? As a compromise, I limit my consumption of fish and dairy, prioritizing wild-caught and higher-welfare sources. (I explain which welfare labels to look for on pages 72 and 73.) Graham still eats poultry and fish from time to time. Our kids have dabbled on and off with vegetarianism. As parents, we feel that our role is to guide and inform so that they can make their own decisions. I encourage them to cook as often as they feel like it, and we educate them about environmental and animal welfare issues. However, we do not impose our dietary choices on them.

My food philosophy is simple: 80 percent is plant-centered, cooked from scratch with wholesome ingredients (vegetables, fruits, whole grains, beans, pulses, nuts, and seeds), while the other 20 percent allows for a little leeway to fit around our busy family life.

Regardless of the path you take on your plant-forward journey, understanding the reasons why you are making changes is motivational and empowering. Awareness is key to forming long-term sustainable habits. Remember that every meal makes a difference.

why we all need to eat more plants

Humans have reared animals for food for thousands of years, but eating meat every day is a relatively new phenomenon that can be traced back to the end of World War II. Meat eating can be regarded as a symbol of wealth and status. So, as incomes grow, so does meat consumption in certain parts of the world. Mass consumption and mass production are negatively impacting our health, the planet, and animal welfare. Whatever your stance on the ethics of eating animals, or the ins and outs of climate change, it seems wise and kind to rethink the way we eat.

for our health

Meat is a cornerstone of the standard Western diet. It has indisputable nutritional value, and there is no good health reason to remove it from our diet altogether. The amount of meat we eat is a different matter. Most of us eat too much of it, and that can have a negative impact on our health.

Meat is a good source of protein, iron, zinc, and B vitamins; however, it contains no dietary fiber. Red meat (such as beef, pork, and lamb) and processed meat (such as ham, bacon, and sausage) in particular can be high in saturated fats. A diet rich in saturated fats is associated with an increased risk of cardiovascular diseases and elevated levels of low-density lipoprotein (LDL) cholesterol in the blood.

The World Health Organization has also linked high consumption of red meat and processed meat with type 2 diabetes and certain types of cancer, especially colorectal cancer. Eating too much red meat and processed meat can also have a negative impact on your waistline—even more reasons to limit your consumption.

The good news is that a varied diet that includes lots of vegetables, fruits, pulses, soy, seeds, nuts, and whole grains can provide all our protein needs while benefiting our health and the planet. As I explain on page 18, we don't need as much protein as you might think.

Packed with dietary fiber, a plant-forward diet also benefits our gut and digestive system, promoting a more diverse and healthier gut microbiome (because the good bacteria in the gut feed on plant-based fiber). The gut microbiome is not only vital for digestion but also plays a central role in supporting a strong immune system. It is believed to help reduce inflammation in our bodies as well. On top of this, emerging research on the brain-gut axis is uncovering connections between gut health and mental health.

The consensus is that eating meat occasionally is unlikely to be bad for you. If you do choose to eat animal products, strive to buy the best quality you can get. For most people, this means buying less meat but better meat—the consistent message of a plant-forward or flexitarian approach. Yes, grass-fed and organic meats cost more than intensively raised ones, but what you get in return is higher quality that translates to tastier and more nutritious products. Grass-fed and pasture-raised beef, for example, has been shown to have less saturated fat and higher amounts of vitamins and omega-3 fats than beef from cows fed on grains in feedlots. It is all about recalibrating what's on your plate and shifting the balance, making plants the centerpiece and meat a garnish or side dish.

The Mediterranean Diet and the Blue Zones Diet are popular examples of the value of plant-rich eating. Both encourage the consumption of plenty of fresh fruits and vegetables, nuts, pulses, whole grains, and healthy fats while limiting red meat, dairy, and processed and refined foods as well as sugar. While nutrient-dense plant food is central to both diets, it is worth noting that the health benefits are also attributed to lifestyle and social factors such as regular physical activity, interaction with nature, a strong sense of community, and conviviality.

The important thing to remember is that when it comes to health, a balanced diet (along with regular exercise) is fundamental, whether you eat animal foods or not.

for the planet

With the world population expected to reach 10 billion by 2050, there will be almost 3 billion more mouths to feed than there were in 2010. Increasing food production will put additional strain on Earth's finite resources. Our growing appetite for meat means that we not only need to produce more meat but also have come to expect lower prices. With meat production being so resource-intensive, cheap and plentiful meat comes at a hefty cost to the planet.

Animal farming has changed a great deal over the past seventy years or so. Traditionally, animals were raised on small-scale farms like the one my grandfather grew up on, in symbiosis with their surroundings. They grazed and roamed the fields, playing a vital role in preserving soil health and biodiversity. Some farmers still operate this way, and I believe it is essential to support them. Organic farming, permaculture, and regenerative agriculture all play a vital role in maintaining a sustainable food system that benefits both the natural world and our health.

By contrast, a lot of the animal products consumed today are produced on large-scale intensive farms where the emphasis is on accelerating animal growth and speeding up production. Corporations strive to produce large quantities of cheap meat as quickly as possible, with little regard for the impacts on the environment or the welfare of the animals raised on those farms.

Intensive animal agriculture requires a large amount of land to grow feed crops for animals, and the need for more and more land leads to deforestation and wildlife displacement. According to the World Wildlife Fund, cattle ranching accounts for 80 percent of current deforestation in the Amazon. With fewer trees to capture carbon dioxide (CO_2), deforestation in turn accelerates climate change.

Factory farming methods that keep large numbers of animals in confined spaces make the problem worse. And while CO_2 gets a lot of attention, intensive animal agriculture produces other greenhouse gases (methane and nitrous oxide) through flatulence, manure, and fertilizer use. According to the EPA, methane is twenty-five times more potent than CO_2 and nitrous oxide almost 300 times more potent than CO_2 at trapping heat in Earth's atmosphere.

The storage of animal waste in open lagoons is another concern because it can contaminate nearby land, groundwater, and waterways. The high quantities of pesticides and fertilizers used on animal feed crops further impact pollution levels.

Intensive farming requires large amounts of water to produce meat, dairy, and eggs. Animals not only have to drink but are typically fed corn and soy, crops that need a lot of irrigation to grow. According to the Water Footprint Calculator, 660 gallons (2,400 liters) of water are required to make just one average-sized burger, including meat, bread, lettuce, and tomato. This is roughly the equivalent of twenty-seven showers (the EPA estimates that the standard showerhead uses 2.5 gallons, or 9.5 liters, of water per minute).

Eating animal foods, and especially red meat, is not an efficient way to feed ourselves because animals consume more food than they produce. For example, it takes 20 pounds (9 kilograms) of grain in modern beef cattle feedlots to produce 1 pound (2.2 kilograms) of edible meat, cut and ready for consumption. Why not use the same amount of land, water, and energy to grow crops for direct human consumption instead?

In 2020, the EAT-*Lancet* Commission, a global science-based platform for food system transformation, published a report titled "Food in the Anthropocene" that brought together thirty-seven leading scientists from across the globe to answer the following question: "Can we feed a future population of 10 billion people a healthy diet within planetary boundaries?" Their answer is yes, on the condition that we transform our eating habits, improve food production, and reduce food waste:

> *Transformation to healthy diets by 2050 will require substantial dietary shifts. Global consumption of fruits, vegetables, nuts and legumes will have to double, and consumption of foods such as red meat and sugar will have to be reduced by more than 50%. A diet rich in plant-based foods and with fewer animal-source foods confers both improved health and environmental benefits.*

for animal welfare

When it comes to animals and taking an ethical stand, it's hard to argue for any position other than vegan. Every other diet is a compromise. More and more people see keeping animal products off the menu as the only way to ensure that their food choices do not contribute to animal suffering. However you look at it, animals are harmed or exploited in any diet that is not vegan.

In the name of profitability, this exploitation often goes too far. On intensive farms, animals are considered commodities. The minimum regulatory standards are often poor. Animals frequently have little or no access to the outdoors and are confined to small spaces. This leads to stress, mutilation, and unsanitary living conditions. To make them grow faster and combat the spread of diseases (many of which can be directly traced to the poor living conditions), animals are pumped with antibiotics that we in turn ingest when the meat ends up on our plates. The overuse and misuse of antibiotics in the meat industry is linked to the rise of antibiotic-resistant bacteria that poses a major threat to human health.

I have only visited a slaughterhouse virtually, but the experience left me in tears and cemented my view that I should change my diet. The dairy industry is plagued by accounts of cows being forcibly impregnated and then separated from their offspring at birth so that their milk can be sold for human consumption. Once the cows are deemed commercially unprofitable because their milk production has dropped below a certain threshold, their lives are cut short.

The treatment of fish is no better. The fishing industry relies only partly on catching fish in their natural habitat, but even fish caught in the wild are not always a sustainable choice. Overfishing depletes fish stocks, while vessels trawling seabeds destroy the fragile marine environment. While some see aquaculture as a good way to maintain wild fish stocks, fish farms are, in fact, no different than factory farms and subject fish to the same cruel conditions that cattle and poultry experience.

Rehoming battery hens has given my family firsthand experience of the appalling conditions under which some of the egg industry operates. Kept in conditions legal under British Welfare Standards (deemed some of the best in the world), the first battery hens we rescued nonetheless arrived exhausted, featherless, and sporting pale floppy combs—a truly shocking sight. While we managed to give them a few months of free roaming, perching, and rolling in dust baths around the garden, two of them died prematurely from poor health linked to their previous exploitation.

A few months later, we welcomed three ex–free-range hens. They looked so much healthier, fully feathered and with more colorful combs. Still, with an average life expectancy of six years, they were being discarded by the egg industry at the ripe old age of eighteen months not because they stopped laying eggs but because they were laying fewer eggs than is considered commercially profitable.

If you are concerned about animal welfare and are going to eat meat, fish, eggs, and/or dairy, making better food choices is essential. Labels and certification schemes are a minefield. Clever marketing adds to the confusion. If and when you buy animal foods, look for certified accreditation schemes that promote quality and better animal welfare and environmental standards, such as grass-fed, pasture-fed, pasture-raised, and organic; I explain which labels to look for on pages 72 and 73. If you can, buy from a local farmer you trust.

chapter 1:

how to get started

It's not unusual to feel overwhelmed at the prospect of embracing a plant-forward diet; it certainly seemed impossible to me at first. You might be concerned about getting enough protein or confused about how to get started. This chapter will help you better understand what protein is, how much our bodies need, and where to get it from. It also looks into how much meat we should eat, whether you consider that question purely from a health stance or you want to incorporate a planetary view.

If you are like me, you will quickly realize that embracing a plant-forward diet is not about what you are eating less of but rather what you are eating more of! My diet is more varied today than it used to be when I was a full-fledged carnivore.

Flexitarianism has allowed me to adapt my lifestyle over the years. I have found this flexibility empowering rather than feeling that I was failing at becoming vegetarian or vegan. Flexitarianism has given me the tools to make long-term sustainable changes. I do not eat meat anymore, and I don't miss it at all; I feel healthier without it. I believe this is because it is not a restrictive diet. There are no forbidden foods. If something is not forbidden, you are less likely to crave it.

Regardless of the diet style you choose—flexitarian, vegetarian, or vegan—you need protein, be it a mix of animal-based and plant-based or solely plant-based. How much protein you need depends on your sex, age, lifestyle, and other factors; after determining quantity, the next step is to decide on the sources and quality of protein you will include in your diet.

let's talk about protein

Is protein a problem? It is if Earth's human population continue to source the largest share of their protein from meat, particularly factory-farmed meat—not only for our health but also for the health of the planet and the welfare of the animals we eat.

Plenty of evidence suggests that for most adults, a diet based mostly on plants can be healthy. However, when you reduce your consumption of certain foods, you need to make sure that you are still meeting your key nutrient needs. Whether exclusively plant-based or not, a balanced diet (along with regular exercise) is essential for good health. In this section, I lay out some parameters to help you craft a balanced plant-forward diet that fits your needs. You may want to consult with a dietitian or healthcare practitioner for further guidance on how best to achieve your goals.

what is protein, and where does it come from?

Protein is an essential macronutrient contained in every cell of our bodies. It helps to repair cells and build new ones. The building blocks of proteins are called amino acids. When we digest proteins, they are broken down into their component amino acids. Our bodies need twenty amino acids to function properly. We need to get nine of those (called essential amino acids) from our diet, while our bodies produce the eleven others.

Foods that contain all nine essential amino acids are known as complete proteins. Complete proteins include meat, fish, shellfish, eggs, and dairy as well as soybeans (which can be made into milk, tofu, and tempeh), quinoa, buckwheat, amaranth, spirulina, chia seeds, and hemp seeds.

While other plant foods, such as lentils, beans, nuts, other seeds, and whole grains, are considered to be incomplete proteins on their own, the good news is that when paired with certain foods, they provide all nine essential amino acids. Incorporating a variety of complete and incomplete protein sources in your diet is key to ensuring you meet your amino acid needs.

Certain vegetables and fruits are also sources of protein and can help you achieve your dietary goals, highlighting the importance of eating a balanced diet focused on nutrient-dense food.

COMPLETE PLANT-BASED PROTEIN COMBOS

WHOLE GRAINS   **PULSES**

- Beans (or lentils) with brown rice

- Bean chili or stew (see the Smoky Sweet Potato Stew recipe on page 270) with added quinoa, or served with tortillas or brown rice

- Falafel with whole-wheat pita (see the Spinach Falafel Bowl recipe on page 156)

- Hummus or bean dip with whole-wheat pita (see the recipe for Curried Chickpea Sandwich on page 168 or Spiced Butter Bean Dip on page 140)

- Lentil pâté with whole-wheat pita or whole-grain crackers (see the Mushroom & Lentil Pâté recipe on page 136)

- Lentil soup with an added whole grain

WHOLE GRAINS   **NUTS OR SEEDS**

- Peanut butter on whole-wheat bread (such as the Peanut Butter & Banana Sandwich with Homemade Raspberry Chia Jam on page 102)

- Brown rice salad or casserole with nuts or seeds

- Stir-fry over brown rice or noodles with peanuts or cashews

PULSES   **NUTS OR SEEDS**

- Bean, lentil, or chickpea salad with raw pumpkin seeds (pepitas) or sunflower seeds

VEGETABLE/ FRUIT (raw unless otherwise noted)	PORTION SIZE	PROTEIN CONTENT
GREEN PEAS	1 cup (145g)	7.8g
SWEET CORN	1 cup kernels (145g)	4.7g
GUAVA	1 cup (165g)	4.2g
MUSHROOMS (shiitake)	1 cup stir-fried (97g)	3.4g
MUSHROOMS (white)	1 cup sliced (70g)	3g
AVOCADO	1 cup cubed (150g)	3g
BRUSSELS SPROUTS	1 cup (88 g)	3g
WHITE POTATOES	1 cup cubed (150g)	3g
ASPARAGUS	1 cup chopped (134g)	2.9g
JACKFRUIT	1 cup sliced (165g)	2.8g
BROCCOLI	1 cup chopped (91g)	2.5g
APRICOTS	1 cup sliced (165g)	2.3g
SWEET POTATOES	1 cup cubed (133g)	2.1g
CAULIFLOWER	1 cup chopped (107g)	2g
BLACKBERRIES	1 cup (144g)	2g
GRAPEFRUIT	1 cup segments (230g)	2g
KIWI	1 cup sliced (180g)	2g
BANANAS	1 cup sliced (150g)	1.6g
SWEET CHERRIES	1 cup pitted (154g)	1.6g
ZUCCHINI	1 cup chopped (125g)	1.5g
RED BELL PEPPER	1 cup chopped (150g)	1.5g
RASPBERRIES	1 cup (123g)	1.5g
CANTALOUPE	1 cup cubed (160g)	1.3g
ORANGES	1 cup segments (185g)	1.3g
CARROTS	1 cup chopped (128g)	1.2g
BOK CHOY	1 cup shredded (70g)	1g
KALE	1 cup chopped (30g)	0.9g
EGGPLANT	1 cup cubed (82g)	0.8g
SPINACH	1 cup (30g)	0.8g
WATERCRESS	1 cup chopped (34g)	0.8g

Source: USDA FoodData Central and Nutritionix

how much protein do we need?

The concern on many people's minds is whether they can get enough protein from vegetarian or vegan food. It is easy to see why. Western society in particular has become so obsessed with protein that it has become a marketing buzzword. Every day we are bombarded with the health benefits of snacks, powders, shakes, and even water enriched with protein. The popularity of low-carb, high-protein diets for weight loss has further cemented the view that our bodies need high levels of protein to function.

The truth is, we need less protein than most people think. Individual protein needs depend on factors such as age, sex, weight, medical conditions, and activity level, but on average, sedentary adults are advised to eat 0.8 gram of protein per kilogram (2.2 pounds) of body weight per day; active people and older individuals need a bit more. For a person who weighs 150 pounds (68 kilograms), this equates to 54 grams of protein. That's about two palm-sized portions of protein-rich food a day. In both the US and the UK, we eat, on average, twice the amount of protein we need and therefore get more than enough.

Some scientists point out that protein quality is more important than quantity and that consuming too much protein can have an adverse effect on health, especially if it comes mainly from animal sources. It is important to point out that the way animals are raised and fed impacts the nutritional value of their meat. For example, several studies have pointed out that grass-fed beef contains more omega-3 fatty acids and lower levels of saturated fats than grain-fed beef—all the more reason to avoid eating factory-farmed meat.

The American Heart Association's lifestyle recommendations for reducing cardiovascular risk emphasize eating a variety of fruits and vegetables, whole grains, nonfat and low-fat dairy products, skinless poultry, fish, nuts, and beans while limiting red and processed meat, sweets, and sugary drinks. Filling our plates with animal proteins leaves little space for nutrient-dense plant foods that are known to be beneficial to health. The focus needs to shift from what we should eat less of to what we should eat more of.

how much meat should we eat?

Both the *Dietary Guidelines for Americans* and the UK Eatwell Guide offer information to support a healthy dietary pattern. Both advise us to diversify our protein intake by eating more plant foods.

According to the *Dietary Guidelines for Americans*, 10 to 35 percent of a sedentary adult's daily calorie intake should come from protein, from both animal and plant sources (such as lean meats, poultry, eggs, seafood, legumes, nuts, seeds, and soy products). So, if you need 2,000 calories a day, this equates to between 200 and 700 calories from protein, or 50 to 175 grams (1¾ to 6 ounces). The UK Eatwell Guide advises us to eat more vegetarian sources of protein while limiting red meat and processed meat to 70 grams (2½ ounces) a day.

If you are just setting out on your plant-forward journey, following either of these sets of guidelines is a good place to begin. Even if you are starting from average meat consumption and reducing the amount of meat you eat to comply with standard dietary guidelines, you could still eat a regular (larger) portion of meat two or three times a week. If you want to eat for the planet, however, neither the *Dietary Guidelines for Americans* nor the UK Eatwell Guide goes far enough, as neither fully takes into account the full environmental impacts of our food choices.

As you continue on your plant-forward journey, you might want to take a look at the EAT-*Lancet* planetary health plate, which consists by volume of approximately half vegetables and fruits; the other half, in terms of contribution to calories, should be primarily whole grains, plant proteins, unsaturated plant fats, and (optionally) minimal amounts of animal protein.

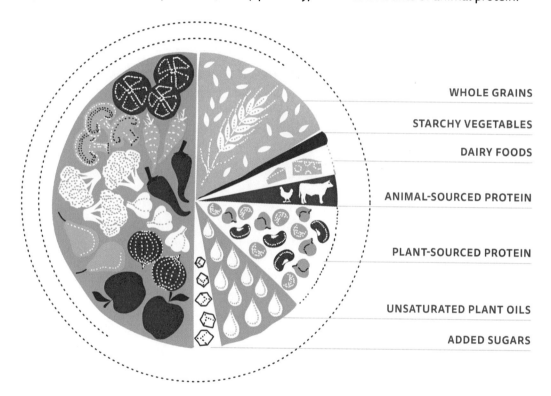

WHOLE GRAINS

STARCHY VEGETABLES

DAIRY FOODS

ANIMAL-SOURCED PROTEIN

PLANT-SOURCED PROTEIN

UNSATURATED PLANT OILS

ADDED SUGARS

The EAT-*Lancet* Commission defines planetary health as "the health of human civilization and the state of the natural systems on which it depends," and its recommendations highlight the critical role that diets play in linking human health and environmental sustainability.

The Commission's "Food in the Anthropocene" report came under criticism for advocating one set of dietary recommendations that may not be suitable for everyone as well as failing to consider local farming methods and diets. Still, if you are going to eat some meat and other animal products, I believe that EAT-Lancet's recommendations are worth aiming for from an environmental sustainability point of view. Speak to a dietitian or healthcare practitioner to decide whether they are right for you.

my top tips

Changing lifelong habits can be tricky, especially when it comes to food. The main advantage of a plant-forward or flexitarian diet is its adaptability, allowing you to tailor the diet to your individual lifestyle choices and health conditions. It is also versatile, so you are unlikely to get bored after a few weeks. It enables you to develop new eating habits that will be easy to stick with for the long term. Here are some suggestions for how to get started.

start *small*

Try to commit to one day a week without meat and sign up to initiatives such as Meat-Free Monday (aka Meatless Monday). Choose a convenient time and stick to it. If, one week, things get out of sync, simply catch up the following day. Gradually build up from there, adding more meat-free (and completely plant-based) days. Some people choose to eat meat only on the weekend to fit with their social lives. Should you wish to challenge yourself further, why not sign up for Veganuary, a popular campaign that encourages people to eat solely vegan food for a month?

If you decide to avoid eating meat, ditching red meat and processed meat is another good starting point.

think more rather than less

Instead of focusing on what you eat less of, focus on what you eat more of. Filling your plate with plenty of wholesome plant foods will effortlessly reduce the amount of meat in your diet. Organize your meals around plant foods and make meat the side dish or garnish. Still hungry? If you are having seconds, go for the vegetables, not the meat.

serve *smaller portions* of meat

If you are watching your meat intake, it is useful to remember that a standard serving of cooked meat is 3 ounces (85g). That's about the size of a deck of playing cards. Share larger cuts between two or three people. Try pounding boneless meat into thinner pieces (see page 54), which not only softens tougher cuts but also gives the illusion that more meat is there. Once you add vegetables or pulses, no one will notice the difference.

learn to cook with *less meat*

There is no denying that meat adds deliciousness to a lot of dishes. If you are not ready to eliminate it entirely, I have compiled some of my favorite techniques to help you cook with less meat without compromising on taste and flavor; see pages 53 to 57. From butterflying and pounding to thinly slicing and shredding, each technique is designed to do more with less. Another easy trick is to replace half (or more) of the meat with lentils, beans, a whole grain, or a vegetable. This technique is called "bulking"; it works perfectly for lasagna, meatloaf, stews, and other dishes.

buy *better meat*

If you are going to eat meat (and other animal products), make sure it has been raised under higher welfare standards. Simply switching to organic, grass-fed, and pasture-raised meats is a great step in the right direction. The Animal Welfare Institute, Compassion in World Farming, Seafood Watch, and the Marine Stewardship Council (MSC) have fantastic resources to help you make more sustainable and ethical choices.

get creative with *leftovers*

Don't waste a single scrap; transform meat leftovers into delicious dishes without the need to buy more. Shred or slice poultry and red meat, as shown on pages 55 and 56, and add them to soups, sandwiches, savory pies, stir-fries, and salads. You can make stock with the bones of a roast or use a chicken carcass as the base of a soup (see page 59). Leftover fish can be flaked and used as a salad, soup, or sandwich topping.

try *meat-alternative* products

When you crave meat but would rather stick to plants, you can turn to meat analogues. An impressive range of vegan and vegetarian alternatives with a similar taste and texture to meat are available on grocery store shelves as well as on restaurant menus. From meat-free burgers, sausages, and ground meat to chicken fillets and nuggets, these products are designed to appeal to meat-eaters and can be so realistic that it is sometimes hard to tell the difference between a meat analogue and real meat.

As tasty as they are, meat analogues are heavily processed and not a substitute for unprocessed whole foods such as vegetables, pulses, nuts, seeds, and whole grains. Enjoy them in moderation. (See page 46 for a more in-depth discussion of meat, fish, and dairy analogues as part of a plant-forward pantry.)

harness *plant-based umami*

Umami is the fifth taste (after sweet, sour, bitter, and salty) that lingers in the mouth and makes us salivate. It is a meaty flavor and is usually found in foods that contain a high level of the amino acid glutamate, like meat, fish, and aged cheese. However, there are plenty of plant-based umami sources that can boost the flavor and depth of meat-free dishes, such as soy sauce, miso, mushrooms, fermented vegetables (such as kimchi), sun-dried tomatoes, olives, capers, balsamic vinegar, onions, and garlic.

eat more *pulses*

Small but mighty, beans and lentils are nutritional powerhouses that not only are filled with vitamins, minerals, and dietary fiber but also are low in fat. Hearty and versatile, they can be eaten on their own or used to bulk up plant or meat dishes so you feel satisfied for longer. To reap all their health benefits, mix them with nuts, seeds, vegetables, or whole grains as shown in the Complete Plant-Based Protein Combos table on page 17. You will find a list of the pulses I keep in my plant-forward pantry on pages 26 and 27. Many are available from supermarkets, already cooked, but in case you prefer preparing them yourself, you will find a concise guide on pages 64 and 65.

know your *whole grains*

Whole grains are good sources of protein and fiber. Swap white rice with brown rice and experiment with quinoa, amaranth, bulgur wheat, barley, and wild rice. All of these can be turned into delicious dishes and mixed with pulses and vegetables to harness their nutritional goodness. See pages 32 to 36 for more on the whole grains I like to use in my cooking.

stock up on *vegetarian & vegan cookbooks*

Lack of inspiration is often an excuse to revert to old habits. There are plenty of vegetarian and vegan cookbooks out there that can help you hone your plant-based cooking skills. Once you have found a recipe you enjoy, make sure to include it in your regular meal rotation.

venture into *world cuisines*

Some cuisines—especially those blending flavors and spices with pulses, tofu, or whole grains—are traditionally well suited to meatless cooking. Take your taste buds on an exciting adventure by trying cuisines such as Indian, Asian, Mexican, Middle Eastern, Mediterranean, and Ethiopian.

buddy up

Team up with a like-minded friend, colleague, or partner so you can support each other. Working towards the same goal, you will be able to motivate one another, share highs and lows, and encourage each other to stay on course.

plan ahead

Weekly meal planning enables you to stick to your plant-forward goal while saving you time and money. Don't forget to take a quick inventory of your fridge and kitchen cupboards before shopping to avoid overbuying.

shop *differently*

When you plan your weekly shopping, check which vegetables are in season and plan your meals around them. Don't make the meat aisle "the destination." Avoid it if you can; if not, limit the amount of meat you buy to one or two higher-welfare pieces a week.

Patronize markets that do their best to offer produce, meat, eggs, and dairy products from farms in your region—within 100 miles is ideal. Or, better yet, buy directly from a farmer; doing so benefits the farmer and guarantees freshness. Pay a visit to your local farmers' market or sign up for a weekly vegetable box from a nearby CSA (community supported agriculture) scheme, which will benefit your local economy. Subscribing to a vegetable delivery service is also a great way to keep up with what is in season and eat vegetables you might not be accustomed to. (See "Choosing Seasonal & Local Food" on pages 76 and 77 for more on this subject.)

batch-cook

Advance preparation of larger batches of plant-based and plant-forward foods like curry, chili, lasagna, Bolognese sauce, and cottage pie can help you keep meat off the menu. You can freeze any extras for later. They will come in handy after a hectic day when you have little time to cook.

chapter 2:

the plant-forward kitchen

Stocking your kitchen with the right ingredients and equipment makes it easier to embrace a plant-forward diet and to prepare nutritious meals even on days when it feels like there is nothing to eat in the house. This chapter gives you an overview of the essentials used throughout this cookbook as well as some optional add-ons.

ingredient essentials

In this section, I have listed my favorite ingredients for cooking and baking plant-forward dishes. Items marked with an asterisk (*) are not required to make the recipes in this book but are great to have on hand.

pulses

When it comes to a healthy diet, pulses are a staple. Put simply, we all should be eating more of them. Pulses are a large food family that includes lentils, dry beans, dry peas, and chickpeas; they fall under the larger umbrella of legumes.

Widely available in stores, canned pulses are precooked and conveniently can be used straight out of the can. Check the ingredient lists to avoid salt, sugar, and flavorings that might have been added during the canning process. Another thing to keep in mind is that many food cans are lined with bisphenol A (BPA), a known hormone disrupter. BPA acts as a protective layer between food and the metal container. If you prefer to avoid it, look for BPA-free cans.

You can also purchase dry pulses, which are easy to prepare from scratch. My cheat sheet on page 64 details the soaking and cooking times for common varieties.

Whether they are canned or dry, pulses not only contain protein, iron, magnesium, zinc, and other micronutrients but also are high in dietary fiber while being low in fat and cholesterol. Aside from their health benefits, pulses have a low carbon footprint, requiring little to no fertilizer to cultivate. They have the ability to draw nitrogen from the air, enriching the soil as they grow. The benefits of pulses even stretch to your wallet, as they are a more affordable source of protein than meat or fish. The following are the pulses I use most often.

dry beans

Red kidney beans, pinto beans, black beans, borlotti (aka cranberry) beans, cannellini beans (technically a white kidney bean), Great Northern beans, and butter beans (to name just a few) are staples of many world cuisines. Delicious on their own or in salads, soups, dips, curries, and stews, they are truly versatile, whether you want to replace the meat in chilis with more beans or add some plant-based creaminess to soups (cannellini beans are perfect for this purpose). You can also use beans as a binding and bulking agent, as in my Fish (or No-Fish) Koftas recipe on page 218. For convenience, I tend to use precooked canned beans in my recipes; however, if you prefer, you can cook dry beans at home for use in all the recipes in this book. Cooking dry beans yourself is more cost-effective and allows you to control seasoning and flavoring (see page 65 for cooking tips).

lentils

Red, yellow, green, brown, or black lentils are ideal in salads, curries, soups, and stews. They can be used to bulk up a dish when you want to use less meat or even replace meat altogether. Split red lentils add creaminess to soups, like my Sweet Potato Chowder (page 194).

For something different, try beluga lentils, a small, dark black lentil that resembles caviar, or French green lentils (my preferred green lentil), a small, dark green variety with a nutty taste and hearty texture. Puy lentils, a type of green lentil grown on volcanic soil in the Auvergne region in France, have a unique peppery flavor and retain their shape after cooking, which makes them ideal for salads and casseroles.

Because lentils cook much more quickly than beans, I often use dried rather than canned, with two exceptions: for convenience, I use precooked canned lentils in my Loaded Sloppy Joe Sweet Potatoes (page 228) and my Mushroom & Lentil Pâté (page 136).

dry peas

Black-eyed peas, green peas, yellow peas, pigeon peas*, and so on are prized ingredients around the world. Green and yellow peas have a sweet flavor and creamy texture, making them perfect for soups, dahls, and dips. Harvested whole, they are also sold split. The splitting process reduces the cooking time. With their delicious earthy taste, black-eyed peas are another favorite of mine. They hold their shape well during cooking and make a welcome addition to dishes such as my Spiced Herb Chicken or Tofu (page 234).

chickpeas

Chickpeas are a staple of plant-based diets. There are two main varieties: desi, a smaller dark-colored chickpea, and the more common kabuli (aka garbanzo bean), which is larger and lighter in color.

Chickpeas have a light and delicate nutty taste as well as a hearty texture. They pair well with a wide range of foods as well as many spices and herbs. They are featured in many world cuisines, from Europe to the Middle East and Asia (think hummus, tagines, and curries). A tasty and inexpensive protein option, they are suitable for a variety of dishes, including salads, soups, stews, curries, burgers, sandwiches, and even desserts.

Chickpeas are available both dry and cooked. They hold their shape well even when simmered, pressure-cooked, or slow-cooked over a long period of time. Once cooked, they can be eaten cold or hot.

Low in fat and high in dietary fiber, chickpeas are a nutrient-dense food. According to a review published in the *British Journal of Nutrition*, the quality of their protein content is considered to be better than other pulses, as they have significant amounts of several essential amino acids. They also provide a variety of vitamins and minerals, especially iron, manganese, vitamin B9 (folate), and copper.

WHAT TO LOOK FOR: *chickpeas*

- **Dry chickpeas**—Cooking your own chickpeas is straightforward and weight-for-weight much cheaper than buying canned chickpeas. For ease, you can batch-cook a larger quantity to keep in the fridge and use throughout the week. (See page 64 for cooking tips.) Once cooked, they can also be frozen in zip-top bags. Stored in an airtight container away from direct light, dry chickpeas should last up to a year.

- **Canned chickpeas**—Widely available, canned chickpeas are precooked for convenience. They can be eaten straight from the can, whizzed into hummus, or added to pretty much any dish. Save the brine (known as aquafaba), as it makes a fabulous egg replacement (see below).

- **Aquafaba**—Aquafaba is the brine, or leftover liquid, from canned chickpeas. High in protein, it is a unique ingredient that is often overlooked or thrown away. It has a fairly neutral taste and is a fantastic binder. What makes it truly special is that it whips like egg white to create perfect snowy peaks that can be used in baking to lighten batters and doughs or create delicious egg-free meringues. The conversion is simple: 3 tablespoons of aquafaba equates to one whole egg, while 2 tablespoons of aquafaba replaces one egg white. Some chickpea cans contain salt, making the aquafaba unsuitable for use in desserts, so make sure to check the ingredients. Note: When cooking dry chickpeas at home, I have had mixed results trying to use the cooking liquid as aquafaba. I find that the brine from cans gives more reliable results.

- **Chickpea flour**—Obtained by grinding dry chickpeas, chickpea flour is gluten-free and high in protein. Its binding properties are ideal for making plant-based fritters and burgers. It has a neutral flavor and can be bought in supermarkets or specialty food stores. You can also make your own by grinding dry chickpeas in a food processor, high-powered blender, or spice grinder.

1. **Hummus**—The king of dips does not need an introduction. Swap plain hummus with something a bit different. Try blending in some roasted red pepper, fresh green peas, or any roasted veg.

2. **Sandwich spread**—Smashed chickpeas make a delicious alternative to cheese, ham, or chicken in sandwiches. Simply mash cooked chickpeas with a fork and then add your favorite spices and seasoning. You can also pulse the chickpeas to a chunky paste using a blender or food processor, as in my Curried Chickpea Sandwich on page 168.

3. **Salads**—Combine chickpeas with vegetables and whole grains for a quick and healthy salad. Mix it up by adding lentils or other pulses.

4. **Curries & tagines**—Including chickpeas in curries or tagines (plant-based or not) is a great way to bulk up and enhance the texture.

5. **Soups & stews**—Chickpeas make a healthy and hearty low-fat addition to soups and stews. As an alternative to cream and dairy, you can even blend them with other ingredients to give soups a thick and creamy texture.

6. **Falafel**—Dry chickpeas soaked in water overnight are the secret to good falafel. Using canned chickpeas can make falafel too crumbly. Check out my Spinach Falafel Bowl on page 156.

7. **Pasta & rice dishes**—Chickpeas are delicious with any kind of tomato-based sauce. When I am in a rush (especially for packed lunches), pasta e ceci (pasta with chickpeas) is my go-to dish. It's a simple, healthy, and absolutely delicious alternative to pasta Bolognese.

8. **Socca**—Socca is a tasty flatbread made from chickpea flour, water, and olive oil that originates from Italy and southeastern France. You can enjoy it plain, but I like to add a mixture of toppings, like in my Spring Soccas with Minty Pea Pesto & Watercress (page 178).

9. **Burgers & fritters**—The texture of vegan burgers and fritters can be a bit soft. Adding chickpeas helps bind the ingredients together and improves texture. You can use a potato masher or pulse cooked chickpeas in a food processor to a slightly coarse texture.

10. **Meatloaf & nut roasts**—Again, if you are looking to give meat-free meatloaf or nut roast a little more of a bite, cooked and mashed or pulsed chickpeas work wonders. As with burgers, texture is key, so do not overmash them.

11. **Snack & salad topping**—For a crunchy and tasty snack, look no further than roasted chickpeas. You can use any herb or spice blend to coat them. I like mine spicy with either smoked paprika, Sriracha sauce, or harissa. They make a great topping for salads as well as a gluten-free alternative to croutons; see my Crunchy Broccoli Salad with Roasted Sriracha Chickpeas on page 146.

12. **Desserts**—Aquafaba, as mentioned previously, is a great egg substitute. I use it for plant-based meringues and mousses, such as my Chocolate Mousse with Passion Fruit Curd on page 288.

13. **Cocktails**—If you are looking to make an egg white cocktail vegan-friendly, simply add aquafaba to the cocktail shaker in lieu of the egg white and mix it with the rest of the ingredients.

14. **Cakes & pancakes**—Just like egg whites, whisked aquafaba will lighten any cake or pancake batter and is also ideal for macaroons, biscuits, and cookies.

nuts & seeds

Small but mighty, nuts and seeds are loaded with protein, healthy unsaturated fats, vitamins, and minerals. They all have their individual nutritional profiles, so keep a wide selection on hand to add to salads, yogurt, smoothie bowls, curries, soups, roasted vegetables, and more. For a quick and healthy energy boost on the go, mix them with dried fruits or whip them into nut and/or seed butter (see page 328). If you are watching your waistline, keep in mind that they are high in calories and enjoy them in moderation.

NUT/SEED (raw)	PROTEIN CONTENT per 1-ounce (30g) serving
HEMP SEEDS, HULLED	10g
PEANUTS	7.3g
SUNFLOWER SEEDS	6.3g
ALMONDS	6g
PUMPKIN SEEDS	6g
FLAX SEEDS	5.7g
CASHEWS	5g
CHIA SEEDS	5g
SESAME SEEDS	4.8g
WALNUTS	4.7g
BRAZIL NUTS	4.3g
HAZELNUTS	4.2g
PECANS	2.8g

Sources: USDA FoodData Central and Nutritionix

nut & seed butters

Nut butter is another staple of a plant-forward pantry that deserves so much more attention than it gets—it has so many more uses than simply being spread between two slices of bread. Whether smooth or chunky, butters made from nuts, seeds, or peanuts are incredibly versatile sources of protein, varying from 4.4 grams per 2-tablespoon serving of hazelnut butter to 7 grams per 2-tablespoon serving of peanut butter. For comparison, the average large egg contains around 6 grams of protein, while a slice of cheddar cheese gives you around 4 grams. Nut butters also provide healthy fats, dietary fiber, vitamins, minerals, and antioxidants while being low in carbs. They are high in calories, so if you are watching your weight, make sure to enjoy them in moderation as part of a balanced diet.

From peanut butter to almond or cashew butter (to name a few), they all have slightly different flavors that suit different types of dishes and cuisines. Add them to curries, stews, dips, dressings, sauces, smoothies, or even baked goods, or use them to top sweet potatoes. If you are allergic to nuts and/or peanuts, sunflower seed butter is a tasty alternative that you might enjoy. Tahini, made from ground sesame seeds, has a delicious creamy texture and can be used in dips, sauces, soups, brownies, and ice creams. I like to use it in salad dressings; see my recipe for Creamy Tahini Dressing—Three Ways on page 303.

Nut butter not only makes a great dairy substitute but can also enhance your cooking and baking in a number of ways. It can replace butter or oil in baked goods or eggs in pancakes and cookies. When a curry or stew requires a bit of creaminess, I like to add nut butter; it also makes a wonderful addition to smoothies and shakes. In this book, I use peanut butter in a tasty dip for my Summer Rolls (see page 114) and as the main binding ingredient for my Puffed Quinoa Chocolate Chip Bars (see page 296).

The three butters I always have in my kitchen are almond, cashew, and peanut. I find plain smooth nut butter—unsalted and unsweetened—to be the most useful and versatile type for general cooking, while I enjoy the texture of crunchy nut butter in cookies, curries, and ice creams.

You can easily make your own butters at home and get creative by mixing nuts, seeds, and sweet or savory flavoring ingredients.

grains

Grains is a broad category that describes the seeds of grasses grown for food. Each grain has three parts: the bran, germ, and endosperm. Sometimes grains are left whole and unprocessed, and sometimes the germ and bran are removed, leaving only the starchy endosperm.

With most of the goodness residing in the outer bran layer and germ of the seed, whole grains retain the nutritional goodness that is often lost in the refining process. They are high in fiber and many vitamins and minerals. This is why I strongly recommend choosing whole grains whenever possible. Easy swaps include whole-wheat bread instead of white bread and brown rice instead of white rice.

Some whole grains, like quinoa and amaranth, are considered complete proteins because they contain all nine essential amino acids, making them invaluable staples in a plant-forward cupboard. I tend to use quinoa more often than amaranth because I prefer its taste and texture.

GRAIN	PORTION SIZE	PROTEIN CONTENT
FREEKEH	1 cup (184g) uncooked	28g
KAMUT	1 cup (186g) uncooked	27g
FARRO	1 cup (240g) uncooked	27g
OATS	1 cup (156g) uncooked	26.4g
AMARANTH	1 cup (193g) uncooked	26.2g
QUINOA	1 cup (170g) uncooked	24g
WILD RICE	1 cup (160g) uncooked	23.5g
SPELT FLOUR	1 cup (150g)	22g
MILLET	1 cup (200g) uncooked	22g
PEARL BARLEY	1 cup (200g) uncooked	19.8g
BULGUR	1 cup (140g) uncooked	17.2g
WHOLE-WHEAT FLOUR	1 cup (120g)	15.8g
POPCORN	1 cup (156g) uncooked	15.6g
BUCKWHEAT FLOUR	1 cup (120g)	15.1g
BROWN RICE	1 cup (185g) uncooked	14g
RYE FLOUR	1 cup (102g)	11.1g
SPELT (GRAIN)	1 cup (194g) uncooked	10.7g
POLENTA	1 cup (240g) cooked	5g

Sources: USDA FoodData Central and Nutritionix

Note: Freekeh, kamut, farro, amaranth, quinoa, wild rice, spelt, millet, barley, bulgur, buckwheat, and rye are also considered ancient grains, a term used to describe grains and pseudo-cereals that have been cultivated in the same way over the last several hundred years without being cross-bred or manipulated.

oats

Incredibly good for you, oats are prized for their nutritional value and health benefits and should be regularly incorporated in your diet. Nutrient-rich oats are a versatile complex carbohydrate that can be included in both sweet and savory breakfasts, mains, snacks, baked goods, and desserts. Gluten-free unless processed in a facility where gluten-containing grains are also present, they are high in a soluble fiber called beta-glucan that helps lower bad cholesterol (LDL) and keeps you fuller for longer while benefiting gut health. Cooked oatmeal is the breakfast of choice in our house, enabling us to start the day filled with energy.

Three main types of oats are sold in grocery stores: rolled (aka old-fashioned), steel-cut, and Scottish oats. All are made from whole oats (known as groats) stripped of their outer layer. In this cookbook, I use rolled oats because they are the most versatile.

WHAT TO LOOK FOR:  *oats*

- **Rolled oats,** also known as old-fashioned oats or as jumbo oats in the UK, are made from groats that have been steamed and then flattened with a roller. They have a lot of texture and are perfect for overnight porridge, cooked porridge, granola, snack bars, cookies, and crumbles.

- **Quick oats** are also precooked but flattened even thinner than rolled oats. As a result, they take less time to cook and have a mushier texture. They work well in cooked porridge as well as baked goods.

- **Instant oats,** designed to be cooked in a microwave in under 1 minute, are precooked and rolled before being sweetened and flavored. They have an extra-smooth texture and are often sold in individual portion packs.

- **Scottish oats,** rather than being rolled or cut, are ground to a coarse texture. They are ideal in porridge, cookies, cakes, and oatcakes. Once cooked, they have a creamier texture than steel-cut oats.

- **Steel-cut oats,** also known as Irish oats, are simply cut with a steel blade into smaller chunks that have a similar appearance to broken rice grains. Less processed than rolled oats, they tend to take longer to cook than other varieties and have a heartier texture. Use them in porridge (they reheat well, so you can batch-cook them in advance to enjoy throughout the week), casseroles, cookies, soups, and so on.

quinoa

Healthy and wholesome, quinoa is a star ingredient in a plant-forward pantry. While it is considered a whole grain, quinoa is botanically closely related to beets, chard, and spinach. Indigenous to the Andes area, it has been a staple food in South America for thousands of years. While most of the quinoa found in stores comes from South America, it is also grown in the US, Canada, and Europe. So, if you looking to reduce food miles, make sure to buy some that was grown close to where you live.

Deemed "the mother of all grains" by the Incas, quinoa is an incredibly nutritious food. It contains all nine essential amino acids, making it a complete protein and a healthy alternative to animal-based protein sources. Naturally gluten-free, it is low in fat and high in dietary fiber. It is also a good source of antioxidants as well as magnesium, iron, and zinc. It is fair to say that quinoa deserves its superfood status. See page 66 for my foolproof method for cooking it.

WHAT TO LOOK FOR: *quinoa*

• **White, red, and black quinoa**—Quinoa is available in three colors. There is not much nutritional difference between them, but they differ in texture once cooked. White quinoa is more delicate and fluffier, black is crunchier and nuttier, while red falls somewhere in between. There is also a slight difference in cooking time; white quinoa cooks a bit quicker than the other two varieties. Overall, it comes down to personal preference, with red and black quinoa looking the most appealing when combined with other ingredients. Tri-color (aka rainbow) quinoa is a mixture of black, white, and red, and it is my favorite. A tasty combination of texture and flavors, it adds vibrancy to many dishes.

• **Puffed quinoa**—Like popcorn, quinoa pops and puffs when heated. Light and crispy, puffed quinoa has a similar texture to puffed rice. I've had mixed success trying to make it at home, so I much prefer buying it already puffed. It makes a crunchy and tasty addition to no-bake desserts (such as the Puffed Quinoa Chocolate Chip Bars on page 296), snacks, breakfast cereals, and granola (such as the Very Berry Granola on page 110). You can also use it as a crispy topping for salads and soups.

• **Quinoa flour**—Made by milling whole white quinoa seeds, quinoa flour is ideal for gluten-free baking. High in protein and dietary fiber, it is extremely versatile and can be used on its own or mixed with other flours to make a wide range of sweet and savory baked goods.

• **Quinoa flakes**—Similar to rolled oats, quinoa flakes are made by rolling quinoa seeds flat. Boasting the same high-quality nutritional value as other quinoa products, the flakes can be added to cookies, snack bars, muffins, and homemade granola. Quick and easy to cook, they also make a tasty alternative to oats in porridge.

8 WAYS TO USE *quinoa*

1. **Slow-cook it.** You can add rinsed quinoa to your favorite plant-based slow cooker recipes, cooking it for four to six hours.

2. **Stir-fry it.** Cooked quinoa makes a tasty alternative to rice in stir-fries. In fact, stir-fries are a fantastic way to use up any leftover grains and vegetables.

3. **Add it to salads.** Quinoa is perfect in salads. You can use it on its own or combine it with another grain. A mixture of two parts quinoa and one part bulgur wheat has a satisfying texture and bite, as in my Quinoa & Edamame Salad on page 152.

4. **Add it to soups.** Quinoa is a great thickener for soups. Simply add dry quinoa when you add the water or stock and cook with the rest of the ingredients for 20 to 25 minutes. Keep in mind that quinoa expands while cooking, so, for best results, use between ½ and ¾ cup (90 to 140g) of quinoa for a total of 6 to 8 cups (1.5 to 2 liters) of liquid.

5. **Add it to stews.** Adding ½ cup (90g) of dry quinoa to a plant-based chili or other stew is a simple way to boost its protein content and texture.

6. **Make pie & tart crusts.** Swap conventional savory pie and tart pastry crusts with a crunchy and chewy quinoa crust. Simply mix cooked quinoa with eggs and shredded cheese to make a delicious and nutritious gluten-free alternative to puff or shortcut pastry. Try my Quinoa Crust Quiches—Two Ways on page 129.

7. **Stuff it into vegetables.** If you are looking to reduce the amount of meat in your diet, try stuffing vegetables with quinoa rather than meat. It works fantastically well with mushrooms, bell peppers, tomatoes, jalapeños, eggplant, zucchini, butternut squash, and other squash.

8. **Make fritters.** Fritters made from quinoa mixed with your favorite vegetables are really versatile. Serve them with a salad or falafel-style with a creamy dipping sauce like any of my Creamy Tahini Dressings on pages 303 and 304.

pasta, noodles & rice

Whether it is Italian pasta, Asian noodles, or rice, the foods in this category are incredibly versatile and used in many world cuisines. I keep a wide selection of rice, pasta, and noodles in my kitchen, choosing whole-grain varieties whenever possible to boost fiber and nutrient intake.

- Italian pasta (all shapes and forms)
- Lasagna sheets
- Long-grain rice (basmati and jasmine)
- Orzo
- Rice noodles
- Short-grain and risotto-style rice (Arborio rice, Carnaroli rice, pudding rice, sticky rice, and sushi rice)
- Soba noodles
- Udon noodles

tofu

Made from soybeans, water, and a curdling agent, tofu is a staple of vegetarian and vegan cuisines. It is available in textures ranging from silken to extra-firm, each suitable for specific culinary uses. A 3-ounce (85g) serving of tofu provides 10 to 17 grams of low-fat protein, depending on the type. I use mainly extra-firm tofu for the savory recipes in this book. Extra-firm tofu freezes well, so you can stock up and always have some on hand.

This versatile ingredient can be used in sweet and savory dishes, such as scrambles, stir-fries, kebabs, and desserts. If you think tofu is bland, think again! Plain tofu may seem unexciting, but with a little bit of preparation, you can easily improve its texture and flavor, and plain firm or extra-firm tofu absorbs the aromas of other foods it is cooked with. The key to unleashing its full potential is to prepare and cook it properly, as explained on pages 67 to 70.

In addition to plain tofu, look for smoked tofu, which can be eaten on its own or added to your favorite dishes to infuse them with a deep, rich flavor.

10 WAYS TO USE  *tofu*

1. **Marinate it.** Cut up some pressed or frozen and thawed firm or extra-firm tofu and place it in a container with your choice of condiments and seasonings. My preferred flavors include smoky BBQ seasonings or a combination of peanut butter and soy sauce. Leave in the fridge for one hour to overnight before cooking using your preferred technique (grilling, baking, stir-frying, etc.).

2. **Bake it.** Bake pressed or frozen and thawed plain or marinated firm or extra-firm tofu in the oven. It becomes crispy on the outside while remaining smooth on the inside. You can use it in salads or stir-fries or as a hot or cold snack.

3. **Grill it.** Grilling works best with marinated tofu. You can grill it on an outdoor grill or on a grill pan on the stovetop. If you don't have a grill or grill pan, you can broil the tofu in the oven on the top rack.

4. **Pan-fry it.** Dice or slice some pressed or frozen and thawed firm or extra-firm tofu. Toss the pieces in flour seasoned with garlic powder and dried herbs until they are coated all over. Then pan-fry the pieces in hot oil over medium-high heat. Fried tofu can be used as a topping for stir-fries, salads, rice, noodles, and vegetables.

5. **Scramble it.** Scrambled firm or extra-firm tofu is a scrumptious alternative to eggs that hits the spot every time. Perfect on toast, tortillas, or in sandwiches.

6. **Stir-fry it.** Pressed or frozen and thawed plain or marinated firm or extra-firm tofu is great in a stir-fry.

7. **Slow-cook it.** Plain or marinated extra-firm tofu can add healthy vegetable protein to slow cooker recipes. Coarser and more absorbent frozen and thawed tofu is ideal here.

8. **Add it to soup.** Dice or scramble some pressed or frozen and thawed extra-firm tofu over a bowl of warming soup. You can also use silken tofu for an ultra-smooth vegetable soup. Simply add it in the last five minutes of cooking and blend with the rest of the ingredients until you have your desired consistency.

9. **Drink it in shakes & smoothies.** Add dairy-free protein to your morning smoothie with thick and creamy silken tofu.

10. **Beat it into mousses, dips & cakes.** Silken tofu can be beaten into light and creamy mousses or dips. It can also replace eggs in vegan cakes or quiches.

tempeh

Like tofu, tempeh is an excellent plant-based meat alternative. Made from whole soybeans that are cooked, fermented, and compacted into a block, it provides 34 grams of protein per cup (166g). It has a firm and meaty texture and a nutty flavor. Like extra-firm tofu, it freezes well, so you can stock up.

Unlike tofu, tempeh cannot be eaten raw. You can cook it in different ways to improve its flavor and texture. If you find it bitter, steam it first and then, according to the consistency you are looking for, cut it into strips or cubes, grind it, grate it, or crumble it. You can then bake, grill, or pan-fry it, which gives it a nice crunchy texture. When grilling, I cut tempeh into ¼-inch (6mm)-thick slices, coat them with a spiced herby rub or marinade, and grill them over medium-high heat for five minutes on each side until charred.

Tempeh is also useful as a garnish to replace bacon or smoked ham, like in the Banh Mi with Smoky Tempeh recipe on page 166 or the Sweet Potato Chowder with Tempeh Bacon recipe on page 194.

jackfruit

Young jackfruit is one of the easiest-to-use plant-based meat substitutes. It doesn't taste like meat, nor is it a good source of protein, but it does a good job of mimicking the texture of pulled meats when cooked with savory spices and herbs and topped with condiments.

Originally from Southeast Asia, jackfruit is the largest fruit to grow on trees. Green and prickly on the outside, it has a dense and fleshy texture. Ripe jackfruit is sweet and can be eaten fresh or added to desserts. In contrast, unripe young (or "green") jackfruit has a neutral taste and is better to cook with. Its fibrous flesh has the appearance and texture of braised steak, pulled pork or chicken, or even duck. It is preserved in brine or water and most often sold in cans, though you may find it in other packaging (for example, boxed). It is increasingly available in conventional supermarkets; otherwise, look for it in Asian markets. Be sure not to purchase jackfruit packed in syrup, which is the sweet, ripe version and is not a suitable meat substitute.

Though similar to meat in texture, young jackfruit is not a nutritional match for meat or for protein-rich meat substitutes, such as pulses, tofu, or whole grains. For a balanced meal, make sure to include some plant-based protein.

1. **Sandwiches**—Paired with BBQ sauce, shredded young jackfruit makes a convincing pulled pork or chicken alternative for sandwiches and sliders.

2. **Tacos & carnitas**—Smothered in a flavorful sauce, jackfruit is a match made in heaven for Mexican dishes. It is even more delicious when served with a creamy avocado sauce (see page 302) or guacamole.

3. **Pizza**—Pan-fry some drained and pulled jackfruit with oil and herbs, then use as a pizza topping.

4. **Curry**—Marinate pulled jackfruit in your favorite spice blend before adding it to your favorite curry recipe. It should cook in 20 minutes or so.

5. **Stir-fry**—Stir-fry pulled jackfruit in a wok with some vegetables, then add your favorite stir-fry sauce.

6. **Chili**—Similar to curry, marinate some pulled jackfruit in your favorite spice blend before adding it to your favorite chili and cooking it for 20 minutes or so.

7. **Meatballs & fish balls**—Pulse jackfruit to a chunky paste in a food processor with spices and/or herbs, breadcrumbs, cooked cannellini beans, and a suitable binder to hold the mixture together, such as egg or flax egg. Shape into small balls and fry or bake until browned. If frying, fry the balls in ¼ cup (60ml) of hot vegetable oil in a frying pan over medium-high heat for about eight minutes; if baking, bake in a 400°F (200°C) oven for about 25 minutes. If making faux fish balls, I opt for classic fish seasoning, like Old Bay; for meatballs, Italian seasoning is always a good choice. Try serving the meatballs with marinara sauce, the fish balls with tartar sauce. Also try my Thai Salmon (or No-Salmon) Cakes on page 204.

herbs

I use a lot of fresh and dried herbs in my recipes. Both are nutrient-dense. A sprinkle of fresh herbs, just before serving, livens up any dish. When added while a dish is cooking, herbs provide layers of depth without the need for extra salt, sugar, or fat. And I have found that herbs play an extra-important role in cooking with less meat, adding an abundance of flavor that makes a diminished quantity of animal protein less noticeable.

Here is a list of the herbs I use most often—jump to page 42 to learn more about how to cook with them:

- Basil
- Bay leaves
- Chives
- Cilantro
- Dill
- Lemon thyme
- Mint
- Oregano
- Parsley
- Rosemary
- Sage
- Thai basil
- Thyme

growing your own herbs

You can easily grow your own herbs no matter where you live. You can keep them in small pots on a windowsill, in containers on a patio or terrace, or plant them directly in your garden. Some, like rosemary, sage, thyme, and bay tree, can be grown into shrubs and become an integral part of your garden. For a more elaborate indoor solution, consider investing in a smart garden appliance that provides plants with light, irrigation, and nutrients.

Having a home herb garden means that you will always have a fresh supply and can grow varieties that are not widely available in stores, such as lemon verbena, lemon thyme, chocolate mint, French sorrel, curry plant, borage, and Mexican tarragon.

storing & preserving fresh herbs

Whether you grow your own herbs or buy them from a grocery store, knowing how to keep them at their best or preserve them for longer will save you both time and money.

- **Store at room temperature.** Once cut, some herbs, especially basil, do not keep well in the fridge. I prefer to store tender herbs at room temperature, upright in a jar filled with water, uncovered, so that the stems can stay hydrated. I keep them out of direct sunlight and heat, making sure to refresh the water regularly.

- **Store in the fridge.** How many times have you found a shriveled bunch of herbs in your fridge just days after buying it? Another method to keep herbs fresh for longer is to wrap them loosely in a damp cloth or paper towel and store them in a zip-top bag at the bottom of the fridge. As the towel dries, dampen it a bit more. This method works for most tender and woody herbs.

- **Freeze for later use.** To preserve tender herbs such as basil, cilantro, parsley, chives, or mint, freezing is the best method to use; it tends to preserve more of the original flavor and vibrancy than drying, and for longer. To freeze tender-stem herbs, simply wash and dry the herbs. Discard the thick stems and chop the leaves and slender stems. You can freeze them, as is, in a zip-top bag, small freezer-safe container, or ice cube tray. There is no need to thaw frozen herbs before use. Simply add them to your recipe during or near the end of cooking, and they will defrost in a couple of minutes.

   If you choose to freeze woody herbs, such as rosemary, sage, and thyme, try pouring a little olive oil or melted butter into the cavities of an ice cube tray, then add the leaves. This will create some flavorful little cubes that you can add directly to food while cooking.

- **Dry for later use.** Though any herb can be dried, woody herbs, such as bay leaves, marjoram, oregano, rosemary, sage, tarragon, and thyme, are ideally suited to this preservation method; their flavor is retained and, in some cases, even enhanced. Tender herbs have a higher moisture content and will develop mold if they are not dried quickly enough.

   To dry herbs, tie small bunches together and hang them upside down in a warm, dry, and well-ventilated area, away from direct sunlight. To keep out the dust, you can wrap them loosely with muslin or thin paper bags. To prevent the development of mold, do not use plastic. After seven to fourteen days, the leaves should be crispy dry. Carefully tear the leaves away, storing them in airtight containers and discarding the stems.

cooking with herbs

Culinary herbs are generally split into two types: tender herbs and woody herbs.

Tender herbs have soft, grasslike stems and include basil, chives, cilantro, dill, mint, and parsley. They have a lighter flavor than woody herbs. They are best used fresh, as a garnish or topping, or added at the end of cooking. They are particularly well suited for salads and pestos. In some recipes, the entire herb sprig is used (both the tender stem and the leaves).

Woody herbs have thicker and harder stems and include marjoram, oregano, rosemary, sage, tarragon, and thyme. They have a stronger flavor than tender herbs and are best added during cooking. They are a great choice for stocks, stews, casseroles, and recipes that require roasting, slow cooking, or braising. You can drop a whole sprig directly into the pan and fish out the stem after cooking, which saves you the effort of removing the leaves from the stem. This technique is often used in stews and saucy recipes. Alternatively, you can use only the leaves, removing them first by running your fingers down the stem from top to bottom and then pushing the leaves off. This approach is better for drier dishes such as roasted vegetables, fish, or meat.

substituting dried herbs for fresh

I generally prefer fresh herbs because they are more nutritious and have a more vibrant flavor. However, if they are added during cooking, you can substitute dried herbs. Dried herbs are useful when you do not have fresh herbs on hand, and they are often cheaper than their fresh counterparts. A simple rule is that 1 teaspoon of dried herbs equates to 1 tablespoon of fresh. Note that over time, even dried herbs lose their potency, and this happens even quicker if the herbs are ground. To check if your dried herbs are still good, crumble some of the leaves between your fingers; if they are no longer aromatic, it's time to buy a new jar.

spices

Spices add flavor and aroma. Some, like turmeric and saffron, can make a dish more appealing by adding color as well.

Ground coriander and cumin are fantastic food enhancers. With its rich and smoky flavor reminiscent of BBQ dishes, smoked paprika is my spice of choice to add a deep, savory umami taste to meat-free dishes. You can use sweet spices such as cardamom, cinnamon, cloves, and nutmeg to give food a subtle sweetness, while hot spices, like cayenne pepper, chipotle flakes or powder, and red pepper flakes add a fiery note.

The best way to preserve spices is to keep them in airtight containers, away from heat and light. Ground spices lose their freshness quickly, so unless you use them a lot, it's better to buy smaller quantities. Whole spices last longer and can easily be ground using a small blender, spice grinder, or mortar and pestle.

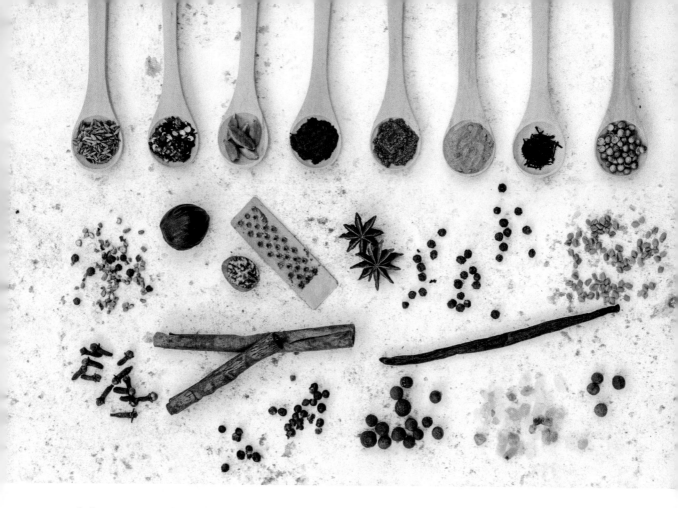

Spices vary greatly in quality and cost. Beware of cheap spices, which generally do not have as much flavor as more expensive ones, resulting in less tasty dishes. Here are some of the spices I keep at hand and use throughout this cookbook, as well as some optional add-ons (which I have marked with an asterisk). Note that for best flavor and freshness, I purchase peppercorns and grind them with my pepper mill whenever ground pepper is called for; if you prefer, you can use pre-ground black pepper in all of the recipes.

- Allspice (ground)
- Caraway (seeds)*
- Cardamom (pods and ground)
- Cayenne pepper (ground)
- Chinese five-spice powder
- Chipotle (flakes)*
- Cinnamon (sticks and ground)
- Cloves (whole and ground)

- Coriander (seeds and ground)
- Crushed red pepper
- Cumin (seeds and ground)
- Curry powder (mild)
- Garam masala
- Ginger powder
- Jerk spice*
- Mustard seeds, yellow

- Nutmeg (whole; for grating)
- Paprika*
- Peppercorns
- Saffron
- Smoked paprika
- Sumac
- Turmeric powder
- Vanilla (pods and extract)

condiments & other flavor boosters

Using quick flavor boosters can often rescue a dish that you find bland or in need of a little more depth or balance. I often use spices (see pages 42 and 43) and, of course, salt as flavor enhancers. I like lemon juice, preserved lemon, vinegar, pickled and fermented vegetables, olives, honey, and aged cheese for injecting a bit of tanginess into recipes, while the fattiness of oil (my favorite being olive oil), avocado, nuts, seeds, eggs, and some dairy is essential to improve texture and convey aromas. Some of these flavor boosters also add umami, which helps deepen the flavor of a dish. When vegetarian or vegan food seems like it is missing something, you can often put it down to a lack of umami.

Here are my favorite condiments and flavor boosters:

- Balsamic glaze
- Capers
- Garlic
- Honey
- Hot sauce*
- Kimchi
- Lemon juice
- Lime juice
- Liquid smoke (hickory)
- Maple syrup

- Marmite*
- Miso, white
- Mustard (Dijon, whole grain)
- Nori (dried seaweed)
- Nutritional yeast
- Olives
- Onions
- Pomegranate molasses
- Preserved lemons

- Roasted red peppers
- Salsa*
- Shallots
- Soy sauce (light/all-purpose, low-sodium)
- Sriracha
- Sun-dried tomatoes
- Sweet chili sauce

- Tahini
- Tamari
- Tamarind paste*
- Tomato paste
- Vegetable stock (any form)
- Vinegars (apple cider, red wine, unseasoned rice, white wine)

tip:
When boiling rice or grains, use vegetable stock instead of water to infuse flavor effortlessly.

oils

I use either olive oil or extra-virgin olive oil in most of the recipes in this book. I reserve the more expensive extra-virgin type for dressings, pestos, salsa, or anything else that is not heated and will benefit from some additional flavor.

In recipes where the flavor of olive oil would not be appropriate, or when an oil with a higher smoke point is needed, I tend to use vegetable oils such as canola oil and sunflower oil. Throughout this book, I use toasted sesame oil to prepare Asian-inspired dishes.

Being the only vegetable oil that is solid at room temperature, coconut oil is invaluable for making raw plant-based desserts. I always use cold-pressed virgin coconut oil.

frozen foods

A well-stocked freezer ensures that you can have a healthy meal on the table even on days when you have limited time to cook. Using the freezer is a great way to economize; not only does frozen produce tend to be cheaper than fresh produce, but you can limit food waste by freezing fresh items that are getting close to their use-by date.

Store-bought frozen vegetables and fruits are harvested and frozen at the peak of freshness to preserve their full nutritional content. Out of season, they make a welcome addition to many savory dishes as well as smoothies and desserts.

If you are looking to stock up on higher-welfare animal products, look for meat subscription services that deliver grass-fed and/or organic meat to your doorstep. If it's not already frozen, you can freeze some of the meat to use later. Conveniently, some suppliers also deliver sustainable fish and seafood as well as organic dairy.

Freezing is also a great tool to preserve homegrown and foraged foods, as well as batch-cooked meals and leftovers. As long as it has not been frozen before, you can freeze pretty much any type of food, even eggs, tofu, cheeses, yogurt, wine, cake, and bread.

According to the FDA (US) and the FSA (UK), food should be stored continuously in freezers at 0°F (–18°C). While freezing allows food to be kept for much longer, frozen food doesn't last forever. As a general rule, most frozen food items will keep for three to six months if packed and stored properly.

Aside from leftovers, here is a list of the frozen foods I regularly keep in my freezer:

- Berries and fruits (for smoothies)
- Edamame
- Green beans
- Green peas
- Herbs (see pages 40 to 42)
- Ice cream and ice pops
- Meat analogues (sausages, ground meat, and burger patties; see page 46)
- Mixed vegetables
- Pastry doughs and wraps
- Spinach
- Tofu (see page 37)

meat & fish analogues

One of the biggest stumbling blocks to adopting a plant-forward diet is the apprehension of missing out on food we enjoy. Over the past few years, an array of meat, fish, and dairy substitutes have appeared on supermarket shelves and on restaurant menus. While fish and cheese have been a bit trickier to replicate, many meat substitutes look and taste like the real thing, and drinking dairy-free milk has become mainstream. The increase in alternative meat products has many advantages, namely having more choices when eating out or, if in a rush to make dinner at home, being able to prepare a quick and easy meal that appeals to everyone.

In a bid to decrease our reliance on animal proteins, plant-based substitutes have gone from strength to strength. A wide range of products that mimic meat and fish in the form of convenience food, such as burgers, sausages, bacon, and nuggets, are available. In addition, exciting developments are paving the way towards a plant-forward future. With more advanced technologies such as 3D printed meat and cultured meat grown in labs by cultivating cells taken from a live animal, there is no doubt that we are on the cusp of major changes in the way our food is produced.

The current plant-based meat analogues receive their share of both good and bad press. On one hand, they are touted as being healthier, as well as more sustainable and ethical than animal products. They are also practical and easy to cook with. On the other hand, almond milk production involves heavy use of pesticides and water, and vegan burgers, deemed healthier because they boast a high protein content and more dietary fiber and less cholesterol than beef, can also contain high levels of salt.

Meat and fish substitutes are typically made of soy, pea, or mushroom proteins processed with other ingredients such as beetroot, coconut oil, wheat, and gluten to replicate the mouthfeel and texture of the real thing. The keyword here, though, is "processed," and in some cases, substitutes can be described as ultra-processed foods, which I generally avoid eating too much of. Simply because a dish is vegan does not make it healthy. Processed food, whether it's plant-based or not, should be eaten in moderation. I strongly believe that an unprocessed diet, cooked from scratch with fresh ingredients, is best. So, I eat meat or fish analogues every now and then, but on a day-to-day basis, my proteins of choice are tofu, tempeh, beans, pulses, quinoa, nuts, and seeds eaten as part of a balanced diet.

That said, I would much rather eat a "fake" burger, sausage, or nugget than the real thing because I believe that, overall, doing so is more sustainable and ethical. Also, when it comes to the amount of processing, I see little difference between a meat and a meat-free sausage.

Here is a list of the meat, fish, and dairy analogues that I turn to most often:

- Beyond Meat burgers, meatballs, and sausages
- Quorn chicken fillets and nuggets, fishless fillets, steak & gravy pies, and meatless grounds
- Cauldron sausages
- Nurishh cheese alternatives
- Naturli' butter, yogurts, and ice creams

dairy-free milks & creams

Dairy-free milk can easily substitute for conventional dairy milk. And the good news is, dairy-free milk has a lower environmental impact than dairy milk. However, depending on where you live, different types of milk (both dairy and dairy-free) must travel varying distances, and some types may be more sustainable than others. For example, almond milk requires more water than any other dairy alternative.

Whether you're in the US, the UK, or elsewhere, there are now a lot of choices to suit both individual tastes and intended uses. The dairy-free milks that I most enjoy drinking and cooking with are almond milk, coconut milk (both in cans for cooking and in cartons for drinking and pouring over cereal), oat milk, and soy milk. Except for coconut milk, which has a distinctive flavor, I use oat and soy interchangeably, reserving almond milk for sweet recipes. (Note that for savory cooking, unsweetened and unflavored milks are best to use, so make sure to double-check the ingredients; otherwise, you could end up with a strange-tasting dish.)

When buying dairy-free milk, my favorite UK brand is Alpro, but I often make dairy-free milk (and cream) at home. To make homemade dairy-free almond milk, see my recipe on page 330. To make homemade oat milk, you can find dozens of recipes online.

Likewise, dairy-free cream can be used in place of conventional cream. To make homemade cashew cream, see my recipe on page 323. The consistency can be adjusted to your needs from heavy cream to half-and-half simply by thinning the base recipe with water. (*Note:* If you'd like to make cashew milk instead of cream, follow the instructions for making homemade nut milk on page 330, using raw cashews.)

The type of store-bought dairy-free cream that I use in the UK is soy-based and is called "soya cream" (my favorite brand is Alpro). This cream is less commonly available in the US. As a substitute, I suggest using the dairy-free heavy whipping cream alternative from the brand Silk.

equipment essentials

Here is an overview of the kitchen equipment that I use most often in my own kitchen, and that you'll need to make the recipes in this book.

kitchen tools

- **Box grater**—the coarse shredding side is ideal for shredding cheese and vegetables, while the finer grating/zesting side is perfect for garlic, ginger, nutmeg, and citrus zest.

- **Cheesecloth**—to make nut milk or labneh.

- **Chef's knife (8 inches/20cm) and paring knife (3 to 4 inches/8 to 10cm)**—I also have a sharpening steel so I can keep my knives razor sharp at home.

- **Citrus juicer**—this tool makes juicing citrus so much easier. I use a lot of lemon and lime juice in my recipes, so this is an often-used tool.

- **Colander**—for rinsing and straining foods.

- **Cooling rack**—for cooling baked goods.

- **Cutting boards**—I use wooden cutting boards for most things; for meat, poultry, and fish, I use plastic boards because they can be sanitized in the dishwasher.

- **Digital scale**—weighing ingredients is more precise for baking.

- **Fine-mesh sieve**—to rinse or strain anything that would pass through the larger holes of a regular colander.

- **Julienne peeler**—ideal for cutting thin strips of vegetables. Can also double as a spiral slicer.

- **Kitchen scissors**—helpful for cutting parchment paper and cheese cloth but also for snipping and chopping fresh herbs, trimming dough, cutting small pieces of meat, or slicing pizza.

- **Mandoline**—the best tool for perfectly cut thin slices of fruits and vegetables.

- **Measuring cups and spoons**—both liquid and dry.

- **Meat mallet**—use this tool to pound and tenderize meat (see page 54). In a pinch, you can use a rolling pin or small cast-iron skillet.

- **Metal spatula (aka pancake turner)**—for flipping and removing food from pans, and for tossing when sautéing or making stir-fries. A fish spatula is handy to have as is a slotted spatula.

- **Microplane zester**—for grating citrus zest as well as garlic, ginger, nutmeg, hard cheeses, and chocolate. Not a required tool, as you can use the fine grating/zesting side of a box grater for the same purpose.

- **Mixing bowls**—a set of glass or ceramic bowls in various sizes.

- **Mortar and pestle**—the traditional tool for pounding spices and fresh herbs. You can use a spice grinder or food processor instead.

- **Parchment paper**—for lining pans to prevent sticking and make cleanup easier.

- **Pastry brush**—for brushing egg wash, glaze, melted butter, or oil on pretty much anything.

- **Rolling pin**—for rolling out flatbreads and pie crusts.

- **Silicone spatula**—to scrape food out of mixing bowls, saucepans, and the food processor and fold ingredients into batter.

- **Spiral slicer**—use this tool to make my Zucchini Noodle Salad with Baked Feta on page 162. It is not required (you can use a julienne peeler instead) but is useful if you are trying to cut down on carbs and make vegetable noodles on a regular basis.

- **Tofu press**—compact and easy to use, it easily fits in the fridge so you can press tofu ahead of time. Again, this is not a required tool, but I use mine often and find it more convenient and secure than a makeshift setup of plates and weights.

- **Vegetable peeler**—for peeling potatoes, carrots, and other produce.

- **Whisk**—essential for making sauces and whipped creams.

- **Wooden spoons and spatulas**—of various sizes.

pots, pans & baking dishes

- **Cast-iron braiser**—I love this super practical and flexible piece of cookware that can go from the stovetop to the oven and the table. Mine has a 3.5-quart (3.5L) capacity and measures 12 inches (30cm) in diameter. I use it for any dish that requires cooking both on the stovetop and in the oven, such as fish pie, shepherd's pie, and my Golden Rice & Cabbage on page 252. Though taller than a braiser, a Dutch oven can be used as a workable substitute.

- **Dutch oven**—I have two enameled cast-iron Dutch ovens that I use almost daily, one 9-inch (24cm) round and one 11-inch (29cm) oval. Many of the recipes in this book were made in the round one. Long-lasting and easy to clean, they are, in my opinion, some of the best pots around as they cook food evenly and can be used on the stovetop—whether induction, electric, or gas—and in the oven to braise, roast, and bake. To my mind, they are also safer to use than other cookware made with nonstick coatings. I use them to make stews, casseroles, soups, and even bread. I'm partial to the Le Creuset brand, but there are other enameled Dutch ovens on the market at various price points.

- **Frying pans**—I use both cast-iron and nonstick frying pans. I like the versatility of cast iron, which can be used both on the stovetop and in the oven. I use an 11-inch (29cm) diameter cast-iron frying pan to fry vegetables, meat, and tofu; a 10-inch (26cm) diameter cast-iron skillet is perfect to make my Spring Soccas with Minty Pea Pesto & Watercress recipe on page 178.

I use a large 12-inch (30cm) diameter nonstick frying pan to fry vegetables, meat, fish, eggs, tofu, and so on. I also have a smaller 8-inch (20cm) nonstick pan for cooking smaller quantities as well as toasting seeds and nuts. Make sure to look for PFOA-free nonstick coatings.

When a nonstick frying pan is required, as in my Quick Flatbreads recipe on page 170, the recipe instructions will specify this type of pan; when nonstick isn't specified, feel free to use another type of pan, such as stainless steel.

- **Loaf pans**—the one I use most often is a 2-pound (900g), 8½ by 4½ by 2¾-inch (21 by 11.5 by 7cm) loaf pan. I also have a couple of 1-pound (450g), 7¼ by 3½ by 2¾-inch (18.5 by 9 by 6.5cm) loaf pans to make smaller loaves of bread and cakes.

- **Muffin tin**—I use a standard-size 12-well muffin tin for most muffin recipes, including the Healthier Carrot Muffins on page 98.

- **Rimmed baking sheets (aka sheet pans)**—for baking and roasting. I have two 15 by 10 by 1-inch (38 by 25 by 2.5cm) rimmed baking sheets.

- **Saucepans with lids**—three in various sizes ranging from small to large, ideally 2 to 4 cups (475ml to 1L), 2 quarts (2 liters), and 4 quarts (4 liters).

- **Square baking dishes**—mine are 8 inches (20cm) and 9 inches (23cm), and I use them interchangeably for recipes such as my Blueberry & Peach Baked Oatmeal on page 94.

- **Stockpot with a heavy bottom**—for soups, stock, and batch-cooking. I have a 6-quart (6-liter) stockpot.

- **Tart pans**—to make my Quinoa Crust Quiches on page 129, you will need two tart pans with removeable bases, either 14 by 4½ by 1-inch (35 by 10 by 2.5cm) or 9-inch (23cm). I also own a larger 12 by 8.5 by 1-inch (31.5 by 22 by 3cm) removeable-base rectangular tart pan that is invaluable for tarts and quiches.

- **Wok**—ideal for stir-fries. Mine is 12 inches (30cm) in diameter. If you don't have one, you can use a large frying pan instead.

small appliances

- **Blender**—for smoothies, batters, and ultra-smooth soups and sauces. For kitchen projects that require extra-powerful extracting or blending, such as making nut milk or nut butter, you will need a high-powered blender or a food processor.

- **Electric mixer**—my indispensable Kitchen Aid stand mixer has been sitting on my kitchen countertop for over twenty years. I use it to knead dough, mix dough, whisk eggs or aquafaba, and whip cream. A handheld electric mixer is a more affordable choice that is perfect for smaller jobs like whizzing egg whites and aquafaba and mixing cake batters.

- **Food processor**—for most of the recipes in this book, a standard-size food processor—between 9 and 12 cups (2.1 and 2.8L)—will do the job. For smaller jobs, a mini food processor with a 3- to 4-cup (710 to 950ml) capacity works better. The smaller bowl of a mini processor is ultra-convenient for making nut butters, dips, and pastes, while a standard-size processor is great for shredding, blending, chopping, and grating bigger quantities of food. There are food processors that come with more than one size of work bowl; for example, my 13-cup (3.1L) food processor comes with a smaller 4-cup (950ml) bowl.

- **Immersion blender**—my preferred tool for blending hot soups (so much safer than a regular blender!). Some models come with extra attachments and double as a whisk, chopper, masher, etc. If you do not have an immersion blender, you can use a countertop blender, working in batches if needed for safety (and with the lid on very securely!).

kitchen guides

Whether you're just starting down the path of a plant-forward lifestyle or you have been at it for some time, the guides in this section will help to ensure your continued success. These guides cover a range of helpful subjects, from reducing the amounts of foods such as meat and dairy in your diet to increasing your consumption of plant foods, such as tofu and pulses. I use a lot of herbs in my cooking, so I have also included a section explaining how to cook with them.

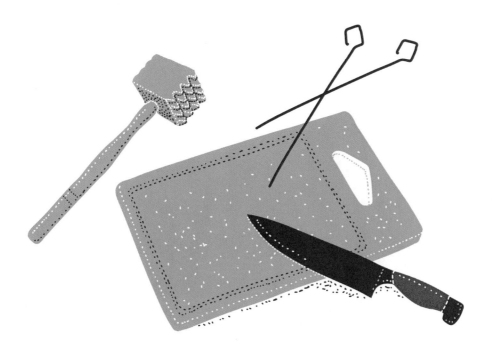

cooking with less meat

This section features simple techniques for cooking with less meat without compromising on taste. Mastering these methods will benefit not only your waistline but also the planet and your wallet while still infusing your meals with meaty flavor.

butterflying and cutting into cutlets

Cutting into cutlets and butterflying are easy techniques used to reduce the thickness of a piece of meat (or fish). They require a very sharp knife, a cutting board, and a steady hand.

For the purpose of reducing meat consumption, slicing in half horizontally works well with thick-cut boneless steaks and poultry breasts. Once halved, forming two cutlets, the thinner pieces of meat spread out over the same area and can easily be split between two people without anyone noticing a significant difference.

Traditionally, the butterflying technique is used when meat is to be stuffed; in that case, the meat is not cut all the way through into two thinner halves but remains connected along one side, allowing it to be opened like a book, or a butterfly—thus the name.

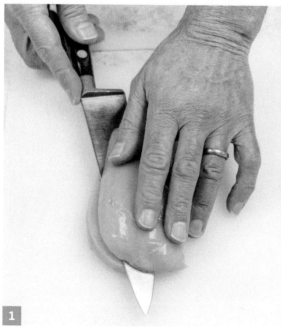

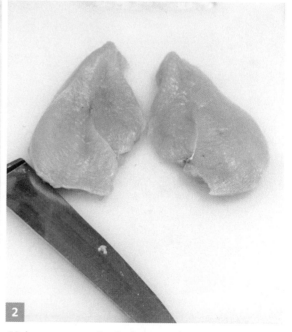

1 Lay the meat flat on a cutting board. Using a very sharp chef's knife positioned parallel to the cutting board, slice the meat in half horizontally. Place your other hand on top of the meat to keep it from moving, with your fingers pointing outward to avoid cutting them.

2 Make sure to cut both pieces to the same thickness so that they cook evenly. If using a cut of meat that is naturally uneven, such as chicken breast, you may wish to use the pounding technique (see page 54) to even out the thickness.

pounding

Pounding, also called tenderizing, is a quick way to break up the connective tissue of a piece of meat to make it more tender. It helps thicker pieces to cook faster and more evenly. This technique works with any kind of meat and is especially great for cheaper cuts that tend to be tougher. Like cutting meat into cutlets and butterflying, pounding makes the meat thinner and bigger (in surface area), giving the illusion that more is there. It can also be used to even out the thickness of uneven cuts, such as chicken breasts, to ensure even cooking. Once cooked, a pounded piece of meat can be shared between two or more people.

Depending on the type of meat and the dish you are preparing, pounding can sometimes be combined with cutting horizontally, butterflying, or slicing (see page 56) for best results.

Pounding requires a heavy food-safe plastic bag or a sturdy piece of plastic wrap (plastic is best to avoid bacterial cross-contamination) and a meat mallet. If you do not have a mallet, you can use a rolling pin or a small cast-iron skillet.

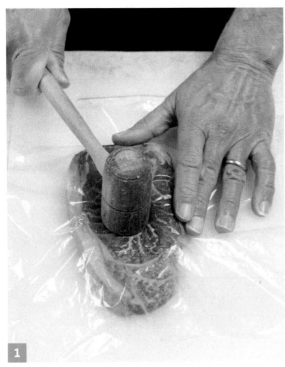

1 Place the meat on a cutting board. Cover it with heavy plastic wrap or place it inside a heavy food-safe plastic bag.

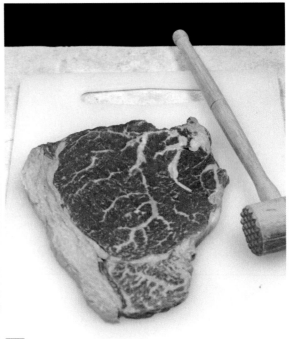

2 Pound the meat gently to your desired even thickness. Depending on the recipe you are making, this can vary from ¼ inch (6mm) to 1½ inches (3.75cm) or more.

shredding

Shredding pork, beef, or poultry not only improves the texture (by breaking through meat tissues) and flavor (by creating more surface area for seasonings and sauces to cling to) but also helps give the impression that there is more meat in the dish. This technique works wonders with leftover meat, immediately retrofitting it for use in sandwiches, soups, stews, salads, stir-fries, pasta dishes, tacos, pizzas, and more.

Shredding meat is easy to do: you use two forks to pull the meat apart and break it into smaller pieces. (This simple technique also works really well for jackfruit, a plant-based meat substitute; refer to pages 38 and 39.) If you're looking for a speedier method, you can use a potato masher or a stand mixer fitted with the paddle attachment on low speed. A stand mixer is a great option when you have a bigger quantity of meat to shred because it works quickly and is even hands-free! But to end up with an even consistency, you need to cut the larger pieces of meat into manageable chunks (no larger than 3 inches/8cm) and work in small batches; otherwise, the chunks of the meat at the bottom of the bowl will end up overworked and puréed while the ones near the top will be too chunky.

1 Using two forks, pull the cooked meat apart and break it into smaller pieces.

2 Cut the cooked meat into smaller chunks and place a small batch in a stand mixer fitted with the paddle attachment. Working on low speed, shred the pieces to your desired size.

slicing

Cutting meat into smaller pieces or strips, either before or after cooking, is another clever trick for using less. If you are working with raw meat, pounding it first will ensure an even thickness.

Stir-frying sliced chicken, pork, or beef stretches a small amount a long way, while a cooked whole chicken breast, loin, or steak can be sliced into strips before serving and divided among several people.

Like shredding, slicing is an ideal way to stretch leftovers. I like to use a few strips of meat to garnish a salad, bowl of soup, or serving of pasta or rice. When you think of meat as a garnish rather than the focal point of a dish and bulk up your plate with vegetables, grains, and/or pulses, plants effortlessly take center stage. See the Roasted Vegetable & Meat Platter with Chimichurri Sauce recipe on page 213 for a perfect example of this practice.

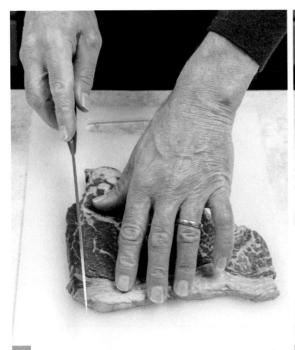

1

Lay the piece of raw or cooked meat (or fish) on a cutting board.

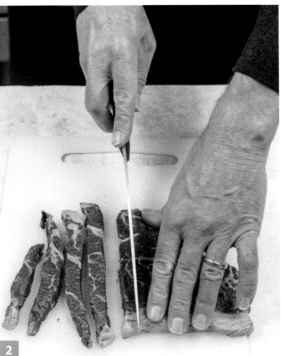

2

Using a sharp knife, cut the meat into strips. If slicing red meat, be sure to slice it against the grain.

bulking

This approach works well with recipes that call for ground meat. The idea is to replace half the quantity of meat with an equal amount of a plant-based filler—such as pulses, grains, and/or vegetables. Doing so not only boosts the fiber content but also reduces the cost of the dish.

Quinoa, barley, and millet work well in chili, meatloaf, shepherd's pie, and casseroles. Finely chopped mushrooms, eggplant, and butternut squash and shredded vegetables such as carrot, sweet potato, and zucchini are ideal complements for chili, spaghetti sauce, lasagna, and casseroles. Pulses are so versatile that they can be used to bulk up almost any recipe that calls for ground meat. Some, like red lentils, are perfect for all kinds of savory dishes because they break down during cooking and go unnoticed.

In my Less-Meat Lasagna recipe on page 220, you replace half of the meat in the Bolognese sauce with lentils and mushrooms.

skewering

Skewers of grilled meat, an archetype of summer barbecues, make impressive starters or mains. Alternating pieces of grilled meat with a variety of vegetables stretches the meat while creating a pretty and colorful presentation. Skewers work well with tender cuts of beef, pork, and lamb as well as chicken, turkey, scallops, shrimp, or chunky/firm fish cuts, such as tuna steak. For best results, you will need to marinate the meat, fish, or seafood beforehand.

Bulk up the skewers with onions, bell peppers, cherry or grape tomatoes, mushrooms, zucchini, or small precooked potatoes, adding just a couple of pieces of meat, fish, or seafood per skewer.

Brighten up a meat or fish skewer with colorful vegetables while making your meat go further. Try my Greek Kebabs on page 210.

making use of leftover meat

Given the environmental impact of meat production, it is obscene to waste meat, especially if you take into account the plight of factory farmed animals. The following are some simple methods to make use of leftover poultry or red meat.

USING LEFTOVER CHICKEN/TURKEY

CHOP OR SHRED AND SERVE AS A:

- Pizza topping
- Salad topping
- Sandwich filling (with mayo and corn)
- Savory pie filling (see my Easy Turkey Pot Pie on page 202)
- Soup topping (see my Gnocchi Soup on page 186)

IT CAN ALSO BE USED TO BULK UP DISHES SUCH AS:

- Chili
- Curry
- Pasta
- Risotto
- Tacos, fajitas, and enchiladas (see my Turkey Enchilada Skillet recipe on page 240)

USING LEFTOVER BEEF/LAMB/PORK

SLICE AND SERVE AS A:

- Salad topping
- Sandwich filling
- Savory pie filling
- Soup topping

IT CAN ALSO BE USED TO BULK UP DISHES SUCH AS:

- Bolognese sauce
- Chili
- Curry
- Pasta
- Risotto
- Shepherd's pie
- Tacos, fajitas, and enchiladas (use beef instead of turkey in the Turkey Enchilada Skillet)

Don't discard the carcasses and bones either, which are filled with flavor and goodness and are perfect for infusing stock or soup with a meaty taste. Here are a few options:

- **Easy Chicken Stock**—Place the carcass in a pot with celery, onions, carrots, and herbs. If available, adding the neck and feet will give the stock extra richness. Cover everything with water and simmer for two to three hours (or overnight in a slow cooker), periodically skimming off any foam that rises to the top. Strain the stock to catch any small bones that might have detached from the carcass before using to flavor soups, cook grains or pasta, and make gravies and sauces.

- **Chicken Carcass Soup**—Don't have time to make stock first? Make chicken carcass soup instead. Cook the carcass in a pot of water for one hour. Remove the carcass and strain the stock to catch any small bones. Return the stock to the pot, add seasonings and vegetables such as tomatoes, potatoes, carrots, onions, celery, and cabbage, and simmer until the vegetables are tender. A whole grain or rice makes a nice hearty addition.

- **Easy Beef or Pork Stock**—Place leftover bones from a beef or pork roast in a pot with celery, onions, carrots, and herbs. Cover everything with water and simmer for two to three hours (or overnight in a slow cooker), periodically skimming off any foam that rises to the top. Strain the stock before using it to flavor soups, cook grains or pasta, and make gravies and sauces.

cooking with less dairy

If you are looking to reduce the amount of dairy in your diet, there are plenty of excellent choices out there. In fact, in many recipes, you can simply replace dairy milk, cream, or cheese with store-bought dairy-free alternatives. There are a few things to watch out for, like added sugars, fillers, and stabilizers. Also take note of the protein and nutritional content; some products are fortified with calcium and vitamins D and B12.

For more wholesome alternatives, make your own. Dairy-free milk, butter, cream, and ice cream are all easy enough to prepare at home and give you the chance to experiment with flavors and textures.

Nuts make delicious and nutritious dairy substitutes when turned into milk, cream, or cheese. While I have not ventured into making my own cheeses yet (aside from the "cream cheese" on page 326 and the labneh on page 131), you can make simple plant-based cheeses such as faux ricotta, chèvre, and feta at home from either nuts or curdled dairy-free milk.

The process of making dairy-free milk or cream from nuts is simple, the sole difference being that milk is strained and cream is not. I always have a batch of cashew cream (see page 323) on hand to add to recipes. While nut milk is widely available in grocery stores, making your own unleashes a world of nut choices and goodness. Best of all, homemade nut milk is easy to make and can be customized in a wide variety of ways. See page 330 for a simple method for making plain and flavored nut milks.

Here are a handful of my favorite dairy-replacement tips.

DAIRY REPLACEMENT	USE IN PLACE OF	*how to use it*
 NUTRITIONAL YEAST	CHEESY TOPPING	Commonly sold in granules or flakes, nutritional yeast is a great source of vitamins, minerals, and amino acids and a fantastic flavor booster that lends a tasty cheesy and nutty note to plant-based dishes. You can add it towards the end of cooking or as a garnish (like grated Parmesan cheese). It is best used to enhance sauces, rice, grains, pasta, soups, scrambled tofu, popcorn, and the like. Keep in mind that nutritional yeast dissolves into liquids and juices rather than melts.
 WHITE BEANS	CREAM	Cooked and drained white beans make a soup or sauce extra-creamy without the need for dairy. Simply add them whole towards the end of cooking and blend them with the rest of the ingredients to your desired consistency.

| **NUTS**  **CREAM** | As with white beans, nuts can be blended into soups and sauces to make them extra-smooth and silky. There is no need to soak them first; simply add them at the same time as the stock or water and leave them to soften while cooking with the rest of the ingredients. My favorite nuts for this purpose are almonds (raw with skins on or blanched) and cashews. |

NUTS **SOFT CHEESE**

Soaked overnight, raw nuts can be blended to a soft cheese consistency, as in my "cream cheese" recipe on page 326. Cashews work best for this purpose.

HOMEMADE PLANT-BASED BUTTERMILK ⟳ **BUTTERMILK**

Replace 1 cup (240ml) buttermilk in baked goods with 1 tablespoon lemon juice or apple cider vinegar whisked into 1 cup (240ml) dairy-free milk and let sit for 10 minutes before using.

HOMEMADE PLANT-BASED CREAM ⟳ **CREAM**

Thinned to your desired consistency, plant-based cream is a great substitute for heavy cream or half-and-half in soups and sauces. See my recipe for homemade cashew cream on page 323.

COCONUT MILK ⟳ **WHIPPED CREAM**

Place a 15-ounce (400ml) can of full-fat coconut milk in the fridge overnight. Scoop out the hardened coconut cream (reserving the coconut water for later use in a smoothie). Whip the cream with an electric mixer until light peaks form. You can add sugar and vanilla extract if desired. (*Note:* The fat content of coconut milk varies greatly from brand to brand, so make sure to use the best-quality full-fat coconut milk you can find.)

COCONUT MILK ⟳ **ICE CREAM**

Canned coconut milk makes a tasty dairy-free ice cream. You can use full-fat or light coconut milk in place of heavy cream.

SILKEN TOFU ⟳ **CREAM**

Whizz silken tofu in a blender, adding some dairy-free milk to achieve your desired consistency. You can then add it to soups, sauces, and desserts to replace dairy cream. (*Note:* Silken tofu does not whip well and is not a good alternative to whipped cream.)

cooking with less eggs

In addition to providing nutritional value, eggs are widely used in cooking and baking to act as an emulsifier, binder, leavening agent, or thickener. They also add structure and moisture as well as flavor and color.

The good news is that if you are trying to reduce the amount of eggs in your cooking, there are plenty of worthy alternatives. You can of course find packaged egg substitutes in grocery stores, but you can make plenty of egg replacements at home using everyday ingredients.

Before choosing an egg replacement, it's best to work out the primary function of the egg(s) you will be replacing. For example, in some recipes, eggs serve primarily as a binder; for those recipes, you need a moist, thick replacement, such as applesauce or mashed banana or nut butter for a sweet recipe or silken tofu for a savory one. A flax or chia egg is neutral and works for both sweet and savory recipes. If the primary role of the egg is leavening, you need to include baking powder and/or baking soda and an acidic ingredient, which is required for the baking soda to act. Also, for best results, make sure that the egg replacement you choose will not overpower the other ingredients and give a flavor that's not wanted. For example, if the taste of nuts doesn't complement what you're making, nut butter would not be a fitting egg substitute.

See the table, opposite, for several easy egg replacements.

EGG REPLACEMENT	MAIN FUNCTION	REPLACE 1 EGG WITH	BEST USED FOR
AGAR AGAR	Binder, thickener	1 tablespoon agar agar + 1 tablespoon water	Cookies, cupcakes, cakes, brownies
GELATIN	Binder, thickener	1 tablespoon unflavored gelatin + 1 tablespoon water	Cookies, cupcakes, cakes, brownies
APPLESAUCE (unsweetened)	Moisture, binder	¼ cup (60ml)	Cookies, cupcakes, cakes, muffins, pancakes, quick breads*
BAKING POWDER	Leavener	2 teaspoons baking powder + 2 tablespoons water + 1 teaspoon vegetable oil	Cookies, cupcakes, cakes, muffins, pancakes, quick breads
BAKING SODA	Leavener	1 teaspoon baking soda + 1 tablespoon white vinegar	Cookies, cupcakes, cakes, muffins, pancakes, quick breads
CARBONATED WATER	Moisture, leavener	¼ cup (60ml)	Cookies, cupcakes, cakes, pancakes, quick breads
CHICKPEA BRINE (aka aquafaba)	To replace whipped egg whites but also binder, thickener, leavener	3 tablespoons	Meringues, cookies, cakes, pancakes
CHICKPEA FLOUR (aka gram flour)	Binder, thickener	2 tablespoons	Baked goods, savory pancakes, burgers, fritters, custards, sauces
FLOURS (arrowroot, tapioca, corn, etc.)	Binder, thickener	2 tablespoons flour + 3 tablespoons water	Baked goods, burgers, fritters, creams, sauces
FLAX SEEDS	Binder	1 tablespoon ground flax seeds whisked in 3 tablespoons water and left to gel for 10 minutes	Cookies, cakes, pancakes, muffins, quick breads
CHIA SEEDS	Binder	1 tablespoon ground chia seeds whisked in 3 tablespoons water and left to gel for 10 minutes	Cookies, cakes, pancakes, muffins, quick breads
MASHED BANANA	Moisture, binder	¼ cup (60g)	Cookies, cakes, pancakes**
NUT BUTTER	Binder	3 tablespoons (60g)	Cookies***
SILKEN TOFU	Texture, binder	¼ cup (60g)	Quiches, custards
EXTRA-FIRM TOFU	Texture	2 ounces (60g)	Scrambles
VEGETABLE PUREE (carrot, pumpkin, butternut squash, sweet potato)	Binder, moisture	¼ cup (60g)	Cakes, pancakes, breads
XANTHAN GUM	Binder, thickener	¼ teaspoon xanthan gum whisked in ¼ cup (60ml) water	Cakes, muffins, ice creams, savory dishes
YOGURT OR BUTTERMILK	Moisture	¼ cup (60ml)	Cakes, quick breads, muffins, biscuits

*You may wish to reduce the quantity of sweetener because applesauce is naturally sweet.

**The taste of banana will dominate the baked good.

***The taste of nut butter will dominate the cookies.

cooking pulses

While canned pulses are practical because they are precooked and can be used straight out of the tin, dry pulses are often cheaper and are available in a wider variety. They taste better too! However, they require more time to prepare. Many types of pulses benefit from presoaking overnight to reduce the cooking time and make them cook more evenly.

To save time and effort, you can cook a large batch of dry pulses and then season with salt before storing in the fridge to use throughout the week. Cooked pulses can also be stored in the freezer for up to six months. For ease, you can store them in portion-sized zip-top bags.

When working out how much to prepare, keep in mind that dry pulses expand when cooked. The typical ratio is 1:3 dried to cooked.

Some pulses, like split peas and red lentils, can be added unsoaked and uncooked to soups, stews, dahls, sauces, and so on. They cook quickly and become creamy by absorbing the liquid around them. Compensate for the absorption of liquid by adding an extra 1½ cups (350ml) of liquid for every 1 cup (about 200g) of dry lentils or split peas.

For convenience, nearly all the recipes in this book (aside from the falafel on page 156 and the primavera on page 256) call for canned pulses. If you are cooking pulses from scratch, simply swap one 15.5-ounce (440g) can of cooked pulses or lentils with 1½ cups (260g) of home-cooked beans or 1½ cups (240g) of home-cooked lentils.

DRY PULSE	SOAKING TIME	COOKING TIME
ADZUKI BEANS	Overnight	45 minutes to 1 hour
BLACK BEANS	Overnight	45 minutes to 1 hour
BLACK-EYED PEAS/BEANS	Overnight	45 minutes to 1 hour
BUTTER BEANS	Overnight	1½ to 2 hours
CANNELLINI BEANS	Overnight	1 to 1½ hours
CHICKPEAS/GARBANZO BEANS	Overnight	1 to 1½ hours
GREAT NORTHERN BEANS	Overnight	1 to 2 hours
KIDNEY BEANS	Overnight	1½ to 2 hours
LENTILS (green and brown)	No need to soak	20 to 30 minutes
LIMA BEANS	Overnight	1½ to 2 hours
MUNG BEANS	No need to soak	25 to 35 minutes
NAVY BEANS	Overnight	45 minutes to 1 hour
PINTO BEANS	Overnight	1½ to 2 hours
SPLIT PEAS (green and yellow)	No need to soak	15 to 20 minutes

Note: Cooking times may vary from one brand to the next. Check the package instructions.

1

Place the pulses in a sieve. Check for and remove any grit, dirt, little stones, and broken pieces, then rinse under cold water.

2

Place the rinsed pulses in a large container, cover with plenty of water, and soak overnight. If you live in a very warm climate, place the container in the refrigerator to soak.

3

Discard the soaking water and rinse the pulses under cold water.

4

Place in a large saucepan and cover with at least 2 inches (5cm) of water. Simmer over medium heat, covered, until just tender, using the cooking time listed on the package or, if not available, in the table opposite. Check the water level periodically and top up with more water if needed to keep the pulses submerged. Drain when done. (Alternatively, you can use a pressure cooker to reduce the cooking time.)

cooking quinoa

If you are unsure of how to make perfect fluffy quinoa worthy of being enjoyed as a stand-alone side dish, the following method will set you straight. To make fluffy quinoa, my preferred ratio is two parts water to one part dry quinoa. Don't skip the rinsing step, which helps remove any bitterness caused by saponins, a naturally occurring soapy substance that protects the quinoa seeds. Please note that in the recipe chapters in this book, where quinoa is incorporated directly into various dishes rather than served as a side dish, the cooking time and method of preparing the grain varies, according to the needs of each recipe.

1. Place the quinoa in a fine-mesh sieve and rinse under cold running water. Drain well.

2. Place the rinsed quinoa in a saucepan and add twice the amount of water.

3. Bring to a boil over medium-high heat. Reduce to a gentle simmer and cook, uncovered, until the quinoa is tender and all the water has been absorbed, ten to fifteen minutes.

4. Remove the pan from the heat and cover with a lid. Leave the quinoa to rest for five minutes, then fluff the grains with a fork.

5. Depending on the recipe you are following, season the quinoa as needed.

6. Any leftover cooked quinoa will keep in an airtight container in the refrigerator for up to five days.

note:

1 cup (190g) of dry quinoa yields about 3 cups (540g) of cooked quinoa, which serves three to four people.

cooking jackfruit

Canned young jackfruit is cut into small chunks and preserved in brine. To get the best texture, you will need to extract as much water as possible from the jackfruit before cooking it. To do so, drain the jackfruit and then transfer it to a clean kitchen towel and squeeze to extract as much water as possible. Don't worry if the jackfruit chunks start breaking up; they will pull apart during cooking anyway.

Simply heat up the jackfruit in your favorite sauce and simmer for 15 to 20 minutes. The jackfruit will soften as it cooks, and all you have to do is pull the flesh apart with two forks. Alternatively, you can pull apart the jackfruit first, mix it with spices, and bake it uncovered in a 400°F (200°C) oven for about 30 minutes. Once done, stir in your favorite sauce and serve.

preparing & cooking tofu

Tofu contains a fair amount of liquid that needs to be extracted in order to improve its texture, flavor, and consistency. If you have ever had a bland, overly moist tofu dish, the tofu likely was not pressed before being cooked. There are two main methods to prepare tofu: pressing and freezing. Both work best with the firm and extra-firm varieties.

Pressing is the more common method. My first tofu pressing experience involved a plate, a chopping board, and a kettle filled with water—a precarious game of Jenga that of course ended up in disaster when it all came crashing down. I have since invested into a tofu press (see page 68), which has made the process much less precarious.

Freezing is another method for extracting water from tofu. It gives the tofu a hearty texture and makes it more absorbent so that it can soak up the flavors of the other ingredients it is being cooked with. This works really well when pan-frying sliced tofu, as in my Spiced Herb Chicken or Tofu recipe on page 234.

Tofu can be frozen precut or whole. It's better to slice or dice it first since frozen tofu can crumble when sliced. If you decide to freeze it whole, simply place the slab in the freezer in its original packaging, where it will keep for up to three months. There is no need to drain it first.

To preserve its creaminess and silky texture, silken tofu is best used as is. If you are short on time, store-bought marinated or flavored tofu will liven up a dish instantly.

pressing

Remove the tofu from the package and drain the excess water. Place the block in a tofu press or on a plate.

Push down on the handles of the tofu press to apply even pressure to the tofu slab. Or, if using a plate, place a second plate on top of the tofu, then place something weighty on top of the plate to put continuous pressure on the tofu and extract the water. A saucepan or bowl with two unopened cans of beans in it should suffice.

Press for 20 minutes to 1 hour. (*Note:* Most of the water will have been expressed after 20 minutes, although you can press the tofu for longer if desired. Typically, the longer you press it, the drier and firmer it will be.)

When you're ready to marinate or cook the tofu, simply remove it from the press or plate and pour off the water. Cut the tofu to size and use straightaway.

freezing

Remove the tofu from the package and drain the excess water. Cut the tofu to size, bag, and freeze overnight. (Tofu can also be frozen whole but will take longer to thaw and may crumble when sliced.)

Defrost the next day by placing in the refrigerator.

Drain the excess water and use the tofu straightaway.

chapter 3:

how to take it a step further

After embarking on your plant-forward journey, you might be looking for additional ways to eat and live more sustainably. There is no doubt that reducing animal products in your diet is one of the best ways to reduce your environmental impact, but there are other things you can do.

As a family, we have adjusted our way of living over the years, trying to strike the right balance between our environmental ethos and the practicalities of modern life. Our view has always been that if we are going to eat animal products, then we should ensure that those animals have been raised according to the best possible welfare standards. We also strive to reduce the amount of food waste we generate by planning our food shopping better and composting. Our rescue hens lend a helping hand by feasting on our food scraps and giving us beautiful eggs in return. While we live on the outskirts of one of the biggest cities in the world, we are lucky to have a community farm right on our doorstep supplying local and seasonal produce free from unnecessary plastic packaging.

This chapter highlights some of the tips we find useful on a daily basis.

eating less meat, but better meat

Since I began my flexitarian journey, I have embraced a "less and better" approach to eating animal products. When it comes to meat, seafood, eggs, and dairy, making higher-welfare food choices is essential. Rearing animals outdoors with plenty of space to roam while eating their natural diets not only promotes their quality of life but also provides tastier, healthier food while benefiting the environment.

If and when you buy animal foods, look for accreditation schemes that promote better animal welfare and environmental standards and higher quality, such as "grass-fed," "pasture-fed," and "organic." If you can, buy from a local farmer who you trust. To find farmers in your area, go to Eatwild (www.eatwild.com, US) or Pasture for Life (www.pastureforlife.org, UK).

Understanding labels and certification schemes is not always easy. Product labels can be deceptive too, which adds to the confusion. Beware of terms such as "cage-free," "free-range," "humane," "natural," "humanely raised," and "hormone-free," which do not always guarantee that the animals were raised using the best humane practices. As mentioned earlier, if you don't see any welfare labels on the packaging, leave it on the shelf!

Some of the higher-welfare labels worth looking out for are listed on the opposite page.

Also, visit Seafood Watch (www.seafoodwatch.org) and the Marine Stewardship Council (www.msc.org) online and check out their guides to buying fish and shellfish that meet high environmental and welfare standards.

Another option is to sign up for a subscription service that delivers sustainably sourced meat and seafood straight to your door. You can limit the amount you eat by freezing some of the products for later use. (Some of these products arrive already frozen.)

UK LABELS

Certified Animal Welfare Approved by AGW

The only USDA-approved third-party animal welfare food certification label that supports and promotes family farmers who raise their animals with the highest welfare standards, outdoors, on pasture or range. A Greener World's standards cover the treatment of breeding animals, animals during transport, and animals at slaughter.

Soil Association Certification

Organic standards that offer many welfare benefits exceeding standard industry practice, including prohibiting confinement systems, ensuring bedding and/or environmental enrichment, ensuring free-range access with shade and shelter, specifying stunning and slaughter practices, and monitoring welfare through outcome measures.

Certified Grassfed by AGW

An optional add-on to the Certified Animal Welfare Approved by AGW program, it requires that products come from animals whose diet is 100 percent grass and forage.

RSPCA Assured + Outdoor Reared or Bred

The Royal Society for the Prevention of Cruelty to Animals' labeling and assurance scheme dedicated to improving welfare standards for farm animals. The standards offer a number of welfare benefits relative to standard industry practice. The scheme covers both indoor and outdoor rearing systems and ensures that greater space, bedding, and enrichment materials are provided. In addition, on-farm health and welfare monitoring is required, and stunning and slaughter processes are specified.

Certified Humane (pasture-raised eggs only)

An additional certification to designate pasture-raised egg-laying hens. Requires 2.5 acres of pasture per 1,000 birds.

Global Animal Partnership (Steps 4, 5, 5+)

Rates producers on a 6-tier scale from low (Step 1) to high (Step 5+) welfare. Feedlots are prohibited and access to pasture is required for all animals at Step 4 and higher. All physical alterations are Prohibited at Steps 5 and 5+.

Free Range or Pasture Raised

Animals benefit from quality outdoor space, but how much space the animals have and the amount of time they spend outside will vary from one farm to the next. Rules also differ depending on the country where the animals are raised.

Regenerative Organic Certified (other than dairy)

Requires USDA Organic certification and certification from either Certified Humane, Global Animal Partnership (at Step 4 or higher), or Certified Animal Welfare Approved by A Greener World. Standards also include the treatment of animals during transport and at slaughter.

Sources: Animal Welfare Institute, Compassion in World Farming, and Farms Not Factories

reducing food waste

In addition to being mindful of what's *on* our plates, we can make the effort to cook and shop thoughtfully. Changing everyday habits like these can help us make even more of an impact.

The United Nations (UN) estimates that roughly one-third of the food produced for human consumption is lost or wasted globally. This amounts to about 1.3 billion metric tons of perfectly good food per year. It's shameful, really, especially when you consider that, as the UN reckons, one in seven people in the world goes to bed hungry, and more than 20,000 children under the age of five die from hunger daily.

Individual households waste a large amount of food, and we all have our part to play to reduce the amount we discard.

When we throw away food, we waste not only money but also water, energy, and other valuable resources that are necessary to bring that food from field to plate. Avoiding this waste is even more critical with animal products, which not only have a higher carbon impact than plant foods but also, in most cases, take the life of a sentient being. If you are going to eat meat, seafood, and/or dairy, make sure you use every bit of what you buy.

Here are some tips to help you reduce food waste:

• **Plan ahead to avoid unnecessary purchases.** Taking regular stock of the food in your fridge, freezer, and pantry is key to wasting less. Plan your weekly meals accordingly, selecting dishes that feature ingredients you already have or make use of leftovers. Another tip is to cook recipes that require some of the same ingredients (two dishes containing tomatoes and mushrooms, for example), thus minimizing any surplus.

• **Love your leftovers.** Week in, week out, we end up with quite a few odds and ends in the fridge. Come Sunday evening, everything gets reheated for a big leftover feast that takes only 10 minutes to prepare.

• **Rotate the items in your fridge, fruit bowl, and pantry.** How many times have you found spoiled food at the bottom of the fridge, in the bottom of the fruit bowl, or at the back of the pantry? When unloading your groceries, put the food that is already there in front of what you just bought so that you use up older items first.

• **Keep your produce drawers and fruit bowl organized.** Did you know that as some fruits and vegetables ripen, they emit ethylene gas? Some varieties, including apples, avocados, bananas, peaches, pears, plums, cantaloupe, honeydew melon, and tomatoes, are ethylene-emitting, while others, including cabbage, carrots, lettuces, various greens, kiwi, and watermelon, are ethylene-sensitive (that is, they will ripen faster if placed near ethylene-emitting produce). To preserve your fruits and vegetables, keep them away from each other. Conversely, you can place a banana near an unripe kiwi to help it mature.

- **Understand date labeling.** Consumers' confusion about what labels such as "sell by," "use by," and "best by" really mean is a major source of food waste. Often, food gets tossed based on these dates, when in fact it is still good. Remember that these labels are guides, and products might still be good to eat beyond those dates. I am wary of keeping meat and fish past their use-by dates. As for the rest, if a food has gone bad, it will generally develop a noticeable funny smell, flavor, or texture or go moldy.

- **Test your eggs.** Before you throw away eggs that are past their use-by date, test them. Fill a large glass with water and gently lower an egg into it. If the egg sinks to the bottom of the glass, it is still good. If it floats, it's time to throw it away.

- **Snap up a bargain.** Every day, supermarkets drop prices on food approaching its sell-by, use-by, or best-by date. This also applies to products with damaged packaging and foods past their season, such as Easter or Christmas chocolates. A browse through the discount bins or discounted cooler section could help you save money as well as prevent perfectly good food from going to waste.

- **Download a food waste app.** Whether you want to share your own food surplus with others or are looking for a deal on food that needs to be eaten right away, technology is there to help. Apps designed to reduce food waste help connect neighbors (check out OLIO) or shops, restaurants, and consumers (check out Too Good To Go and YourLocal). Others, like Flashfood, locate groceries near you that are close to their expiration dates and can be purchased at a discount. Sharing and buying surplus food is a great way to save money and keep perfectly good food from going to landfill.

- **Freeze extras.** Most food can be frozen unless it has been frozen before. Even the smallest amounts of wine, cream, cheese, yogurt, butter, citrus fruit, pesto, and herbs can be preserved in ice cube trays to be used later. To help you keep track, don't forget to label the contents and put dates on the food you are freezing. To prevent freezer burn, occasionally rotate the items in your freezer, bringing food that has been in there the longest to the front/top so you don't forget to use it.

- **Compost.** Making your own compost is easy, and it's a great way to reduce the amount of food waste that would otherwise go to landfill. You can compost almost anything, from vegetables and fruits to meat, fish, and bread scraps. We have two compost systems at home: a wormery, where worms quickly turn our food scraps into a nutrient-rich soil fertilizer, and a hot composter for food and garden waste that cannot go into the wormery. As a result, we produce most of our garden compost from the food waste we generate. If you are limited by space or live in an apartment building, check if your community garden has a compost bin. Alternatively, you can look into indoor composting solutions such as a bokashi bin. Another option is to sign up with Sharewaste.com and find someone in your neighborhood who is willing to accept extra scraps to compost or feed to their worms or animals.

choosing seasonal & local food

With so many fruits and vegetables available in stores all year, it's hard to keep up with what is actually in season or has not traveled thousands of miles before ending up in your store's produce section. It is also easy to forget that seafood and meat can be seasonal too. While intensively farmed animals are available year-round, those caught in the wild or raised using traditional methods are subject to seasonal fluctuations due to factors such as temperature, gestation, and how long it takes them to mature. For example, commercial fishing during spawning season can have a negative effect on future stocks, while pasture-raised, grass-fed beef is at its peak in fall and early winter. Buying seafood and meat in season supports the natural life cycles of animals and ensures that you are getting the best flavor and texture.

When allowed to fully ripen before being harvested, seasonal produce is fresher, tastier, and more nutritious than produce grown halfway around the world, picked before it is fully ripe, and shipped a great distance. When it comes to flavor and nutritional value, the ideal is produce that has been picked at the peak of freshness; buying local and seasonal produce gets you closer to that ideal, diminishing the window of time between harvest and your cutting board, allowing you to harness the fruit or vegetable's natural goodness.

In order to maximize profits and efficiency, modern agriculture has sacrificed biodiversity and flavor and made us reliant on a few crops. Many heirloom fruits and vegetables, ancient grains, and other foods have either almost or entirely disappeared from our plates. The Food and Agriculture Organization of the United Nations estimates that "of more than 50,000 edible plant species in the world, only a few hundred contribute significantly to food supplies. Just 15 crop plants provide 90 percent of the world's food energy intake, with three—rice, maize and wheat—making up two-thirds of this."

Striving to cook with local and seasonal food is a way to reconnect with the abundance of food that nature puts at our disposal.

buying directly from local farmers

Seasonal food will vary according to where you live, and this is why it is important to buy as much as you can from local farmers. Over time, you will learn what is in season and what is not. Lower food miles benefit the environment while supporting small independent producers, which helps strengthen the local economy and community.

Farmers' markets are fantastic places to source seasonal foods and specialties as well as meet local producers. The USDA provides online Local Food Directories (www. usdalocalfoodportal. com) where you can find nearby community supported agriculture (CSA), farmers' markets, food hubs, on-farm markets, and even agritourism farms. In the UK, Sustain (sustainweb.org) and Local Food Britain (localfoodbritain.com) run similar initiatives.

Local food markets are a thriving tradition around the world, so even if you are on holiday or abroad, there is always an opportunity to visit one. When visiting my family in the South of France, I never miss a chance to enjoy sun-ripened produce and stock up on local delicacies like garlic braids, olive oil, herbs, honey, and sun-dried tomatoes.

getting a weekly produce box

Getting a weekly produce box from a nearby producer is another way to eat seasonally and locally. Not always knowing what's ready for harvest and discovering unfamiliar ingredients can bring excitement to your weekly meal routine. Conveniently, some schemes offer other products such as bread, milk, and eggs, as well as pantry essentials, and will deliver them straight to your door. Whether you are looking for organic, ethically sourced, or sustainably farmed produce or you wish to rescue fruit and vegetable cast-offs from going to waste, there is a weekly delivery scheme out there for you.

Living on the outskirts of London, we are fortunate to have a CSA farm on our doorstep. From humble beginnings as an empty field, it has become an inspiring place that brings together people from many different walks of life through a common love of healthy food.

I encourage you to find out if there are CSAs in your area. They not only offer the shortest supply chain—straight from farm to table—but also can have a positive environmental and social impact on local communities.

growing your own

You may wish to grow your own fruits and vegetables. Nothing can compare to the freshness! Depending on your skill level and the time you can dedicate to gardening, your venture could range from keeping potted herbs on your windowsill, growing tomatoes in a patio container, or having a few raised beds to cultivating your own plot in your backyard or a community garden.

Growing and harvesting your own food is so rewarding. It is a great way to reduce your carbon footprint and help preserve biodiversity in your area, as it gives pollinators and insects access to a wider variety of plants. It also gives you the opportunity to experiment with heirloom vegetables that might not be widely available in stores. From rainbow carrots to purple beans to white eggplants, there are so many rare varieties to choose from.

limiting your use of plastic

In the name of convenience, we have become reliant on plastic—a phenomenon that can be traced back to the 1950s. Somehow, until then, people seem to have managed fine, with little to no plastic in their lives.

Our addiction has come at a hefty price for the planet, wildlife, and our health. After putting plants center stage on our plates, reducing our use of plastic is one of the next best things we can do for the future of the planet. The majority of the plastic we discard ends up in landfills rather than being recycled, no matter how it is labeled. As a result, millions of tons of it are swirling around the world's oceans. Gyres are large systems of natural currents that help ocean waters circulate around the globe. Unfortunately, they also draw garbage in the water to concentrated areas known as garbage patches. Debris get stuck there, polluting the marine life. The most famous one is the Great Pacific Garbage Patch that stretches between California and Japan.

After we dispose of plastic, it takes a really long time to fully decompose—twenty years for a single-use bag, 200 years for a straw, and 500 years for a toothbrush, according to World Wildlife Fund Australia. Plastic breaks down into tiny particles known as microplastics that pollute our soil and water. Birds, fish, and other marine animals ingest these plastics. Apparently, we do too. Recent research found nanoplastics to be present in human stool and placentas, suggesting that exposure may be widespread in our food chain.

For good reasons, we are being asked to reduce the amount of plastic we use. And so we should, especially when it comes to single-use plastic (shopping bags, straws, takeaway cups and food containers, drink bottles, coffee pods, and so on). We are presented with compostable plastics as an alternative, but these are no panacea either, as they require the right conditions to biodegrade and can end up contaminating other plastic recycling.

At the same time, avoiding plastic altogether can be tricky and may be counterproductive. For example, reusable food storage containers such as Tupperware® can last for years and help limit food waste. It is worth noting, though, that there is a wide range of good arguments for avoiding some constituents of plastic, such as BPA (bisphenol A) and phthalates, which are known hormone disrupters. While the Tupperware Corporation has declared that the products it has sold since 2010 are free of BPA, glass storage containers with bamboo lids are a good alternative if you wish to steer clear of plastic.

I strive to limit the amount of plastic in my life and say no to single-use plastic as much as I can. If I am going to use a container over and over, however, I feel that BPA- and phthalate-free plastic is okay. When it comes to food shopping, preparation, and storage, here are my top tips for using less plastic:

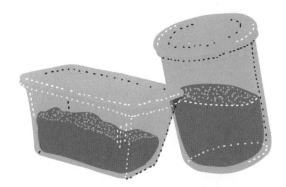

- **Use reusable shopping bags.** Keep a few large reusable bags in the trunk of your car and a smaller folding or collapsible one in your handbag or satchel.

- **Shop for loose produce.** Forget shrink-wrapped cucumbers, bagged lettuce, and tomatoes in plastic containers. Grab a few cotton mesh produce bags and buy these items loose instead. If your grocery store sells little produce free of packaging, make the commitment to shop at a farmers' market, where all the produce will be sold loose.

- **Buy in bulk.** Strive to buy staples in bulk to reduce packaging. I concentrate on the dry foods we consume regularly, such as oats, pasta, rice, lentils, flour, nuts, and coffee beans. Bulk bins used to be found only in natural foods stores, such as food co-ops, but today they are increasingly a fixture in conventional supermarkets.

- **Embrace zero-waste grocery stores.** A relatively new phenomenon, packaging-free stores are gaining momentum. At these one-stop shops, you can refill your own glass jars and reusable plastic containers with pasta, cereals, coffee, flour, nuts, and other pantry essentials as well as restock on personal care and cleaning products.

- **Avoid plastic wrap.** Preserve food items in airtight lidded containers or wrap them in damp tea towels (ideal for extending the freshness of leafy green vegetables), parchment paper, wax paper, or reusable beeswax wraps instead. For a vegan alternative, look for soy wax wraps or rice bran wax wraps.

- **Invest in reusable storage containers.** Invest in some reusable glass storage containers in various sizes. Easily stackable, they save space on refrigerator shelves and are freezer-safe.

- **Choose reusable serveware.** Avoid unnecessary plastic waste when you are on the go by investing in quality lunch boxes, insulated food jars, reusable cutlery, water bottles, and coffee cups.

- **Sign up for a milk delivery service.** How many plastic milk jugs do you dispose of every week? Why not switch to reusable glass bottles instead? Some companies even offer dairy-free milk alternatives in glass bottles.

- **Avoid packaging-heavy meal kit delivery services, aka recipe boxes.** Subscription services that deliver individually portioned ingredients for specific recipes are a convenient way to cook without having the hassle of planning and shopping. Some boxes come with a lot of extra plastic packaging, unfortunately, which takes some of the fun out of the experience. If you use one of these services, search for one with a high green/eco or sustainable rating, and try not to rely on the service regularly.

- **Cook from scratch.** Preparing your own food is not only healthier but also reduces the packaging waste incurred when eating ready-made meals.

- **Bring your own doggy bags to restaurants.** Avoid food waste when eating out by taking any leftovers home to enjoy for lunch or dinner the next day. Don't hesitate to bring your own container to fill.

the recipes:
before you begin

With this book, I've tried to anticipate all of your questions about a plant-forward lifestyle and get you started down your path. But I also hope to help you learn new cooking skills and explore new cuisines while enjoying tasty food and having fun along the way. And that's where the following recipe chapters come in! To ensure your success with the recipes, please read this short introduction before diving in.

what to expect

When developing the recipes for this book, I aimed to put plants center stage, from breakfast through dessert, without ever compromising on taste, as well as to help you replace old habits with new, better ones. The range of dishes and flavors in these recipes is very much influenced by my upbringing in France, my Mediterranean roots, my travels, and my having lived in two cosmopolitan metropolises, New York and London.

Many of the recipes are vegetarian or vegan. Some do call for animal products but are structured to be flexible, and I have highlighted easy swaps so that you can make them plant-based if you prefer. To show you how versatile plant-forward cooking can be, without the need for specialized products, I deliberately chose not to use meat or fish analogues, although you are welcome to swap them in if you wish.

To reflect the way my family eats, I created two chapters for main dishes: Less Meat, More Plants Mains includes recipes with fish or meat, and Meat-Free Mains features vegetarian and vegan dishes. I have two full-time carnivore kids at home, and preparing meals to cater to different diets can be challenging and time-consuming. So I designed some of the recipes in Less Meat, More Plants Mains so that they can be cooked either with or without meat or fish, or so that one half is made with meat or fish and the other half is vegetarian or vegan. These hybrid recipes save me the extra work of cooking two different dishes. If your family's food preferences are as varied as mine, I'm sure you will find these flexible recipes as useful as I do.

I share my love for hearty salads, soups, and anything on bread or flatbread by dedicating a chapter to each category. I also devote a chapter to sauces, dressings, and other basic recipe components that are used throughout the book and that you will be able to use in other recipes.

My recipes are generally designed to be accessible no matter what your cooking skills are. They call for ingredients that should be widely available at local supermarkets or online. Working within my budget, I always strive to use the best ingredients I can find—whether they are local, seasonal, fair trade, or organic. If and when I buy animal products, I look for higher-welfare labels (see pages 72 and 73). I suggest you do the same whenever possible.

The recipes are written to work not just in the United States but also in the UK, where I currently reside, and in any other metric-using country—thus the inclusion of temperatures in degrees Celsius, weights in grams, liquid volume measurements in milliliters and liters, and dimensions in centimeters. You can find a table of handy conversions on page 335. If you are British and are confused by some of the American cooking terms used in the recipes, such as "zucchini" instead of "courgette," please see the "American to British Cooking Terms" chart on page 334.

practical tips

To make this cookbook easy for you to use, here are explanations of how I use certain key ingredients in my cooking, along with a breakdown of the sizes of dice and cubes.

cheeses

I prefer to grate and shred my own cheeses because I find that they taste better than their store-bought equivalents. If you prefer to buy pregrated and preshredded cheeses, make sure to measure them by weight rather than volume.

dairy-free milk

If you opt for a dairy-free milk such as almond, oat, or soy, make sure to use an unsweetened, unflavored product for the recipes in this book.

cream

In several recipes, I say to drizzle cream over the dish at the end as a finishing touch. To give you flexibility, I simply call for "cream" in these instances. You can use any type of dairy cream or the dairy-free cream of your choice, including my Simple Cashew Cream on page 323.

eggs

Egg sizes vary throughout the world, so a "large" egg in one country will not necessarily correspond to what is considered a large egg in another country. In this book, I call for large eggs, the standard size used in American cooking. One US large egg weighs 2 ounces (55g). If you live outside the US, be sure to use eggs that weigh as close to 2 ounces (55g) as possible; in the UK, the closest equivalent is a medium egg.

herbs

To make herb quantities consistent between US and UK measurements, all cup quantities are listed as packed cups. Simply press the herbs down into the cup with your fingers as much as possible. Unless I specify just the leaves, I intend for you to use the leaves and tender stems of the herb.

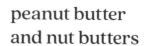

peanut butter and nut butters

I use natural peanut butter and nut butters in all of my cooking and baking. Here, "natural" means 100 percent peanuts or nuts with no salt or sweetener added. To make your own peanut or nut (or seed) butters, see my recipe on page 328.

lemon and lime juice

I use a lot of citrus juice in my cooking because it enhances flavors; lemon juice is also a great alternative to salt. The recipes in this book often express quantities of citrus juice as a range—1 to 2 tablespoons, for example—to allow you to adjust according to your personal taste. Start with the smaller amount; you can always add more if needed.

I prefer fresh citrus juice because it is more natural and has a sharper taste, but you can substitute bottled juice if you wish. The flavor of the bottled stuff is not as citrusy, so you might need to use a little more.

sizes of cuts

Finely diced = ¼ inch (6mm)

Diced = ½ inch (1.25cm)

Cubed = ¾ inch (2cm) to 1 inch (2.5cm)*

*Some recipes require an exact cube size; in those cases, the size will be noted. When not specified, anything between ¾ inch (2cm) and 1 inch (2.5cm) is fine.

breakfast

chocolate cherry smoothie bowl

serves

1

prep time:
10 minutes

One of our freezer drawers is dedicated to frozen fruits so I can whizz up a smoothie before the kids leave for school. I often sneak in a few vegetables too! For a more substantial breakfast, I like to top my smoothie bowls with fresh fruit, seeds, nuts, and muesli or granola.

This recipe can also be enjoyed as a snack or healthy dessert. Feel free to get creative and play around with the toppings.

¼ cup (60ml) orange juice

1 teaspoon pure vanilla extract

1¼ cups (150g) frozen dark sweet cherries, pitted

1 packed cup (35g) baby spinach

1 medium banana

⅓ cup (50g) scrubbed and chopped raw beetroot

3 dates, pitted

1 tablespoon unsweetened cocoa powder, plus more if desired

SUGGESTED TOPPINGS:

½ medium banana, sliced

6 raspberries

4 blackberries

3 cherries, pitted

2 tablespoons muesli or granola

1 tablespoon hulled hemp seeds (aka hemp hearts)

1 tablespoon unsweetened coconut flakes

2 teaspoons cacao nibs

Pour the orange juice into a blender. Add the rest of the ingredients and blend on high speed until smooth and creamy. Taste to check the flavor; if you'd like it more chocolatey, add another teaspoon of cocoa powder and blend.

Transfer the smoothie to a serving bowl. Serve immediately with the toppings of your choice.

overnight porridge

serves
2

prep time:
10 minutes, plus
overnight to soak

Overnight porridge is the ultimate make-ahead breakfast. Topped with dried and fresh fruits, nuts or nut butter, seeds, or whatever you like, it's a healthy and nutritious start to the day. If you are rushed for time in the morning, individual portions prepared in Mason jars are a perfect grab-and-go breakfast to eat in transit or at work.

I've included two options for the porridge base. The first is our standard mix, while the addition of yogurt gives a lovely tang and creamier texture to the second. Both versions will keep in an airtight container in the fridge for a couple of days. For those of you who appreciate golden milk for its flavor and touted health properties, I've also included a Golden (Turmeric) Porridge variation.

PORRIDGE BASE #1:

½ cup (50g) rolled oats

¾ cup (180ml) dairy-free milk, plus more if needed

1 tablespoon chia seeds

PORRIDGE BASE #2:

½ cup (50g) rolled oats

⅔ cup (160ml) dairy-free milk, plus more if needed

⅓ cup (80ml) plain dairy-free yogurt

1 tablespoon chia seeds

suggested toppings (for either base)

CHOCOLATE BANOFFEE:

2 medium bananas, sliced

¼ cup (70g) Five-Minute Date "Caramel" Spread (page 318)

2 tablespoons unsweetened shredded coconut

1 tablespoon cacao nibs

TROPICAL FRUIT:

2 kiwis, sliced

Pulp of 1 passion fruit

⅔ cup (100g) diced pineapple

2 tablespoons unsweetened shredded coconut

6 raw almonds

Sprig of fresh mint

MANGO RASPBERRY DREAM:

1 small mango, chopped

12 raspberries

2 tablespoons unsweetened shredded coconut

1 tablespoon cacao nibs

1 tablespoon goji berries

1 tablespoon hulled hemp seeds (aka hemp hearts)

1 tablespoon fresh mint leaves, thinly sliced

In a 1-pint (500ml) lidded jar, thoroughly combine all of the ingredients for your chosen porridge base. Seal the jar and leave to soak in the fridge overnight.

The next morning, stir the porridge; add a splash of milk if it is too thick. Divide into 2 equal portions and serve with your chosen toppings.

mango raspberry dream porridge

golden (turmeric) porridge

tropical fruit porridge

chocolate banoffee porridge

variation:

golden (turmeric) porridge

After putting the ingredients for the porridge base in the jar, add the following flavorings and stir to combine: 1 teaspoon turmeric powder, ½ teaspoon ginger powder, ½ teaspoon ground cinnamon, ¼ teaspoon ground cardamom, a pinch of black pepper, and ½ teaspoon pure vanilla extract. The next morning, top the servings equally with 1 small apple, thinly sliced; 10 blackberries; 8 raw hazelnuts, halved; 1 tablespoon raisins; 1 tablespoon unsweetened dried cranberries; and 1 tablespoon hulled hemp seeds (aka hemp hearts).

apple & cranberry bircher muesli

serves

2

prep time:
10 minutes, plus
at least 2 hours
to soak

Bircher muesli is the original overnight porridge. As food history goes, Maximilian Bircher-Benner, a Swiss physician and proponent of raw food diets, developed the recipe around the year 1900 to serve as a light evening meal. This version contains more oats and less apple, but the principle is the same: grated apple soaked overnight with oats, milk, and nuts.

I've adapted the original recipe by adding unfiltered 100% apple juice, warming spices, and dried fruits as well as seeds and swapping conventional milk for dairy-free milk, which I find more digestible. But feel free to use dairy milk if you prefer.

This is an ideal breakfast if you are in a rush, as you can prepare it ahead and grab a portion for feasting on the go.

½ cup (50g) rolled oats

½ cup (120ml) dairy-free milk, plus more if needed

¼ cup (60ml) unfiltered apple juice (not from concentrate)

1 medium Granny Smith apple, shredded

1 tablespoon chopped raw walnuts

3 tablespoons unsweetened dried cranberries

1 tablespoon raw sunflower seeds

1 tablespoon raw pumpkin seeds (pepitas)

¾ teaspoon ground cinnamon

½ teaspoon ginger powder

SUGGESTED TOPPINGS:

½ medium banana, sliced

¼ medium apple, cut into strips

4 raw walnuts

A few berries of choice

In a 1-pint (500ml) lidded jar, combine the oats, milk, apple juice, apple, walnuts, dried cranberries, sunflower seeds, pumpkin seeds, cinnamon, and ginger. Seal the jar and leave to soak in the fridge for at least 2 hours or preferably overnight.

After soaking, add a splash of milk if the texture needs loosening up. Divide the muesli into 2 equal portions and serve with your chosen toppings.

spiced oatmeal with caramelized bananas & pecans

serves
4

prep time:
5 minutes

cook time:
9 minutes

Most mornings, especially when it's cold outside, Graham makes steaming hot bowls of porridge for the entire family—even the dog gets one. Over the years, he has perfected the ratio of oats to milk using a pastis glass and an old wooden scoop. I finally standardized his recipe to use as a base for my own, jazzing it up with warming spices as well as caramelized bananas and pecans. I like to top it off with fresh raspberries and maple syrup. When berries are out of season, I swap the raspberries for a few peeled orange slices.

CARAMELIZED BANANAS & PECANS:

2 teaspoons virgin coconut oil, melted

2½ tablespoons pure maple syrup

¼ teaspoon ground cinnamon

2 large bananas, cut into ¾-inch (2cm) slices

¼ cup (30g) raw pecans

OATMEAL:

1½ cups (150g) rolled oats

3¼ cups (760ml) dairy-free milk, plus more if needed

¾ teaspoon ground cinnamon

½ teaspoon ginger powder

½ teaspoon freshly grated nutmeg

SUGGESTED TOPPINGS:

1 cup (125g) raspberries

1 tablespoon cacao nibs

1 tablespoon unsweetened shredded coconut

Pure maple syrup, for drizzling

Make the caramelized bananas and pecans: Bring the oil, maple syrup, and cinnamon to a boil in a large frying pan over medium-high heat. Add the bananas and pecans in a single layer and cook for 2 to 3 minutes, just until the banana slices are light golden brown on the underside; be careful not to overcook them. Gently flip the bananas and cook for a minute on the other side. The pecans should be lightly browned and coated in caramel. Remove the pan from the heat.

Make the oatmeal: In a medium saucepan over medium-high heat, stir the oats, milk, cinnamon, ginger, and nutmeg until well combined. Bring to a steady simmer and cook, stirring regularly, for 5 to 6 minutes, until the milk has been absorbed and the oatmeal is creamy. Add a splash more milk if you'd like the oatmeal thinner.

Divide the oatmeal into 4 equal portions. Serve with the caramelized bananas and pecans and the additional toppings of your choice.

blueberry & peach baked oatmeal

serves
4 to 6

prep time:
15 minutes

cook time:
40 minutes

Graham introduced me (and my mother) to porridge, and I introduced him to baked oatmeal. We keep a constant supply of oats on hand and favor rolled oats (aka old-fashioned oats) for their hearty texture.

This baked oatmeal is deliciously fruity with undertones of coconut. I like serving it warm with some vanilla yogurt on the side. Leftovers reheat brilliantly in the microwave.

2 cups (200g) rolled oats

¼ packed cup (45g) light brown sugar

2 tablespoons ground chia seeds (see notes)

1 teaspoon baking powder

1 teaspoon ground cinnamon

¾ teaspoon freshly grated nutmeg

½ teaspoon salt

Grated zest of 1 lemon

2 cups (475ml) refrigerated unsweetened coconut milk (see notes)

3 tablespoons virgin coconut oil, melted, plus more for greasing

1½ teaspoons pure vanilla extract

1¼ cups (175g) blueberries, fresh or frozen, divided

1¼ cups (240g) sliced peaches in light syrup, drained and cut into bite-size pieces, divided

¾ cup (45g) unsweetened coconut flakes

Vanilla yogurt, for serving

Preheat the oven to 350°F (180°C) and grease a 9-inch (23cm) square baking dish with melted coconut oil.

In a large bowl, stir together the oats, brown sugar, chia seeds, baking powder, cinnamon, nutmeg, salt, and lemon zest.

In a medium bowl, whisk together the coconut milk, coconut oil, and vanilla until well combined.

Add the wet ingredients to the dry and mix with a wooden spoon until well combined. Let rest for 5 minutes.

Spread 1 cup (140g) of the blueberries and 1 cup (200g) of the peaches in the prepared baking dish. Pour the oatmeal mixture over the fruits and spread evenly. Scatter the remaining blueberries and peaches on top.

Bake for 10 minutes. Remove from the oven and sprinkle with the coconut flakes. Bake for an additional 25 to 30 minutes, until the top is crisp and golden and the oatmeal is completely set. Let cool for at least 10 minutes, then serve warm or at room temperature with yogurt on the side.

notes:

If you prefer using eggs, omit the chia seeds and mix 2 beaten eggs into the coconut milk mixture.

The coconut milk to use here is the type that's packaged in cartons, not cans, and kept in the refrigerated section of the grocery store.

plant swap:

Make it vegan by swapping the yogurt for a plant-based alternative.

tofu scramble on toast

This tofu scramble is a tasty high-protein, plant-based alternative to scrambled eggs. Tofu is also cholesterol-free, making it a great choice if you are watching your cholesterol.

Tofu is pretty bland on its own, so I like to perk it up with flavorful seasonings like nutritional yeast, garlic powder, turmeric powder, and salt. Turmeric also gives the scramble a yellowish color, reminiscent of eggs.

I admit I was skeptical at first, but I now prefer this tofu scramble to scrambled eggs, especially when it is served with fresh toppings like spinach, avocado, and tomato. It's a delicious and healthy start to the day.

serves
2

prep time:
20 minutes, plus 20 minutes to press tofu

cook time:
15 minutes

8 ounces (225g) extra-firm tofu

3 tablespoons olive oil

1 small red onion, finely diced

3 packed cups (105g) baby spinach

1 clove garlic, grated

Dash of freshly grated nutmeg

Salt and pepper

1 tablespoon dairy-free milk

1 tablespoon nutritional yeast

¼ teaspoon garlic powder

¼ teaspoon turmeric powder

2 slices bread

1 large avocado, sliced

2 cherry tomatoes, quartered

FOR SERVING:

½ lemon

Sriracha sauce

Start by pressing and marinating the tofu. To press it, you can use either a tofu press or a makeshift setup involving a weight to press out the water. (For a tofu pressing tutorial, see page 68.) Press the tofu for 20 minutes, discarding as much liquid as possible.

When the tofu is nearly done being pressed, make the spinach topping: Heat the oil in a large nonstick frying pan over medium heat. Add the onion and cook gently, stirring from time to time, until it starts to soften, 6 to 8 minutes. Add the spinach and garlic and cook for another 2 to 3 minutes, until the spinach has wilted. Season with the nutmeg and salt and pepper to taste. Transfer to a bowl, cover with foil, and place in a low oven to keep warm. Wipe out the pan and return it to the stovetop.

Place the pressed tofu in the frying pan and mash with a fork until it resembles a scramble. Add the milk, nutritional yeast, garlic powder, turmeric powder, and ¼ teaspoon of salt. Mix well. Cook over medium heat, stirring often, until the scramble is warm and golden, about 5 minutes.

Toast the bread, then top each slice with the tofu scramble, spinach mixture, avocado slices, and quartered tomatoes. Serve straightaway with a squeeze of lemon juice and Sriracha sauce on the side.

healthier carrot muffins

makes
12 muffins

prep time:
10 minutes, plus
20 minutes to
soak oats

cook time:
25 minutes

I love a healthy treat for breakfast, and these carrot muffins hit the spot every time. They are made with whole-wheat flour and no refined sugar. The combination of cinnamon, ginger, nutmeg, and cloves gives them a lovely warm flavor, and the soaked oats add just the right amount of moisture. You can easily make this recipe vegan by following the Plant Swap below.

1 cup (100g) rolled oats, plus more for topping

1 cup (240ml) whole or 2% milk

1½ cups (190g) whole-wheat flour

1 teaspoon baking powder

1 teaspoon baking soda

2 teaspoons ground cinnamon

1 teaspoon ginger powder

¼ teaspoon freshly grated nutmeg

¼ teaspoon ground cloves

½ teaspoon salt

½ cup (120ml) light-colored honey

1 large egg

⅓ cup (80ml) vegetable oil

⅓ cup (80ml) orange juice

1½ teaspoons pure vanilla extract

1½ cups (150g) peeled and shredded carrots

¾ cup (75g) raw walnuts, chopped

½ cup (70g) raisins

In a medium bowl, stir together the oats and milk. Leave to soak for 20 minutes.

After the oats have soaked for about 10 minutes, preheat the oven to 400°F (200°C). Line a standard-size 12-cup muffin tin with cupcake liners.

In a large bowl, whisk together the flour, baking powder, baking soda, cinnamon, ginger, nutmeg, cloves, and salt.

In a separate medium bowl, stir the honey, egg, oil, orange juice, and vanilla until well combined.

Add the soaked oats and the honey mixture to the dry ingredients and mix thoroughly with a wooden spoon. Fold in the carrots, walnuts, and raisins.

Divide the batter evenly among the muffin cups, filling each about three-quarters full. Top each muffin with a sprinkle of rolled oats.

Bake for 20 to 25 minutes, until a metal skewer inserted into the center of a muffin comes out clean. Leave the muffins to cool in the pan for 5 minutes, then transfer to a wire rack to cool completely. The muffins can be frozen for up to 3 months.

plant swap:
Make it vegan by opting for dairy-free milk and substituting maple syrup for the honey. Omit the egg and instead mix 1 tablespoon of ground chia seeds into the oats and milk and leave to soak.

zucchini chocolate pancakes

My kids love these fluffy silver dollar pancakes for breakfast or as a midafternoon snack. I've added chocolate for extra indulgence while sneaking in some vegetables for a healthy twist. The batter is sweetened with sugar and banana, so there's no need to pour a lot of maple syrup on top.

makes
18 to 20 silver dollar pancakes

prep time:
10 minutes

cook time:
2 to 3 minutes per batch

2 cups (250g) all-purpose flour

2 tablespoons baking powder

3 tablespoons granulated sugar

½ teaspoon salt

1 teaspoon ground cinnamon

1 teaspoon ginger powder

¼ teaspoon freshly grated nutmeg

1¼ cups (300ml) dairy-free milk

1 packed cup (125g) shredded zucchini

½ cup (100g) mashed overripe banana (about 1 medium banana)

3 tablespoons vegetable oil, plus more for the pan

1 teaspoon pure vanilla extract

½ cup (80g) dark chocolate chips

SUGGESTED TOPPINGS:

Dairy-free vanilla yogurt

Fresh fruits (sliced banana, blackberries, raspberries, sliced strawberries, etc.)

Natural almond butter

Unsweetened coconut flakes

Cacao nibs

Pure maple syrup

In a large bowl, whisk together the flour, baking powder, sugar, salt, cinnamon, ginger, and nutmeg.

In a medium bowl, stir the milk, zucchini, banana, oil, and vanilla until well combined.

Add the wet ingredients to the dry and, using a wooden spoon, mix until well combined. Fold in the chocolate chips.

Heat a large frying pan over medium-high heat and lightly grease with oil. Add 1 heaping tablespoon of batter to make the first pancake. Depending on the size of your frying pan, you can cook 2 to 4 pancakes at once. Lower the heat to medium and cook until bubbles form on the surface of the pancakes, 1 to 2 minutes. Flip the pancakes and cook for another minute or so, until cooked through. Repeat with the rest of the batter, regreasing the pan as needed.

Serve straightaway with your chosen toppings.

peanut butter & banana sandwich with homemade raspberry chia jam

makes
1 sandwich

prep time:
5 minutes

Living in the US, I fell in love with peanut butter and jelly sandwiches—such a scrumptious combination! This is a healthier (but no less delicious) version, made with my low-sugar raspberry chia jam that's got superfood status. It's perfect for breakfast or as a snack.

1 small ripe banana

2 slices whole-wheat bread

2 tablespoons smooth natural peanut butter

1 tablespoon Raspberry Chia Jam (page 324)

In a small bowl, roughly mash the banana with a fork and set aside.

Toast the bread, then spread an even layer of peanut butter followed by an even layer of jam on each bread slice.

Spoon a layer of mashed banana on one of the bread slices. Top the sandwich with the other slice of bread and eat straightaway.

veggie breakfast bowls

serves
2

prep time:
15 minutes

cook time:
25 minutes

Since moving to England, I haven't become a fan of the "full English." As much as I like a savory breakfast, I much prefer a lighter veggie option, like these breakfast bowls. The eggs are baked in avocado halves and served on a bed of gluten-free millet and fiery kimchi. Sautéed mushrooms and kale, fresh beetroot and tomatoes, and a slice of my Fruity Nut & Seed Loaf complete this hearty meal.

If you've never tried cooked avocados, you are in for a treat. Roasting makes them extra creamy—a delicious way to power your day.

KIMCHI-SPICED MILLET:

½ cup (90g) millet (see note)

1 cup (240ml) water

¼ teaspoon salt

1½ teaspoons olive oil

¼ cup (50g) drained kimchi

BAKED EGGS:

1 large avocado

2 lemon wedges

Salt and pepper

2 large eggs

SAUTÉED MUSHROOMS & KALE:

2 tablespoons olive oil

1 medium red onion, finely diced

8 ounces (225g) mushrooms (any kind), sliced

2 cups (60g) stemmed and roughly chopped kale

2 cloves garlic, grated

½ teaspoon dried herb blend of choice

FOR SERVING:

1 small beetroot, scrubbed, trimmed, and shredded

4 cherry or grape tomatoes, halved

2 sprigs fresh parsley

2 slices Fruity Nut & Seed Loaf (page 108) or other bread of choice

Prepare the millet: Toast the millet in a medium saucepan over medium heat for 3 to 4 minutes. Pour in the water and bring to a boil, then add the salt and reduce the heat to low. Cover the pan and simmer for about 15 minutes, until the millet is tender and has absorbed all of the water. Fluff with a fork and stir in the oil. Cover and set aside.

Preheat the oven to 400°F (200°C).

Prepare the baked eggs: Slice the avocado in half lengthwise and remove the pit. For each half, scoop out some of the flesh with a spoon, making a hole large enough to contain an egg. Place the extra flesh in a bowl, squeeze a lemon wedge on top, and mash with a fork; set aside.

Fit the avocado halves snugly in a small baking dish so they stay flat. Season with salt and pepper. Break an egg into each cavity; do not worry if some of the egg white overflows. Squeeze the other lemon wedge over the avocado halves. Bake for 15 minutes for set egg whites and still runny yolks; for set yolks, bake for another 5 minutes.

Meanwhile, prepare the mushrooms and kale: Heat the oil in a medium frying pan over medium heat. Add the onion and cook gently, stirring from time to time, until it starts to soften, 6 to 8 minutes. Add the mushrooms and cook for an additional 4 to 5 minutes, until the mushrooms are soft. Add the kale, garlic, and herb blend and cook for another 4 to 5 minutes, until the kale has wilted. Slide the pan off the heat.

Stir the kimchi into the millet.

To serve, divide the millet and kale mixtures evenly between 2 serving bowls. Add an avocado half to each bowl. Top evenly with the reserved avocado flesh, beetroot, tomatoes, and parsley. Serve each bowl with a slice of bread.

note:

You can swap the millet for quinoa, bulgur wheat, or barley.

plant swap:

Make it vegan by skipping the eggs. Brush the avocado with oil and season with salt and pepper. Bake for 12 to 15 minutes, until the center is soft. Be sure to use a vegan kimchi or simply omit it and serve your favorite hot sauce at the table instead. Serve the vegan bread of your choice, or follow the Plant Swap for a vegan version of my Fruity Nut & Seed Loaf.

butter bean & feta shakshuka

serves
4

prep time:
10 minutes

cook time:
40 minutes

When it comes to cooking breakfast or brunch, shakshuka is one of my favorite recipes. The eggs are poached in a smoky tomato and red bell pepper sauce and served with bread to soak up the rich flavors. This easy one-pot dish is hearty enough to be a scrumptious lunch or dinner, especially since my version includes butter beans and feta for added protein, as well as olives and plenty of fresh parsley. The original dish, which comes from North Africa, doesn't include butter beans or feta, so feel free to omit them if you'd like to make a more traditional version, or change the beans and cheese to other types of your choosing. This recipe is very versatile!

3 tablespoons olive oil

1 cup (125g) finely diced red onions

2 medium red bell peppers, cut into thin strips

1 (28-ounce/800g) can diced tomatoes

1 cup (240ml) water

4 cloves garlic, grated

2 teaspoons smoked paprika

1½ teaspoons ground cumin

½ teaspoon cayenne pepper

½ teaspoon salt

1 (15.5-ounce/440g) can butter beans, drained and rinsed

Sugar, if needed (depending on acidity of tomatoes)

4 large eggs

½ cup (55g) crumbled feta cheese

½ cup (70g) pitted Kalamata olives

2 tablespoons chopped fresh parsley

4 slices bread, for serving

Heat the oil in a large frying pan over medium-high heat and sauté the onions and bell peppers for 8 to 10 minutes, until the peppers start to soften and the onions are translucent.

Add the tomatoes, water, garlic, smoked paprika, cumin, cayenne pepper, and salt and stir to combine. Lower the heat to medium-low and simmer, uncovered, for 15 to 20 minutes, until the sauce has thickened.

Stir in the beans and taste for seasoning. Add some sugar if the sauce is too acidic (1 to 2 teaspoons should do it) and season with more salt if needed.

Make 4 shallow wells in the tomato mixture and crack an egg into each well. Simmer for another 8 to 10 minutes, until the egg whites have set but the yolks are still runny. (You can cover the pan with a lid to help cook the tops of the eggs.)

Serve topped with the feta, olives, and parsley, with a slice of bread on the side.

plant swap:
Make it vegan by using plant-based feta and omitting the eggs or swapping them for scrambled tofu.

fruity nut & seed loaf

This hearty Paleo loaf is a nutritious alternative to bread, perfect for when you need a break from gluten and wheat. It contains no flour and can be eaten on its own or topped with butter, jam, sliced avocado, fresh fruit, or cream cheese (see my plant-based "cream cheese" recipe on page 326).

You can adapt this recipe to use whatever nuts and seeds you have on hand. Just make sure to use the same proportions and a nice variety of ingredients.

makes
one 9 by 5-inch
(25 by 11cm) loaf
(14 to 18 slices)

prep time:
10 minutes

cook time:
1 hour

1¼ cups (175g) raw almonds

1¼ cups (175g) raw cashews

¼ cup (45g) chia seeds

¼ cup (35g) flax seeds

¼ cup (35g) hulled hemp seeds (aka hemp hearts)

¼ cup (35g) raw pumpkin seeds (pepitas)

¼ cup (35g) sesame seeds

¼ cup (35g) raw sunflower seeds

1 cup (140g) raisins

1 teaspoon salt

4 large eggs, lightly beaten

¼ cup (60ml) vegetable oil

1 medium Granny Smith apple, peeled and grated

Preheat the oven to 350°F (180°C). Grease a 9 by 5-inch (25 by 11cm) loaf pan and line it with parchment paper.

In a large bowl, stir together the nuts, seeds, raisins, and salt.

In a medium bowl, stir together the eggs, oil, and grated apple.

Add the wet ingredients to the dry and thoroughly combine using a wooden spoon.

Pour the mixture into the prepared loaf pan and press with the spoon into an even layer; make sure the top is flat. Bake for 1 hour, or until the loaf is firm and browned.

Let cool completely in the pan, then remove the loaf from the pan before slicing. It will keep in the fridge for up to a week or can be frozen for up to 3 months.

plant swap:
Make it vegan by swapping the eggs for psyllium husk (not to be confused with psyllium husk powder). Simply add ¼ cup (18g) of psyllium husk to the large bowl with the nuts and seeds and replace the eggs with 1¼ cups (300ml) of water. (You can find psyllium husk in health food stores, the supplement aisles of grocery stores, or online.) Once you have mixed the dry and wet ingredients, leave the mixture to rest for 30 to 60 minutes before pouring it into the pan. Bake for 60 to 70 minutes.

very berry granola

Growing up in France, I never put much thought into breakfast. For years, my first meal of the day consisted mostly of butter and jam on either toast or, sometimes on the weekend, croissants. Living in the US, I discovered breakfast cereals and fell in love with granola. Since I started making my own, I rarely go back to store-bought granola; many are shockingly high in sugar.

Easily customizable, homemade granola is a thrifty way to use up odds and ends, such as dried fruits, nuts, and seeds, that might be lurking in your kitchen cupboards. It is also the perfect opportunity to create a unique "house mix" that you can call your own.

This granola is lightly sweetened with maple syrup. I also include some nutritious and incredibly tasty freeze-dried berries as well as crispy puffed quinoa. It makes a wonderful breakfast or snack. Enjoy it with milk, yogurt, pancakes, or waffles.

makes
5 cups (500g)

prep time:
10 minutes, plus 1 hour to dry in oven

cook time:
30 minutes

2 cups (200g) rolled oats

½ cup (70g) raw almonds

¼ cup (35g) raw pumpkin seeds (pepitas)

¼ cup (35g) raw sunflower seeds

1 teaspoon ground cinnamon

½ teaspoon salt

¼ cup (60ml) virgin coconut oil, melted

¼ cup (60ml) pure maple syrup

1 teaspoon pure vanilla extract

½ cup (30g) unsweetened coconut flakes

1 cup (30g) mixed freeze-dried berries (I used equal amounts of strawberries, raspberries, and blueberries)

½ cup (15g) puffed quinoa

Preheat the oven to 350°F (180°C). Line a rimmed baking sheet with parchment paper.

In a large bowl, stir together the oats, almonds, pumpkin seeds, sunflower seeds, cinnamon, and salt.

In a medium bowl, mix together the coconut oil, maple syrup, and vanilla.

Using a wooden spoon, stir the oil mixture into the dry ingredients until well combined.

Tip the mixture into the prepared pan and spread into a 1-inch (2.5cm)-thick rectangle. Having a thick layer will help the granola clump together.

Bake for 15 minutes. Remove from the oven, add the coconut flakes, and give the granola a gentle stir. Return to the oven for another 10 to 15 minutes, until the granola has a nice golden color. Switch off the oven and leave the granola to cool in the oven with the door closed for 45 minutes to 1 hour.

Stir in the freeze-dried berries and puffed quinoa until well combined. Transfer to an airtight container. The granola will keep for up to 3 weeks at room temperature.

small bites

summer rolls

These Vietnamese-style summer rolls are made with rice paper wrappers and eaten fresh. Served with a creamy peanut dipping sauce and my zingy Sweet Chili Dipping Sauce, they are ideal on a day when it's just too hot to cook. The kids like them with shrimp, whereas Graham and I prefer the tofu version.

This recipe makes four tofu rolls and four shrimp rolls. If you prefer just one kind, you can double the quantity of either tofu (no need to increase the amount of marinade) or shrimp. Alternatively, you can skip both and make the rolls with just rice noodles, vegetables, mango, and herbs.

When serving these as an appetizer or small bite, one roll per person is sufficient; two per person is perfect for lunch or dinner.

makes

8 rolls (4 tofu and 4 shrimp)

prep time:

1 hour, plus 50 minutes to press and marinate tofu

cook time:

10 minutes

TOFU SUMMER ROLLS:

7 ounces (200g) extra-firm tofu

2 tablespoons toasted sesame oil

2 tablespoons low-sodium soy sauce

2 tablespoons honey

1 tablespoon fresh lime juice

1 teaspoon garlic powder

½ teaspoon ginger powder

1 tablespoon vegetable oil, for the pan

SHRIMP SUMMER ROLLS:

12 large shrimp, cooked and peeled

FOR BOTH TYPES:

2 ounces (60g) vermicelli rice noodles

1 tablespoon toasted sesame oil

2 cups (90g) shredded green leaf lettuce

½ large mango, cut into thin strips

1 small cucumber, cut into thin strips

1 small to medium carrot, peeled and cut into thin strips

½ medium red bell pepper, cut into thin strips

⅛ small head red cabbage, cut into thin strips

4 medium scallions, thinly sliced

¼ packed cup (12g) finely chopped fresh cilantro

¼ packed cup (12g) finely chopped fresh mint

8 (8½-inch/22cm) round spring roll rice paper wrappers

PEANUT DIPPING SAUCE:

¼ cup (65g) smooth natural peanut butter

2 tablespoons unseasoned rice vinegar

1 to 2 tablespoons tamari, according to taste

1 tablespoon fresh lime juice

1 tablespoon dark brown sugar

1 clove garlic, grated

1 tablespoon water

FOR SERVING/GARNISH:

Sweet Chili Dipping Sauce (page 314)

Lime wedges

Fresh mint sprigs (optional)

note:

To cut the cucumber and carrot into thin strips, I use a julienne peeler, discarding the seedy core of the cucumber. For the mango, bell pepper, and cabbage, I use a very sharp knife.

time-saving tips:

To be more efficient, you can prepare all of the ingredients and dips while you press and marinate the tofu. Stay organized by placing the ingredients used to fill the wrappers in separate bowls around your workspace.

To save some prep and cooking time, buy precooked peeled frozen shrimp for the shrimp rolls.

Start by pressing and marinating the tofu: To press it, you can either use a tofu press or a makeshift setup involving a weight. (For a tofu pressing tutorial, see page 68.) Cut the pressed tofu into 8 strips. Put the tofu strips in a shallow bowl.

Marinate the tofu: In a small bowl, whisk together the sesame oil, soy sauce, honey, lime juice, garlic powder, and ginger. Pour the marinade over the tofu and toss gently to coat the strips. Cover and set aside for 30 minutes.

Meanwhile, make the peanut dipping sauce: Mix the ingredients for the sauce in a small bowl until combined. If the sauce is too stiff, thin it with a little water. If you don't have the Sweet Chili Dipping Sauce already prepared, make it at this time as well. Set the sauces aside.

When the tofu is ready, heat the vegetable oil in a large frying pan over medium-high heat. Add the tofu strips and marinade to the pan and fry until the tofu is crispy on all sides, 8 to 10 minutes. Set aside on a paper towel–lined plate.

While the tofu is frying, prepare the rice noodles: Place the noodles in a bowl and cover with boiling water; let soak for 5 minutes. Drain and rinse under cold water. Toss the noodles in 1 tablespoon of sesame oil. Set aside.

When you're ready to assemble the rolls, set up your workstation, placing the lettuce, prepared rice noodles, mango, vegetables, herbs, and shrimp in separate bowls. Fill a large shallow dish (it needs to be at least 9 inches [23cm] wide so the rice paper wrappers can lie flat in it) with 1 inch (2.5cm) of warm water. Have the wrappers at hand.

Dip a wrapper in the warm water for about 5 seconds, until it is pliable but not too soggy. Remove from the water and place on a flat surface.

Pile one-eighth of the lettuce on the bottom half of the wrapper, leaving a 1-inch (2.5cm) border along the bottom and sides. Be sure to orient the lettuce shreds, as well as the rest of the fillings, so the long sides are parallel to you. Follow with the same quantity of the rice noodles, mango, cucumber, carrot, bell pepper, and cabbage, dividing the ingredients evenly among the wrappers. Top with some scallion, cilantro, mint, and either 2 tofu strips or 3 shrimp. Do not overload the wrapper; otherwise, the contents will spill out and the wrapper might rip when you roll it up.

Fold the bottom edge of the wrapper up and over the filling, then tuck in the sides of the wrapper, as if you were making a burrito. Keeping the contents as tight as possible, roll everything up to close. Set aside and cover with a wet towel.

Repeat with the remaining rice paper wrappers and fillings.

Serve the rolls whole or cut in half, with the dips and lime wedges on the side. For a pretty presentation, garnish with fresh mint.

loaded polenta fries

Crispy on the outside and soft on the inside, these loaded fries are one of our family's favorite things to eat. Sometimes we enjoy them as a starter and sometimes as a main meal. The kids like them with chicken, and Graham and I eat them with jackfruit. Topped with black bean salsa, guacamole, pickled jalapeños, and sour cream, these irresistible fries are perfect for movie or game nights.

The polenta needs a couple of hours to set before you can cut it into fries, so you do need to plan ahead. You can make the polenta in the morning and leave it to set until mealtime. Alternatively, you can buy ready-made polenta in tubes and cut it into fries; you will need two 18-ounce (500g) tubes for this recipe. Reflecting how my family likes to eat this dish, this is written as a hybrid recipe, but you can easily make the fries with just the meat option or the vegan option; see the note on page 119.

serves

6 to 8 as an appetizer, 4 to 6 as a meal

prep time:

25 minutes, plus 1 to 2 hours for polenta to set

cook time:

30 minutes

POLENTA FRIES:

4 cups (950ml) vegetable stock

2 cups (290g) quick-cooking (aka instant) polenta

1 cup (60g) grated Parmesan cheese

¼ cup (60g) unsalted butter

1 teaspoon dried oregano leaves

1 teaspoon dried parsley

¼ teaspoon salt

Olive oil, for the baking dishes and brushing the fries

SUGGESTED TOPPINGS:

Pickled jalapeño slices

Sour cream or mayonnaise

Lime halves

Fresh cilantro sprigs

Halved cherry tomatoes

BLACK BEAN SALSA:

¾ cup (125g) canned black beans, drained and rinsed

½ cup (75g) cherry tomatoes, cut into eighths

½ cup (50g) finely diced orange bell peppers

½ packed cup (10g) roughly chopped fresh cilantro

¼ cup (50g) canned corn kernels, drained

¼ cup (30g) finely diced red onions

1 clove garlic, grated

1 tablespoon extra-virgin olive oil

1 tablespoon fresh lime juice

¼ teaspoon ground coriander

¼ teaspoon ground cumin

¼ teaspoon chili powder

Pinch of salt

BBQ CHICKEN/JACKFRUIT:

2 tablespoons olive oil

½ cup (60g) finely diced red onions

3 cloves garlic, grated

2 teaspoons smoked paprika

½ teaspoon ground cumin

1 (14-ounce/400g) can young green jackfruit in brine, drained

1 cup (240ml) BBQ sauce, divided, plus more if needed

½ cup (120ml) water, divided

8 ounces (225g) boneless, skinless chicken breasts, cut into chunks

QUICK GUACAMOLE:

2 large ripe avocados

½ teaspoon ground cumin

¼ teaspoon ground coriander

¼ teaspoon garlic powder

2 tablespoons fresh lime juice, plus more if desired

Salt, to taste

plant swap:

Make it vegan by omitting the chicken and doubling the jackfruit, as outlined in the note on page 119. You will also need to swap the cheese, butter, and sour cream or mayonnaise for plant-based alternatives. (See page 320 for my vegan mayonnaise recipe.)

Bring the stock to a boil in a heavy-bottomed stockpot over medium-high heat. Pour in the polenta and whisk constantly until thickened, 2 to 3 minutes. Turn the heat to low and stir in the Parmesan, butter, herbs, and salt until everything is well combined. Slide the pot off the heat and cover.

Line two 8-inch (20cm) square baking dishes with greased parchment paper. Divide the polenta evenly between the dishes and spread it to an even thickness. Allow to cool, then place in the fridge until completely firm, 1 to 2 hours.

When the polenta is nearly firm, make the salsa: Place all of the ingredients in a bowl and stir gently until combined. Taste and season with additional salt if needed; set aside.

When the polenta has set, place one oven rack in the bottom position and a second rack in the middle position and preheat the oven to 425°F (220°C). Line 2 rimmed baking sheets with parchment paper.

Carefully cut the polenta into ½ by 3-inch (1.25 by 8cm) fries. Scatter the fries on the prepared baking sheets. Brush each fry with oil and bake until golden, 20 to 25 minutes.

While the fries are in the oven, prepare the base for the BBQ chicken and jackfruit: In a medium saucepan, heat the oil over medium heat, then add the onions and cook gently, stirring from time to time, until they just start to soften, about 6 minutes. Stir in the garlic, smoked paprika, and cumin. Transfer half of the onion mixture to another medium saucepan.

Make the BBQ jackfruit: Put the drained jackfruit in a kitchen towel and squeeze to extract as much water as possible. Break up the chunks with your fingers. Add the jackfruit to the first saucepan and cook gently over medium heat for 2 to 3 minutes, until slightly browned. Stir in half of the BBQ sauce and half of the water. Simmer for 10 to 15 minutes, using 2 forks to pull the jackfruit apart as it cooks and becomes tender. If it gets too dry, add more BBQ sauce.

Make the BBQ chicken: Add the chicken chunks to the second saucepan and cook over medium heat until golden brown and the juices run clear, 6 to 8 minutes. Shred the chicken with 2 forks. Stir in the remaining half of the BBQ sauce and half of the water, then lower the heat and simmer gently for 5 minutes. If it gets too dry, add more BBQ sauce.

Meanwhile, make the guacamole: Mash the avocado flesh in a bowl with the cumin, coriander, garlic powder, lime juice, and salt. Taste and add more lime juice, if desired. Set aside.

When the polenta fries are done, remove them from the oven and allow to cool for 2 to 3 minutes.

Serve the fries directly from the baking sheet or transfer them to a serving platter. Top with the salsa, guacamole, and additional toppings of your choice. Serve with the BBQ chicken and jackfruit.

notes:

This hybrid meat/vegan recipe is written to make 3 to 4 appetizer portions each of BBQ jackfruit and BBQ chicken, yielding 6 to 8 servings total. (Or, if serving as a main meal, it makes 2 to 3 portions each of the BBQ jackfruit and BBQ chicken, 4 to 6 servings total.)

To make this recipe vegan, skip the chicken and use 2 cans of jackfruit; to make the recipe with just chicken, double the amount of chicken, using 1 pound (450g). When preparing the base, use a large saucepan instead of a medium one, and leave all of the onion mixture in the pan (do not divide it). Follow the instructions for the jackfruit or chicken version as written, but use the full 1 cup of BBQ sauce and full ½ cup (120ml) of water.

crispy baked egg rolls

Swap takeout for these healthy egg rolls, which are baked rather than fried. They are deliciously crispy on the outside and soft on the inside, and are served with a tasty sweet chili dipping sauce—the same one that's served with my Summer Rolls (page 114) and Kimchi Fritters (page 124).

Packed with satisfying flavor, these rolls can double as a main. The filling is made with vegetables, vermicelli rice noodles (the ones that look like angel hair), and a little chicken, which you can easily skip or replace with tofu if you prefer a meat-free version. If you cannot find egg roll wrappers, you can use spring roll pastry sheets instead; if you do, the yield will be 24 rolls. Once cooked, any leftover rolls will keep in the fridge for up to 3 days and can be reheated in the microwave.

makes
16 egg rolls
(8 servings as an
appetizer, 4 as a
meal)

prep time:
45 minutes

cook time:
30 minutes

1½ ounces (45g) vermicelli rice noodles

2 tablespoons plus 2 teaspoons toasted sesame oil, divided

⅓ cup (50g) thinly sliced shallots

4 cloves garlic, grated

2 cups (125g) finely chopped mushrooms (any type)

1 cup (100g) peeled and shredded carrots

1 cup (55g) thinly sliced green cabbage

1 teaspoon Chinese five-spice powder

1 teaspoon ginger powder

¼ cup (60ml) low-sodium soy sauce

8 ounces (225g) cooked boneless chicken (dark or light meat), shredded

Vegetable oil, for brushing the baking sheet and egg rolls

16 square egg roll wrappers (see note)

FOR GARNISH/SERVING:

4 medium scallions, sliced on the bias

2 or 3 fresh mint sprigs, cut into small sections

1 batch Sweet Chili Dipping Sauce (page 314)

1 lime, cut in half (optional)

Make the filling: Place the rice noodles in a bowl and cover with boiling water; allow to soak for 5 minutes. Drain and rinse under cold water. Toss the noodles in 2 teaspoons of the sesame oil. Set aside.

Heat the remaining 2 tablespoons of sesame oil in a large frying pan over medium heat, then add the shallots and garlic and cook until they start to soften, about 2 minutes. Add the mushrooms, carrots, cabbage, five-spice powder, ginger, soy sauce, and chicken. Cook until the vegetables start to soften, about 5 minutes. Remove from the heat and mix in the noodles until everything is well combined.

Preheat the oven to 425°F (220°C). Brush a rimmed baking sheet with about 2 tablespoons of vegetable oil.

Assemble the egg rolls: Place an egg roll wrapper on a flat surface with one corner pointing towards you. Spoon 2 heaping tablespoons of filling in the center of the wrapper, leaving a ¾-inch (2cm) edge on the right and left sides. Brush the edges of the wrapper with water. Fold the bottom part of the wrapper over the filling, then fold in the right and left corners. Roll up the wrapper completely, making sure it is tight and secure. Brush the top corner with more water if needed to securely seal. Brush the egg roll all over with vegetable oil and place on the greased baking sheet.

Repeat with the rest of the filling and wrappers to make a total of 16 egg rolls.

Bake for 10 minutes, then flip the egg rolls. Bake for 10 to 12 minutes more, until golden and crisp. While the egg rolls are in the oven, make the dipping sauce if you don't already have it prepared.

To serve, garnish the egg rolls with scallions and mint sprigs, and offer the dipping sauce on the side as well as lime halves, if desired, for squeezing over the top.

plant swap:
Make it vegan by using vegan egg roll wrappers and either swapping the chicken for pressed firm or extra-firm tofu or omitting the chicken and increasing the amount of chopped mushrooms to 5½ cups (340g).

note:
Traditionally, the dough for egg roll wrappers included egg, but many wrappers today are egg-free. Egg roll pastry can be bought either frozen or fresh. The number of wrappers per pack varies from one brand to the next, but if you buy them fresh, any extra can be frozen. For this recipe, I use a 16-ounce (454g) pack of 16 wrappers.

tomato & tapenade tart

This tomato tart has summer written all over it. It can be enjoyed warm or at room temperature, and as a starter or a main meal. It is inspired by my mom's tapenade, one of her signature dishes. She has a batch ready for us to enjoy whenever we visit and another batch for us to take home when we leave. My dad is in charge of the crostini. They are the perfect team! I adapted her recipe to add a tasty twist to another Mediterranean classic, the irresistible tomato tart. Traditionally, it is made with a thin layer of Dijon mustard, replaced here with some of Mom's flavorful tapenade. To help the pastry stay crispy, I bake the base and the tomatoes separately. I like to use different colors and shapes of heirloom tomatoes, but if you can't find them, conventional red tomatoes work just as well.

serves
6 to 8 as an
appetizer,
4 to 6 as a meal

prep time:
10 minutes

cook time:
35 minutes

TOMATOES:

1½ pounds (700g) mixed heirloom tomatoes, sliced into ¼-inch (6mm)-thick rounds

1 tablespoon olive oil

1 tablespoon fresh marjoram leaves, or 2 teaspoons fresh oregano leaves

1 tablespoon fresh thyme leaves

1 sheet frozen puff pastry, thawed

TAPENADE:

1 cup (140g) pitted Kalamata olives

⅓ cup (55g) capers

1 clove garlic, grated

1 tablespoon fresh lemon juice

1 to 2 anchovy fillets (packed in oil), according to taste

Ground black pepper

FOR GARNISH:

Fresh basil leaves, whole or cut into chiffonade

Good-quality balsamic glaze (see note)

Have one oven rack in the bottom position and a second rack in the middle position. Preheat the oven to 400°F (200°C). Line 2 rimmed baking sheets with parchment paper.

Put the tomatoes on one of the prepared baking sheets and toss gently by hand with the oil, marjoram, and thyme. Spread the tomatoes out into a single layer.

Place the baking sheet on the middle rack in the oven and bake for 30 to 35 minutes, until the tomatoes have shriveled.

Unfold the puff pastry on the other prepared baking sheet. To create a border, using a sharp knife, score a line ½ inch (1.5cm) from the edge on all four sides of the pastry. Avoiding the border, prick the pastry all over with a fork.

After the tomatoes have baked for 10 minutes, place the baking sheet with the pastry on the bottom rack in the oven and bake for 20 minutes, until crisp and golden.

Meanwhile, make the tapenade: Place the olives, capers, garlic, lemon juice, and anchovy fillets in a blender or mini food processor and blend to a smooth consistency. Season to taste with pepper.

To assemble the tart, use a spatula to gently flatten the center of the pastry, which will have puffed up during baking. Spread the tapenade evenly over the pastry, avoiding the border.

Arrange the tomatoes on top of the tapenade. Sprinkle with basil and drizzle with balsamic glaze before serving. Serve warm or at room temperature.

kimchi fritters

Crispy and slightly spicy, these fritters are quick and easy to make, and they're also great for lunch or a light dinner. I serve them with my zingy Sweet Chili Dipping Sauce and some Miso Sesame Mayonnaise, which makes them truly hard to resist. If serving these fritters as a small bite, two per person should be plenty; serve three or four for a main meal.

This recipe uses chickpea flour, which is high in plant-based protein and helps bind the ingredients together without the need for eggs.

makes
12 fritters
(6 servings as
an appetizer,
3 to 4 as a meal)

prep time:
10 minutes

cook time:
16 minutes

1 cup (200g) drained kimchi

1½ cups (150g) peeled and shredded carrots

½ cup (75g) canned corn kernels, drained

¾ cup (95g) chickpea flour

¾ teaspoon salt

½ cup (120ml) vegetable oil, plus more if needed, for the pan

FOR GARNISH/SERVING:

Sesame seeds

Sliced scallions

Sweet Chili Dipping Sauce (page 314)

Miso Sesame Mayonnaise (page 322)

Lime quarters

Fresh mint sprigs

Place the kimchi in a large bowl. Stir in the carrots, corn, chickpea flour, and salt until everything is well combined and you have a thick batter. Set aside to rest for 5 minutes.

Heat the oil in a large frying pan with at least 2½-inch (6.5cm)-high sides over medium-high heat. When the oil is shimmering, gently drop heaping tablespoons of batter into the pan to form 3 or 4 fritters; don't overcrowd the pan. Flatten the fritters with a spatula and cook until firm and golden, about 2 minutes. Flip the fritters and cook until firm and golden on the other side, about 2 minutes more. Transfer the fritters to a paper towel–lined plate, cover with foil, and keep warm in a low oven.

Repeat until you have used all of the batter. Add more oil to the pan as needed to maintain a depth of 1 inch (2.5cm), making sure to heat the oil until it's shimmering before cooking more fritters.

Sprinkle the fritters with sesame seeds and scallions and serve warm with the dipping sauce, mayonnaise, lime quarters, and mint sprigs on the side.

carrot & cilantro quinoa fritters

When my daughter was younger, she refused to eat any type of vegetable but loved soups and fritters, so I became pretty skilled at making both with whatever seasonal produce I could get my hands on. Fritters are a particular favorite of mine because they are so versatile. These quinoa fritters pair beautifully with my Creamy Avocado Sauce and make a tasty meat-free and gluten-free starter, lunch, or dinner. If serving them as a starter, one or two fritters per person should do it; if serving them for lunch or dinner, allow for three or four per serving. The fritters hold together much better with eggs, so if you need an egg-free alternative, try my Kimchi Fritters on page 124 instead.

makes
10 fritters (5 to 10 servings as an appetizer, 3 as a meal)

prep time:
15 minutes

cook time:
40 minutes

4 cups (950ml) vegetable stock

½ cup (90g) white quinoa

⅔ cup (160ml) plus 1 tablespoon vegetable oil, divided, plus more if needed

¾ cup (90g) finely diced onions

2 cloves garlic, grated

2 cups (200g) peeled and shredded carrots

2 large eggs, beaten

2 tablespoons chickpea flour

1½ teaspoons ground coriander

1 teaspoon ground cumin

1 teaspoon salt

¾ packed cup (15g) roughly chopped fresh cilantro, plus more for garnish

FOR GARNISH/SERVING:

4 cherry tomatoes, quartered

1 batch Creamy Avocado Sauce (page 302)

Handful of arugula

1 lime, halved or cut into wedges

Bring the stock to a boil in a medium saucepan. Add the quinoa and cook, uncovered, over medium-high heat until just soft, about 10 minutes. Drain thoroughly and transfer to a large bowl.

Heat 1 tablespoon of the oil in a large frying pan with at least 2½-inch (6.5cm)-high sides over medium heat. Add the onions and cook gently, stirring from time to time, until they start to soften, 6 to 8 minutes. Stir in the garlic and cook for 1 minute more, until fragrant. Transfer the onions and garlic to the bowl with the quinoa. Wipe out the pan and set aside.

To the bowl with the quinoa and onions, add the carrots, eggs, chickpea flour, coriander, cumin, and salt. Mix until well combined, then stir in the cilantro. Set aside to rest for 10 minutes.

In the same frying pan, heat the remaining ⅔ cup (160ml) of oil over medium-high heat. When the oil is shimmering, add ¼ cup (60ml) of batter to the pan and flatten with a spatula to make a 3-inch (8cm) round fritter. If there is room in the pan, repeat to make a second fritter. Fry the fritters until firm and golden, about 2 minutes. Flip the fritters over and cook until firm and golden on the other side, about 2 minutes more. Transfer the fritters to a paper towel–lined plate, cover with foil, and keep warm in a low oven.

Repeat with the remaining batter. Add more oil to the pan as needed to maintain a depth of 1 inch (2.5cm), heating the oil until it's shimmering before cooking more fritters.

Serve the fritters warm, topped with chopped cilantro, cherry tomato quarters, and dollops of avocado sauce. Offer the remaining avocado sauce, arugula, and lime halves or wedges on the side.

quinoa crust quiches— two ways

These quiches have a signature gluten-free crust that's wonderfully crunchy and chewy thanks to the ancient grain quinoa. You can serve them as a small bite or for lunch or a light supper, ideally with a crisp salad. (If serving as a small bite, cut each quiche into eight to ten pieces; if serving as a meal, cut them into larger pieces.) So that you can prepare two options at once with just a little extra work, this recipe makes one quiche with smoked salmon and another with beetroot. To make the quiches easier to unpan, I use tart pans with removable bottoms; if you prefer, you can make the quiches in two round tart pans rather than rectangular ones, or make one larger round quiche (see notes, next page).

makes

two 14 by 4½ by 1-inch (35 by 10 by 2.5cm) rectangular quiches, or two 9-inch (23cm) round quiches

prep time:

15 minutes, plus 40 minutes to chill/cool crusts

cook time:

75 minutes

CRUST:

Salt

1¼ cups (235g) tri-color quinoa

3 large eggs, beaten

1 cup (75g) shredded cheddar cheese

FILLING:

2 tablespoons olive oil

1 cup (125g) finely diced onions

2½ packed cups (85g) baby spinach

2 cloves garlic, grated

½ cup (90g) jarred roasted red peppers, thinly sliced

¾ cup (180ml) heavy cream (see notes, next page)

¾ cup (180ml) 2% milk

2 large eggs, beaten

½ teaspoon salt

¼ teaspoon ground black pepper

FISH OPTION:

5 ounces (140g) smoked salmon, roughly chopped

½ cup (35g) shredded cheddar cheese

Fresh dill fronds, roughly torn

VEGGIE OPTION:

4 ounces (115g) peeled cooked beetroot, shredded

½ cup (55g) crumbled fresh (soft) goat cheese

Fresh dill fronds, roughly torn

Make the crusts: Fill a medium saucepan halfway with water and bring to a boil. Season the water with a pinch of salt and add the quinoa. Cook, uncovered, over medium-high heat until just soft (do not overcook it), about 10 minutes. Drain, transfer to a bowl, and let cool.

Using a fork, mix the eggs and cheddar cheese into the cooled quinoa until well blended.

Line two 14 by 4½ by 1-inch (35 by 10 by 2.5cm) rectangular removable-bottom tart pans with parchment paper. Alternatively, line two 9-inch (20cm) round tart pans with removable bottoms.

With a spoon, divide the quinoa mixture evenly between the prepared pans and spread it to evenly cover the bottom and sides of each pan. The mixture will be soft, so it may take some patience, and you will have to press firmly. Chill the crusts in the fridge for 30 minutes.

(recipe continues on next page)

To make one large quiche, use a 12- to 13-inch (30 to 33cm) round tart pan. Simply double the amount of ingredients for the fish option or the veggie option.

For a lighter version, swap the heavy cream for 1 cup (240g) of crème fraîche and reduce the amount of milk to ½ cup (120ml).

About 10 minutes before the crusts are fully chilled, preheat the oven to 400°F (200°C).

Remove the chilled crusts from the fridge and place another sheet of parchment on top of each one. Put some pie weights or dry beans on top and blind-bake for 20 minutes. Carefully remove the weights and the top sheet of parchment. Return the crusts to the oven to bake for another 10 minutes, until slightly golden and firm. Remove from the oven and let cool.

While the crusts are in the oven, start preparing the filling: Heat the oil in a large frying pan over medium heat. Add the onions and cook gently, stirring from time to time, until they start to soften, 6 to 8 minutes. Add the spinach and garlic and cook until the spinach has wilted, about 3 minutes. Mix in the roasted red pepper, then transfer the vegetable mixture to a large bowl and let cool.

Whisk the cream, milk, and eggs into the cooled vegetable mixture until well combined. Season with the salt and pepper.

Scatter two-thirds of the smoked salmon evenly over one of the crusts. Scatter the beetroot over the other crust. Divide the vegetable filling evenly between the quiches. Top the salmon quiche with the cheddar cheese.

Bake until the tops are golden, 25 to 30 minutes.

Remove the quiches from the oven and allow to cool for 10 minutes. To unpan, while wearing an oven mitt, use your hand to push the bottom up and slide the tart ring off, then slide each quiche from the metal bottom onto a serving dish. Top the salmon quiche with the remaining smoked salmon and some fresh dill. Top the beetroot quiche with the crumbled goat cheese and some fresh dill. Serve warm.

Store leftover quiche, covered, in the fridge for up to 3 days; to reheat, place in a preheated 350°F (180°C) oven for about 15 minutes. Alternatively, you can freeze the quiche for up to 3 months, reheating it straight from frozen for about 30 minutes, until the internal temperature reaches 165°F (75°C).

labneh

Thick and creamy labneh is the easiest cheese you can make at home. This delicious tangy dip doubles as a spread for toast, pita, and flatbread and will liven up any salad or roasted vegetable. Using whole-milk yogurt is best, as it improves the taste and texture of the labneh.

makes

2 cups (425g)

prep time:

5 minutes, plus 24 to 48 hours to strain

4 cups (1kg) plain whole-milk yogurt

¾ teaspoon salt

SUGGESTED TOPPINGS:

Za'atar

Crushed pink peppercorns

Extra-virgin olive oil

Olives

Grapes

Figs, halved

Mixed cherry and/or grape tomatoes, halved

Fresh mint and/or oregano sprigs

Line a fine-mesh strainer or small colander with a double layer of cheesecloth. Set the strainer over a saucepan.

Mix together the yogurt and salt and tip the mixture into the lined strainer. Fold the cheesecloth over the top, place the pan in the fridge, and leave to strain for 24 to 48 hours. The longer you strain it, the thicker and creamier the labneh will be.

Once you are happy with the consistency, transfer the labneh to a serving bowl. If using it as a dip, decorate it with your chosen toppings.

Store in an airtight container in the fridge for up to a week.

eggplant dip

roasted red bell
pepper dip

zucchini dip

three mediterranean dips

Whenever you need a burst of sunshine on your plate, try these Mediterranean dips. All are made with tahini, lemon juice, and olive oil, and all are smooth, creamy, and incredibly flavorful. They can be served together or separately; I like to serve all three at parties on a meze board with breadsticks and crackers. They are also ideal for a quick lunch or with flatbread and raw vegetables as a snack.

zucchini dip

This is a great dip to make when you have a glut of homegrown zucchini that needs to be eaten. No need to peel the zucchini; the peel adds specks of beautiful green color to the dip.

makes
1⅓ cups (350g)

prep time:
15 minutes

cook time:
30 minutes

1 pound (450g) zucchini, cubed

Olive oil, for the zucchini

¼ cup (60g) tahini

2 cloves garlic, roughly chopped

2 tablespoons chopped fresh mint leaves, plus more leaves for garnish if desired

1 tablespoon chopped fresh parsley leaves

½ teaspoon ground coriander

½ teaspoon ground cumin

1 to 2 tablespoons fresh lemon juice

Salt

Pinch of smoked paprika, for garnish

Handful of raw walnuts, for garnish

Drizzle of extra-virgin olive oil

Preheat the oven to 425°F (220°C).

Spread the zucchini on a rimmed baking sheet and drizzle with oil. Cover with foil and bake until soft, 25 to 30 minutes.

Put the zucchini and its cooking juices in a food processor. Add the tahini, garlic, mint, parsley, coriander, and cumin and whizz or pulse until the mixture has a smooth consistency.

Transfer to a bowl and stir in 1 tablespoon of lemon juice, then taste and add up to another tablespoon, if desired. Season with salt to taste. Just before serving, garnish with the smoked paprika, walnuts, extra-virgin olive oil, and some additional mint, if desired.

Store in an airtight jar in the fridge for up to 3 days.

roasted red bell pepper dip

You can almost think of this dip as hummus, except that roasted red bell peppers replace the chickpeas. It has a mild flavor and an extra smooth texture thanks to the tahini. If you prefer a roasted red bell pepper dip that's a little bit spicy, try my Quick Muhammara (page 138) instead.

makes
1 cup (200g)

prep time:
15 minutes

cook time:
45 minutes

1 pound (450g) red bell peppers, quartered

Olive oil, for the peppers

¼ cup (60g) tahini

¼ cup (60ml) fresh lemon juice

2 cloves garlic, roughly chopped

2 tablespoons chopped fresh basil leaves, plus more for garnish

2 tablespoons chopped fresh parsley leaves, plus more for garnish

½ teaspoon ground coriander

½ teaspoon ground cumin

Salt

Pinch of smoked paprika, for garnish

2 tablespoons pine nuts, for garnish

Drizzle of extra-virgin olive oil

Preheat the oven to 425°F (220°C).

Spread the bell peppers on a rimmed baking sheet, drizzle with oil, and bake until soft, 40 to 45 minutes.

Put the peppers and their cooking juices in a food processor. Add the tahini, lemon juice, garlic, basil, parsley, coriander, and cumin and whizz or pulse until the mixture has a smooth consistency.

Transfer to a bowl and season with salt to taste. Just before serving, garnish with the smoked paprika, pine nuts, extra-virgin olive oil, and some additional basil and/or parsley.

Store in an airtight jar in the fridge for up to 3 days.

eggplant dip

This is my simplified version of baba ghanoush. Traditionally, the eggplant is grilled over an open flame until charred and imbued with a smoky flavor, but here it is roasted in the oven. A pinch of smoked paprika gives the dip its signature smoky flavor.

makes
1¾ cups (430g)

prep time:
15 minutes

cook time:
45 minutes

2 pounds (900g) eggplants

Olive oil, for the eggplants

¼ cup (60g) tahini

2 cloves garlic, roughly chopped

2 tablespoons chopped fresh cilantro leaves, plus more for garnish

2 tablespoons chopped fresh parsley leaves, plus more for garnish

½ teaspoon ground coriander

½ teaspoon ground cumin

1 to 2 tablespoons fresh lemon juice

Salt

Pinch of smoked paprika, for garnish

2 tablespoons pomegranate seeds, for garnish (see note)

Drizzle of extra-virgin olive oil

Preheat the oven to 400°F (200°C).

Using a sharp knife, cut the eggplants in half lengthwise and score the flesh in a crisscross pattern. Place on a rimmed baking sheet, flesh side up, and drizzle with oil. Bake until soft, 40 to 45 minutes.

When the eggplants are cool enough to handle, scoop out the flesh and place it in a food processor; discard the skins. Add the tahini, garlic, cilantro, parsley, coriander, and cumin and whizz or pulse until the mixture has a smooth consistency.

Transfer to a bowl and stir in 1 tablespoon of the lemon juice, then taste and add up to another tablespoon, if desired. Season with salt to taste. Just before serving, garnish with the smoked paprika, pomegranate seeds, extra-virgin olive oil, and some additional parsley.

Store in an airtight jar in the fridge for up to 3 days.

note:

To remove the seeds from the pomegranate, cut it in half horizontally. Pull the sides of each half to loosen the seeds slightly. Then place one half cut side down in your hand and position that hand over a bowl. Using a wooden spatula, whack the top of the pomegranate firmly to release the seeds. If you are too gentle, the seeds will not fall out.

mushroom & lentil pâté

Growing up, I watched my mom and grandfather make dozens of pâté recipes that we enjoyed as appetizers or snacks. In this version, I have replaced the meat with green lentils and mushrooms. Green lentils are key here: once cooked, they lend a heartier texture to the pâté than brown lentils would. Flavored with fresh herbs, lemon juice, and a splash of brandy, it is delicious spread on toast or crackers. You do not have to include the alcohol, but it does add authenticity, as does the buttery topping, which is also optional. Enjoy the pâté with some crunchy cornichons or gherkins.

makes
2¼ cups (500g)

prep time:
10 minutes, plus
3 hours to set

cook time:
15 minutes

2 tablespoons olive oil

⅔ cup (100g) thinly sliced shallots

3 large cloves garlic, grated

7 ounces (200g) white or baby bella mushrooms, roughly chopped

1 cup (125g) raw pecans

1 (15-ounce/425g) can green lentils, drained and rinsed (see note)

2 tablespoons chopped fresh parsley leaves

2 tablespoons chopped fresh thyme leaves

1 tablespoon chopped fresh rosemary leaves

1 tablespoon fresh lemon juice

1 tablespoon brandy or Marsala wine (optional)

1 to 2 tablespoons tamari

Salt and pepper

2 tablespoons unsalted butter, for topping (optional)

FOR SERVING:

Crackers, toasts, or bread

Cornichons or small gherkins

In a large nonstick frying pan, heat the oil over medium heat. Add the shallots and cook gently until they start to soften, about 3 minutes. Add the garlic and mushrooms and cook until the mushrooms are soft and have released their moisture, 6 to 8 minutes. (*Note:* If the mushrooms you've used aren't super fresh, they may not release much moisture and may require less cooking time.)

Meanwhile, toast the pecans in a small dry saucepan over medium heat until fragrant and lightly browned, shaking the pan often, about 5 minutes. Remove from the pan and set aside.

Put the mushroom mixture in a food processor. Add the toasted pecans, lentils, parsley, thyme, and rosemary and whizz or pulse until the mixture has a smooth consistency.

Add the lemon juice, brandy (if using), and 1 tablespoon of tamari. Pulse once or twice to combine, then stop the processor and taste. Add up to another tablespoon of tamari, if desired, then season with salt to taste and plenty of pepper. Transfer to a 1-pint (500ml) lidded jar or 2 smaller lidded jars.

If including the optional topping, melt the butter in a small saucepan over low heat. Pour over the pâté, then seal the jar, place in the fridge, and allow to set for at least 3 hours.

Serve spread on crackers, toast, or bread with cornichons or gherkins.

Store in the fridge for up to 4 days.

plant swap:
Make it vegan by swapping the butter for a plant-based alternative or skipping it altogether.

note:
If you can't find canned green lentils, you can use 1½ cups (240g) of drained, cooked lentils that you've prepared using dry lentils, following the instructions on the package. You'll need about ½ cup (100g) of dry lentils. If cooking dry lentils, look for French green lentils, and in particular Puy lentils, or lentilles du Puy, for their superior flavor and texture.

quick muhammara

makes
2 cups (500g)

prep time:
10 minutes

This dip is one of my favorites. I love it scooped onto pita bread, crackers, or raw vegetables or as a sandwich spread. If you are fond of red bell peppers, you might also enjoy my Roasted Red Bell Pepper Dip (page 134). Traditionally, muhammara recipes call for roasting red bell peppers; to speed things up, I use roasted red peppers from a jar. Aleppo pepper originates from Syria and is milder than crushed red pepper. You can find it in specialty food stores or Middle Eastern grocery stores. Otherwise, you can substitute crushed red pepper.

8 ounces (225g) jarred roasted red bell peppers, drained and roughly chopped

1 cup plus 2 tablespoons (115g) raw walnuts

1 clove garlic, grated

2 tablespoons pomegranate molasses

2 tablespoons tomato paste

1 teaspoon Aleppo pepper, or ¾ teaspoon crushed red pepper

1⅓ cups (75g) panko breadcrumbs

1 teaspoon ground cumin

1 teaspoon ground sumac

¼ cup plus 2 tablespoons (90ml) extra-virgin olive oil

2 tablespoons fresh lemon juice

½ teaspoon salt

FOR GARNISH (OPTIONAL):

Extra-virgin olive oil

Raw walnuts

Pomegranate seeds

Chopped fresh parsley

Place the roasted red peppers in a mini food processor. Add the walnuts, garlic, pomegranate molasses, tomato paste, Aleppo pepper, panko, cumin, and sumac. Pulse until the ingredients are combined and the mixture has a chunky texture; do not overprocess.

Transfer to a serving bowl. Mix in the oil, lemon juice, and salt.

Just before serving, drizzle some extra-virgin olive oil on top and garnish with walnuts, pomegranate seeds, and parsley.

This dip is best served at room temperature. It will keep in an airtight container in the fridge for up to 3 days.

spiced butter bean dip

makes
1 cup (275g)

prep time:
5 minutes

Whenever I get bored of hummus, I make this bean dip. It is bursting with the wonderful flavors of lemon juice, smoked paprika, and cumin and is topped with crunchy dukkah. You can serve it with any scooper you like, such as raw vegetables, crackers, or flatbread.

1 (15.5-ounce/440g) can butter beans, drained and rinsed

1 clove garlic, roughly chopped

¼ cup (60ml) fresh lemon juice

1 tablespoon tahini

1 teaspoon ground cumin

1 teaspoon smoked paprika

1 tablespoon extra-virgin olive oil, plus more for garnish

3 tablespoons finely chopped fresh parsley leaves, plus more for garnish

Salt, if needed

Dukkah (page 310), for garnish

Place the beans in a food processor. Add the garlic, lemon juice, tahini, cumin, and smoked paprika and whizz or pulse until smooth. If the mixture is too thick to process, add a little water.

Transfer to a serving bowl and stir in the oil and parsley. Season to taste with salt if needed, keeping in mind that the dukkah will add a touch of salt.

Top with one or two generous pinches of dukkah, a drizzle of oil, and a scattering of additional parsley.

tzatziki—two ways

This refreshing yogurt dip or sauce is traditionally made with cucumber. For a colorful twist, I sometimes make it with beetroot. Both options are included here. I love the versatility of tzatziki and serve it as a dip with crackers or as a sauce with meat, fish, or vegetables.

makes

1½ cups (350g)

prep time:

10 minutes

1 cup (250g) plain Greek yogurt

1 clove garlic, grated

2 tablespoons chopped fresh dill, plus more for garnish if desired

2 tablespoons chopped fresh mint, plus more for garnish if desired

1 tablespoon fresh lemon juice

¼ teaspoon salt

1 cup (150g) shredded cucumber, or 1 cup (200g) peeled and shredded cooked beetroot

Extra-virgin olive oil, for drizzling

Put the yogurt in a medium bowl. Stir in the garlic, dill, mint, lemon juice, and salt.

Squeeze the cucumber or beetroot with your hands to extract any excess water. Mix the cucumber or beetroot with the yogurt mixture until well combined.

Transfer to a serving bowl. Top with a drizzle of extra-virgin olive oil and, if desired, a bit of fresh dill and/or mint. Store leftovers in an airtight container in the fridge for up to 3 days.

hearty salads & bowls

beetroot & orange salad

serves

4 to 6

prep time:

10 minutes

cook time:

35 minutes

Dotted with creamy labneh and candied walnuts and pumpkin seeds, this salad makes a hearty winter lunch. The base is a mix of quinoa, lentils, and wild rice combined with roasted beetroot, juicy orange slices, and peppery arugula. Try playing around with the herbs in the vinaigrette—this salad pairs well with chives, dill, tarragon, parsley, or mint. You can swap the labneh for plain Greek yogurt.

1 pound (450g) beetroots, peeled and cut into ½-inch (1cm)-thick wedges

2 tablespoons olive oil

¾ teaspoon ground cumin

½ teaspoon salt

½ cup (90g) tri-color quinoa

½ cup (100g) French green lentils, picked over and rinsed (see note)

½ cup (90g) wild rice blend

1 large orange, peeled and cut into thin rounds

1 cup (25g) arugula

½ to ⅔ cup (120 to 160ml) Herby Vinaigrette (page 308)

¼ to ½ cup (50 to 100g) labneh, homemade (page 131) or store-bought

CANDIED WALNUTS & PUMPKIN SEEDS:

½ cup (50g) raw walnuts

2 tablespoons raw pumpkin seeds (pepitas)

3 tablespoons dark brown sugar

½ teaspoon smoked paprika

1 tablespoon water

Pinch of salt

Preheat the oven to 400°F (200°C).

Toss the beetroot wedges in the oil, cumin, and salt. Scatter on a rimmed baking sheet and roast until soft, 25 to 30 minutes.

Fill three 2-quart (2L) saucepans halfway with water and bring to a boil. Add ½ teaspoon of salt to each pan. Add the quinoa to the first pan, the lentils to the second, and the rice to the third.

Cook the quinoa, lentils, and rice until soft: 12 to 15 minutes each for the quinoa and lentils and 20 to 24 minutes for the rice blend. Do not overcook the grains and lentils or they will become mushy.

When the grains and lentils are done, rinse under cold water, drain well, and place in a large salad bowl or on a serving platter.

When the beetroots are cooked, start making the candied walnuts and pumpkin seeds: In a small frying pan over medium heat, stir together the walnuts, pumpkin seeds, brown sugar, smoked paprika, water, and salt until the nuts and seeds are coated with a sticky golden brown caramel, about 5 minutes. Lay a large sheet of parchment paper on the counter, then spread the walnuts and pumpkin seeds on the parchment in one layer and let cool completely.

Mix the cooked beetroots, orange, and arugula with the cooked grains and lentils. Generously drizzle with the vinaigrette and top with the candied walnuts and pumpkin seeds and dollops of labneh.

note:

French green lentils are slightly smaller and darker than other green lentils. They hold their shape nicely when cooked, making them ideal for salads, but I use them in both hot and cold recipes for their flavor and texture. Look for authentic green lentils from Puy, France, which have a lovely peppery taste and a nuttier flavor than other types.

plant swap:
Make it vegan by
swapping the labneh for
a plant-based yogurt.

crunchy broccoli salad with roasted sriracha chickpeas

serves
6

prep time:
15 minutes

cook time:
30 minutes

Fresh and crunchy, this raw broccoli salad is packed with plant goodness. It's tossed in my flavorful Asian-style dressing and topped with spicy roasted chickpeas and creamy avocado. Serve it as a light lunch or pair it with my Crispy Baked Egg Rolls on page 120. Allowing the salad to rest for half an hour while you roast the chickpeas helps the vegetables soak up the flavors of the dressing.

1 medium head broccoli (about 1 pound/450g), cut into bite-size chunks

1⅓ cups (100g) thinly sliced red cabbage

1 cup (100g) peeled and shredded carrots

1 medium red bell pepper, finely diced

⅔ cup (160ml) Asian-Style Dressing (page 309)

½ packed cup (10g) roughly chopped fresh cilantro

3 tablespoons chopped fresh mint leaves

ROASTED SRIRACHA CHICKPEAS:

1 (15-ounce/425g) can chickpeas, drained and rinsed

1 tablespoon olive oil

1½ teaspoons Sriracha sauce

¼ teaspoon salt

¼ teaspoon garlic powder

FOR SERVING:

1 large avocado, sliced into 6 wedges

1 lime, sliced into rounds

A couple of fresh mint sprigs

Crushed red pepper

In a large salad bowl, combine the broccoli, cabbage, carrots, and bell pepper. Pour the dressing over the vegetables, then add the herbs. Toss until everything is combined and coated in the dressing. Set aside.

Preheat the oven to 425°F (220°C).

Dry the chickpeas with a paper towel. Place the chickpeas in a bowl and toss with the oil, Sriracha, salt, and garlic powder.

Spread the chickpeas on a rimmed baking sheet and roast in the oven until browned and crispy, 25 to 30 minutes.

Serve the salad topped with the roasted chickpeas, avocado wedges, lime slices, mint sprigs, and crushed red pepper to taste.

kale & grilled corn salad

serves

4

prep time:

15 minutes

cook time:

15 minutes

With its sweet and tangy lime dressing, this colorful Mexican-inspired salad is the perfect blend of flavors and textures. Grilling fresh corn enhances its sweetness, while the charring complements the natural sugars, giving it an incredible taste.

The secret to a tender kale salad is to massage the leaves with oil and salt. It might seem like overkill, but massaging helps soften the kale by breaking down the fiber. For the best-tasting kale salad, be sure to use lacinato kale (aka cavolo nero, Tuscan, or dinosaur kale), which has a deeper color and a milder flavor than conventional curly kale.

KALE:

8 ounces (225g) lacinato kale, stemmed and roughly chopped

1 tablespoon olive oil

½ teaspoon salt

2 large ears corn, husked

Olive oil, for brushing the corn

8 ounces (225g) cherry and/or grape tomatoes, halved or quartered depending on size

1 (15-ounce/425g) can black beans, drained and rinsed

1 small red onion, finely diced

1 medium orange bell pepper, diced

½ packed cup (10g) roughly chopped fresh cilantro

1 large avocado, diced

DRESSING:

¼ cup (60ml) extra-virgin olive oil

3 tablespoons fresh lime juice

2 teaspoons pure maple syrup

2 cloves garlic, grated

¾ teaspoon ground cumin

¼ teaspoons chili powder

Salt and pepper, to taste

Preheat a grill to high heat.

While the grill heats up, prepare the kale: Place the kale in a large salad bowl. Drizzle the oil on top and sprinkle with the salt. Using your hands, scrunch the leaves until they are soft and tender, about 1 minute. Set aside for 15 minutes.

Brush the ears of corn with oil. Grill the corn until charred all over, 10 to 15 minutes. Remove from the grill and set aside until cool enough to handle.

Meanwhile, make the dressing: Whisk together all of the ingredients in a small bowl.

Slice the grilled corn kernels off the cobs and add to the bowl with the kale. Then add the tomatoes, beans, onion, bell pepper, and cilantro.

Pour in the dressing and toss to combine, then add the avocado and toss gently once more. Serve at room temperature.

mediterranean orzo salad

serves
6

prep time:
15 minutes

cook time:
15 minutes

Bursting with Mediterranean flavors and colors, this salad can be enjoyed on its own or as a side dish. (My Tomato & Zucchini Soup on page 196 would be a great pairing.) Orzo is a tiny pasta that makes a tasty alternative to rice. Make sure to keep it al dente and not overcook it. You can use either feta or queso fresco instead of goat cheese. If using feta, skip the salt in the dressing to prevent the salad from being too salty.

Salt

1 cup (165g) orzo

½ cup (100g) French green lentils, picked over and rinsed (see note, page 144)

1 tablespoon extra-virgin olive oil

2 cups (300g) halved cherry tomatoes

½ cup (70g) pitted Kalamata olives, halved

1 medium yellow or orange bell pepper, finely diced

1 small red onion, finely diced

3 tablespoons chopped fresh basil

3 tablespoons chopped fresh dill

1 cup (110g) crumbled fresh (soft) goat cheese

DRESSING:

¼ cup (60ml) extra-virgin olive oil

2 tablespoons fresh lemon juice

1 tablespoon apple cider vinegar

2 cloves garlic, grated

2 teaspoons Dijon mustard

2 teaspoons pure maple syrup

¼ teaspoon salt

Fill 2 medium saucepans halfway with water and bring to a boil. Salt each pan of water with ½ teaspoon of salt. Add the orzo to one pan and the lentils to the other.

Reduce the heat to medium and cook the orzo until al dente, 7 to 9 minutes; cook the lentils just until soft (do not overcook or they will become mushy), 12 to 15 minutes.

Rinse the orzo under cold water, drain well, and place in a large salad bowl. Drizzle with the oil and stir with a fork to coat; this will keep the orzo from sticking together. Set aside to cool.

When the lentils are done, drain well and mix with the cooled orzo.

Make the dressing: Whisk together all of the ingredients in a small bowl.

Add the tomatoes, olives, bell pepper, and onion to the orzo and lentil mixture and give it a good mix. Pour the dressing over the salad and add the herbs and goat cheese. Toss well and serve at room temperature.

plant swap:
Make it vegan by swapping the cheese for a plant-based alternative or skipping it altogether.

quinoa & edamame salad with lime ginger dressing

serves
4

prep time:
20 minutes

cook time:
12 minutes

Tossed in a piquant dressing, this salad is perfect on its own or as a side to my Summer Rolls (page 114). It's quick to make and packed with energizing plant-based protein. Quinoa and bulgur are ancient grains, and together they make a tasty and hearty combo that is delicious with buttery edamame and crunchy raw vegetables. Fresh, flavorful, and ever so tasty!

Salt

1½ cups (210g) frozen shelled edamame

½ cup (90g) tri-color quinoa

¼ cup (50g) bulgur wheat

½ large red bell pepper, finely diced

½ cup (50g) peeled and shredded carrots

⅔ cup (50g) thinly sliced red cabbage

3 tablespoons chopped fresh cilantro

3 tablespoons chopped fresh mint

3 medium scallions, sliced on the bias

½ cup (75g) roasted and salted peanuts, roughly chopped

DRESSING:

1 tablespoon extra-virgin olive oil

1 tablespoon toasted sesame oil

2 tablespoons fresh lime juice

1 tablespoon unseasoned rice vinegar

1½ tablespoons light brown sugar

2 teaspoons tamari

2 teaspoons peeled and grated ginger

1 large clove garlic, grated

½ teaspoon crushed red pepper

Fill 2 medium saucepans halfway with water and bring to a boil over high heat. Season each pan of water with ½ teaspoon of salt. Add the edamame to one pan and the quinoa and bulgur to the other. Lower the heat to medium-high and cook the edamame until just tender, 4 to 5 minutes; cook the quinoa and bulgur until soft (do not overcook or they will become mushy), 10 to 12 minutes.

Make the dressing: Whisk together all of the ingredients in a small bowl.

When the edamame, quinoa, and bulgur wheat are done, drain well and place in a large bowl.

Add the bell pepper, carrots, cabbage, cilantro, mint, scallions, and peanuts to the bowl and toss to combine. Just before serving, pour the dressing over the salad. Give it a good mix, transfer to a salad bowl or platter, and serve at room temperature.

roasted butternut squash & cabbage salad with pearl barley

serves
6 to 8

prep time:
15 minutes

cook time:
40 minutes

This salad is a celebration of the wonderful flavors of fall tossed in a mild curry lime dressing. It's hearty enough to be enjoyed on its own, but it also makes a wonderful side dish for the holiday season.

1 small butternut squash (about 1½ pounds/700g)

Salt and pepper

1 cup (190g) pearl barley

2 tablespoons olive oil, divided

1 teaspoon ground cinnamon

¾ small head green cabbage (about 12 ounces/340g), cut into ½-inch (1cm)-wide strips

½ cup (60g) raw pecans

2 tablespoons raw pumpkin seeds (pepitas)

1 large Honeycrisp apple or similar variety, halved and thinly sliced

Seeds from ½ pomegranate (see note, page 135)

3 tablespoons chopped fresh parsley

DRESSING:

¼ cup plus 2 tablespoons (90ml) extra-virgin olive oil

2 teaspoons Dijon mustard

½ teaspoon mild curry powder

1 teaspoon peeled and grated ginger

1 clove garlic, grated

1 tablespoon apple cider vinegar

1 tablespoon fresh lime juice

1 teaspoon pure maple syrup, or more to taste

Salt

Peel the butternut squash, then cut it in half lengthwise and remove the seeds. Cut the squash halves crosswise into ½-inch (1cm)-thick half-circles. Set aside.

Have 2 oven racks placed in the bottom half of the oven. Preheat the oven to 400°F (200°C).

Fill a medium saucepan halfway with water and bring to a boil. Add ½ teaspoon of salt and the pearl barley. Cook until the grains are tender but still chewy, 25 to 30 minutes. Drain and transfer to a large serving bowl; set aside.

Meanwhile, roast the vegetables: On a rimmed baking sheet, toss the squash slices in 1 tablespoon of the oil and the cinnamon and roast for 30 to 35 minutes, until golden brown and tender. On another rimmed baking sheet, toss the cabbage in the remaining tablespoon of oil and roast for 20 to 25 minutes, until slightly browned and tender. Switch the pans midway through baking to promote even cooking.

Make the dressing: Whisk together the oil, mustard, curry powder, ginger, and garlic until well combined. Add the vinegar and lime juice and whisk to combine. Sweeten with the maple syrup and add salt to taste. Set aside.

In a small frying pan, dry-toast the pecans and pumpkin seeds over medium heat for about 3 minutes, until golden and fragrant. Stir often to prevent them from burning. Slide the pan off the heat and set aside.

Toss the pearl barley and roasted vegetables in the dressing until well combined. Season to taste with salt and pepper. Top with the apple slices, pomegranate seeds, toasted pecans and pumpkin seeds, and parsley. Serve warm or at room temperature.

spinach falafel bowl

serves

4

prep time:

20 minutes, plus
overnight to soak
chickpeas and
1 hour to rest
falafel mixture

cook time:

30 minutes

Crunchy on the outside and soft on the inside, these spinach falafel are deliciously moist. I serve them on a bed of mixed greens with olives and an assortment of crisp raw vegetables. A scoop of my Zucchini Dip and a drizzle of my Herby Tahini Dressing top the whole thing off. Truly a vibrant salad packed with plant-based goodness.

You need to plan ahead to make the falafel because the chickpeas need to soak overnight. Other than that, falafel are straightforward to make. If you have any left over, they will keep in an airtight container in the fridge for up to 3 days and reheat easily in the oven or microwave. Enjoy them cold or warm.

FALAFEL:

(Makes 16 falafel)

1 cup (200g) dry chickpeas, picked over and rinsed

3 packed cups (105g) baby spinach

½ packed cup (10g) roughly chopped fresh basil

½ packed cup (10g) roughly chopped fresh dill

½ packed cup (10g) roughly chopped fresh mint leaves

½ cup (60g) finely diced onions

4 cloves garlic, roughly chopped

2 tablespoons chickpea flour

¼ cup (60ml) plus 1 tablespoon olive oil, divided

1 teaspoon salt

1 teaspoon ground coriander

1 teaspoon ground cumin

BOWLS:

9 ounces (255g) mixed salad greens

1 cup (140g) pitted olives of choice

½ medium cucumber, sliced

½ small red onion, sliced

16 cherry tomatoes, quartered or halved

4 radishes, sliced

1 batch Zucchini Dip (page 133) or store-bought Mediterranean dip/ hummus

1 batch Herby Tahini Dressing made with yogurt (page 304) or other homemade tahini dressing of choice

Soak the chickpeas overnight in plenty of cold water. The next day, drain and rinse well.

Place the chickpeas in a food processor. Add the spinach, herbs, onions, garlic, chickpea flour, 1 tablespoon of the oil, the salt, coriander, and cumin. Pulse until the mixture is smooth and the ingredients are well blended.

Leave the falafel mixture in the fridge to rest for 1 hour.

When you are ready to bake the falafel, preheat the oven to 400°F (200°C).

Pour the remaining ¼ cup (60ml) of oil onto a rimmed baking sheet, making sure it is coated all over.

Working with 2 tablespoons at a time, shape the falafel mixture into small balls and place them, not touching, on the oiled baking sheet.

Bake until golden all over, about 30 minutes, carefully flipping the falafel over with a spatula after 15 minutes so they cook evenly.

Transfer the cooked falafel to a paper towel–lined plate to absorb any excess oil.

Assemble the bowls: Divide the salad greens among 4 serving bowls. Arrange the olives and the rest of the vegetables on top of the greens. Add 4 falafel to each bowl, then top with some dip and a drizzle of dressing.

"sushi" bowls with carrot ginger dressing

These Buddha bowls make a generous lunch or dinner for two. The zingy dressing makes them really tasty, and you can enjoy all of the delicious flavors of sushi without the fish! Best of all, you can easily customize them with any vegetables you have in your fridge.

serves
2

prep time:
15 minutes, plus 20 minutes to soak rice and press tofu

cook time:
30 minutes

¾ cup (150g) sushi rice or other short-grain rice

1 (14-ounce/400g) package extra-firm tofu

2 tablespoons cornstarch

1 tablespoon vegetable oil

1 tablespoon toasted sesame oil

Sriracha sauce (optional)

TOFU GLAZE:

¼ cup (60ml) tamari

3 tablespoons pure maple syrup

2 tablespoons unseasoned rice vinegar

1 tablespoon toasted sesame oil

1 tablespoon peeled and grated ginger

3 cloves garlic, grated

1 cup (140g) frozen shelled edamame

1 packed cup (35g) baby spinach

⅔ cup (50g) shredded red cabbage

1 avocado, sliced

1 small carrot, peeled and shaved into ribbons

½ medium cucumber, sliced

2 large radishes, sliced

2 teaspoons sushi ginger

½ nori sheet, cut into small strips

⅓ cup (80ml) Carrot Ginger Dressing (page 309)

2 teaspoons black sesame seeds

Place the rice in a fine-mesh sieve and rinse thoroughly under cold water for a couple of minutes. Transfer the rice to a bowl and leave to soak in cold water for at least 20 minutes.

Meanwhile, press the tofu for 20 minutes (see page 68).

Cut the pressed tofu into ½-inch (1cm) dice. Place in a medium bowl and carefully toss in the cornstarch to coat.

Heat the vegetable oil and sesame oil in a large frying pan over medium-high heat. Pan-fry the tofu until golden all over, about 8 minutes.

Meanwhile, prepare the glaze: Whisk together all of the glaze ingredients in a small bowl.

When the tofu is golden, add the glaze to the pan. Stirring from time to time, simmer briskly until the tofu is sticky and the glaze has completely reduced, about 10 minutes. Add a squirt of Sriracha sauce if desired.

Meanwhile, cook the rice according to the package instructions.

Fill a medium saucepan halfway with water and bring to a boil. Blanch the edamame for a couple of minutes. Drain and set aside.

To serve, divide the cooked rice between 2 serving bowls. Top evenly with the tofu, edamame, spinach, cabbage, avocado, carrot, cucumber, radishes, sushi ginger, and nori. Drizzle with the dressing and sprinkle with the black sesame seeds.

watermelon panzanella

Whenever I have some stale bread on hand, I like to make a panzanella. This one is a twist on the Italian classic with juicy watermelon and cannellini beans for added plant-based protein. Fresh, hearty, and summery, this salad can be served as a main or a side.

The croutons will be slightly crispy at first and then soften as they absorb the flavorful juices. For maximum flavor, I like to use a nice fruity extra-virgin olive oil for the dressing; for the salad, a selection of vine-ripened heirloom tomatoes in a mix of hues adds a beautiful burst of color.

serves
6 as a side,
4 as a main

prep time:
10 minutes, plus
30 minutes to
rest

cook time:
15 minutes

5 cups (300g) cubed day-old sourdough bread

¼ cup (60ml) olive oil

2 teaspoons dried thyme leaves

4 cups (500g) cubed watermelon

1 pound (450g) tomatoes, cut into eighths

1 (15.5-ounce/440g) can cannellini beans, drained and rinsed

1 small red onion, thinly sliced

¾ packed cup (15g) roughly chopped fresh basil

Salt and pepper

DRESSING:

½ cup (120ml) extra-virgin olive oil

3 tablespoons red wine vinegar

2 teaspoons Dijon mustard

2 cloves garlic, grated

Salt, to taste

Preheat the oven to 350°F (180°C).

Toss the bread cubes in the oil and thyme. Spread on a rimmed baking sheet and bake for 10 to 15 minutes, until just crispy.

Make the dressing: Whisk together all of the ingredients in a small bowl.

Place the watermelon, tomatoes, beans, and onion in a large bowl. Add the croutons.

Pour in the dressing and top with the basil. Toss well and leave to rest at room temperature for 30 minutes. Season with salt and pepper to taste before serving.

zucchini noodle salad with baked feta

serves
4

prep time:
10 minutes

cook time:
35 minutes

A feast for the eyes and the taste buds, this gluten-free and low-carb zucchini salad is topped with roasted mini sweet peppers, cherry tomatoes, Kalamata olives, and creamy baked feta cheese. It is perfect with some crusty bread on a hot day. The zucchini is raw and cut into thin noodles (aka zoodles) using a julienne peeler or spiral slicer. Quick, healthy, and absolutely delicious.

2 cups (300g) mixed cherry tomatoes, halved

8 ounces (225g) mini sweet peppers, seeded and halved

8 ounces (225g) feta cheese, cut into 8 pieces

¾ cup (105g) pitted Kalamata olives

Leaves from 3 sprigs fresh thyme

2 tablespoons olive oil

1 pound (450g) zucchini

DRESSING:

¼ cup plus 1 tablespoon (75ml) extra-virgin olive oil

2 tablespoons apple cider vinegar

2 tablespoons honey

1 tablespoon fresh thyme leaves

2 teaspoons Dijon mustard

1 clove garlic, grated

Salt and pepper, to taste

Preheat the oven to 350°F (180°C).

Spread the tomatoes, sweet peppers, feta, olives, and thyme on a rimmed baking sheet. Drizzle with the oil.

Bake for 30 to 35 minutes, until the vegetables are soft and the feta has golden edges.

Meanwhile, using a julienne peeler or spiral slicer, cut the zucchini into noodles. Discard the seedy core. Set aside.

Make the dressing: Whisk together all of the ingredients in a small bowl.

When the vegetables and feta are ready, spread the zucchini noodles on a serving dish. Scatter the vegetables, feta, and olives on top. Pour on the dressing and toss well. Serve while the feta is still warm.

plant swap:
Make it vegan by swapping the cheese for a plant-based alternative or skipping it altogether. You can also use light-colored, or golden, maple syrup instead of honey for the dressing.

sandwiches & flatbreads

banh mi with smoky tempeh

makes

2 sandwiches

prep time:

10 minutes, plus
30 minutes to
pickle vegetables

cook time:

15 minutes

The banh mi, a fusion of French and Vietnamese cuisines and a classic street food in Vietnam, is hearty, filling, and very messy. The original sandwich is filled with meat and ham, so I developed a plant-based version that replaces the meat with a flavorful smoky tempeh. It is really delicious and easy to make. The sweet and spicy pickled vegetables bring a nice tangy contrast that is balanced out by the Sriracha mayonnaise and crunchy cucumber.

PICKLED VEGETABLES:

1 small carrot, peeled and cut into matchsticks (about ¾ cup/55g)

3 radishes, sliced

1 jalapeño pepper, seeded and sliced

½ cup (120ml) unseasoned rice vinegar or apple cider vinegar

½ cup (120ml) water

¼ cup (50g) granulated sugar

2 teaspoons finely ground sea salt

SMOKY TEMPEH:

1 (8-ounce/225-g) package tempeh

2 tablespoons vegetable oil

¼ cup (60ml) tamari

2 tablespoons pure maple syrup

1½ teaspoons hickory liquid smoke

1 teaspoon smoked paprika

½ teaspoon garlic powder

2 (8-inch-/20cm-long) sections French baguette, sliced in half lengthwise

4 tablespoons Sriracha Mayonnaise (page 322)

8 slices cucumber

6 sprigs fresh cilantro

Leaves from 3 sprigs fresh mint

1 scallion, cut lengthwise into long strips

Make the pickled vegetables: Put the carrot, radishes, and jalapeño in a 12-ounce (350ml) heatproof jar.

Heat the vinegar, water, sugar, and salt in a medium saucepan over medium-high heat. Stir until the sugar dissolves and bring to a boil. Remove from the heat and pour into the jar to cover the vegetables. Set aside for at least 30 minutes.

In the meantime, make the smoky tempeh: Cut the tempeh lengthwise into ¼-inch (6mm) thick slices. Heat the oil in a large frying pan over medium-high heat. Add the tempeh slices and fry until brown and crispy on the underside, 3 to 4 minutes, then flip and fry until brown and crispy on both sides, another 3 to 4 minutes.

In a small bowl, stir the tamari, maple syrup, liquid smoke, smoked paprika, and garlic powder until well combined. Pour the mixture over the fried tempeh, coating the slices all over. Continue to cook over medium-high heat, stirring often, until all the liquid has been absorbed. Slide the pan off the heat and set aside.

When you are ready to assemble the banh mi, toast the baguette halves lightly under the broiler or in a grill pan. Drain the pickled vegetables.

To assemble the sandwiches, spread the mayonnaise on each baguette half. Layer the smoky tempeh on the bottoms of the baguette sections, dividing it equally between them. Top evenly with the pickled vegetables, cucumber slices, cilantro, mint, and scallion strips. Top each sandwich with its matching baguette top.

curried chickpea sandwich

makes

4 sandwiches

prep time:

10 minutes

Give your lunch box a tasty makeover with this curried chickpea sandwich. Warm and fragrant garam masala gives it a lovely and delicate flavor. If you prefer, you can substitute a mild curry powder (in that case, reduce the amount of turmeric powder to ¼ teaspoon). This recipe makes enough for four sandwiches, making it a great option for lunches throughout the week. I suggest you store the filling and bread separately and assemble each sandwich the day you plan to eat it. The filling will keep in an airtight container in the fridge for up to four days.

FILLING:

1 (15-ounce/425g) can chickpeas, drained

1 clove garlic, grated

2 tablespoons extra-virgin olive oil

2 tablespoons fresh lemon juice, plus more if desired

1 tablespoon garam masala

½ teaspoon turmeric powder

½ teaspoon ground cumin

½ teaspoon salt

½ medium red bell pepper, finely diced

½ small red onion, finely diced

½ cup (70g) raisins

¼ packed cup (12g) finely chopped fresh cilantro

1 packed cup (35g) baby spinach, roughly chopped

8 slices of your favorite sandwich bread

Make the filling: Place the chickpeas in a blender or mini food processor along with the garlic, oil, lemon juice, garam masala, turmeric, cumin, and salt. Whizz or pulse just until you have a chunky paste; do not overprocess.

Transfer the chickpea mixture to a bowl. Stir in the bell pepper, onion, raisins, and cilantro. Taste the filling and add more lemon juice if you'd like it to be zingier.

To assemble the sandwiches: Arrange some spinach on a slice of bread. Spread one-quarter of the filling on top. Sprinkle with more spinach and place another slice of bread on the sandwich. Repeat with the remaining filling, bread slices, and spinach. Slice the sandwiches in half and serve.

quick flatbreads

I love making all types of bread, but when I'm short on time, I make these flatbreads. They are delicious with soups, curries, chilies, stews, or dips or on their own topped with roasted vegetables, salad, fried eggs, or cheese. The dough requires hardly any kneading and needs to rest for only 20 minutes. The flatbreads are cooked in a very hot dry pan, without cooking oil, making things even more streamlined.

makes
4 flatbreads

prep time:
10 minutes, plus 20 minutes to rest dough

cook time:
16 minutes

1 cup (125g) all-purpose flour, plus more for dusting

1 cup (125g) whole-wheat flour

2 teaspoons baking powder

½ teaspoon salt

1 cup (250g) plain Greek yogurt

In a large bowl, mix together the flours, baking powder, and salt until well combined. Stir in the yogurt to make a soft dough.

Transfer the dough to a lightly floured surface and knead until you have a smooth and elastic ball of dough. This should take just a few minutes. Add a bit more flour if the dough is too wet or a bit more yogurt if the dough is too dry.

Transfer the dough to a bowl lightly dusted with flour. Cover with a plate and set aside to rest for 20 minutes.

After the dough has rested, cut it into 4 equal sections, then form each into a ball. Lightly dust a clean work surface with flour. Using a rolling pin also dusted with flour, roll out each dough ball to an oval or round shape 1/16 to 1/8 inch (2 to 3mm) thick and about 10 inches (25cm) in diameter.

Heat a large nonstick frying pan over high heat. When the pan is very hot, place the first flatbread in it. Cook until it begins to char, about 2 minutes, then flip and cook until the other side begins to char, about another 2 minutes. Keep the flatbread in a warm oven, covered with foil, while you cook the rest.

plant swap:
Make it vegan by replacing the Greek yogurt with a plain dairy-free alternative such as coconut, soy, or oat yogurt.

spiced mushroom flatbreads

serves
4

prep time:
20 minutes

cook time:
15 minutes

These tasty flatbreads make a fantastic lunch or light dinner. They're piled with muhammara—a delicious roasted bell pepper spread—along with smoky sautéed mushrooms and peppery arugula. Pickled red onions and tahini dressing top them off. Fresh homemade flatbreads are always preferable, but if you're short on time, you can use store-bought ones.

4 flatbreads, homemade (page 170) or store-bought

SAUTÉED MUSHROOMS:

2 tablespoons vegetable oil

½ cup (60g) finely diced red onions

14 ounces (400g) baby bella mushrooms, sliced

2 cloves garlic, grated

1½ teaspoons smoked paprika

1 teaspoon ground cumin

¾ teaspoon ground allspice

1 tablespoon fresh lemon juice

Salt

OTHER TOPPINGS:

½ cup (125g) Quick Muhammara (page 138)

1 cup (25g) arugula

3 tablespoons Pickled Red Onions (page 315)

½ cup (120ml) Herby Tahini Dressing (page 304) or other homemade tahini dressing of choice, or plain yogurt

Place the flatbreads in a low oven to keep warm (or to rewarm them if made the day ahead or using store-bought) while you prepare the mushrooms.

Make the sautéed mushrooms: Heat the oil in a large frying pan over medium heat. Add the onions and cook gently, stirring from time to time, until they start to soften, 6 to 8 minutes. Stir in the mushrooms, garlic, smoked paprika, cumin, and allspice and sauté over medium-high heat until the mushrooms are soft and starting to brown, about 8 minutes. Add the lemon juice and season to taste with salt.

To build the flatbreads, spread 2 tablespoons of the muhammara on the first flatbread. Top with one-quarter of the arugula, sautéed mushrooms, and pickled onions. Finish with a drizzle of dressing or a dollop of yogurt. Repeat with the rest of the flatbreads and toppings. Eat immediately.

spinach & artichoke flatbread pockets

Spinach and artichoke is one of my favorite combinations, and I have tried it in almost every dish I can think of. This is a lighter dairy-free recipe made without cheese, mayonnaise, or cream, and it makes a perfect filling for toasted flatbread pockets. Enjoy them for lunch, as a snack, or as a light dinner. They are best eaten warm, and any leftovers can easily be heated up in the microwave. The recipe comes together more quickly if you make the filling while the flatbread dough is resting.

I use my homemade plant-based "cream cheese," but you can swap it for another dairy-free alternative. (If you can't find ready-made herbed dairy-free cream cheese, you could buy your favorite plain option and mix in fresh herbs, following my recipe.) If you're not averse to dairy, regular cream cheese works too.

makes

4

prep time:

15 minutes, plus
20 minutes to
rest dough

cook time:

45 minutes

1 batch Quick Flatbreads dough
(page 170)

SPINACH & ARTICHOKE FILLING:

3 tablespoons olive oil

½ cup (60g) finely diced onions

2 cloves garlic, grated

4 packed cups (140g) baby spinach

1 cup (155g) marinated artichoke
hearts, finely chopped

3 large sun-dried tomatoes packed
in oil, finely chopped

¾ cup (150g) herbed dairy-free
cream cheese, homemade (page
326) or store-bought

Salt and pepper

After you've mixed the flatbread dough per the recipe on page 170 and set it aside to rest, prepare the spinach and artichoke filling.

Heat the oil in a large frying pan over medium heat. Add the onions and cook gently, stirring from time to time, until they start to soften, 6 to 8 minutes. Stir in the garlic and spinach and cook until the spinach has wilted, about 3 minutes.

Pull the pan off the heat and mix the artichoke hearts, sun-dried tomatoes, and cream cheese into the spinach mixture until the cream cheese has completely softened and everything is well combined. Season to taste with salt and pepper. Set aside.

Cut the rested dough into 4 even pieces, then form each into a ball. Lightly dust a clean work surface with flour. Using a rolling pin also dusted with flour, roll out each dough ball into a circle about 10 inches (25cm) in diameter.

Place a quarter of the spinach and artichoke filling on half of one dough circle. Spread the filling to a semicircle shape, leaving a ¾-inch (2cm) edge. Brush the edge with water. Fold the other half of the dough over the filling and firmly press the edges to seal the flatbread and gently pat the filling down so it is evenly distributed.

Heat a large nonstick frying pan over medium-high heat. Transfer the first flatbread pocket to the frying pan. Cook for 3 to 4 minutes on each side, until lightly charred. Watch that the flatbread does not burn and lower the heat if necessary. Remove from the pan and keep warm in a low oven, covered with foil, while you prepare the remaining flatbread pockets.

Cut each flatbread pocket in half just before serving.

roasted vegetable sandwich with basil hummus

makes
2 sandwiches

prep time:
10 minutes

cook time:
35 minutes

Filled with juicy roasted vegetables, creamy burrata cheese, and a tasty basil-flavored hummus, this is the ultimate summer sandwich. I love it on ciabatta, but you can also use sourdough bread. It can be eaten warm or at room temperature and is perfect for lunch boxes as well as picnics. If you are firing up the grill, you can grill the vegetables and bread and enjoy this sandwich as part of your cookout. You can swap the burrata for sliced fresh mozzarella.

3 tablespoons olive oil, plus more for the rolls

1 clove garlic, grated

1 tablespoon fresh lemon juice

1 tablespoon fresh thyme leaves

½ teaspoon salt

1 medium to large zucchini (about 8 ounces/225g), cut lengthwise into ¼-inch (6mm)-thick planks

1 small eggplant (about 8 ounces/225g), cut lengthwise into ¼-inch (6mm)-thick planks

1 medium red bell pepper, quartered

2 (6-inch/15cm-long) ciabatta sandwich rolls

1 cup (25g) arugula

1 (4-ounce/120g) burrata cheese, drained

BASIL HUMMUS:

1 (15-ounce/425g) can chickpeas, drained and brine reserved

1 packed cup (25g) roughly chopped fresh basil

2 cloves garlic, grated

¼ cup (60ml) fresh lemon juice

2 tablespoons tahini

½ teaspoon salt

Have 2 oven racks positioned in the bottom half of the oven. Preheat the oven to 400°F (200°C).

In a small bowl, whisk together the oil, garlic, lemon juice, thyme, and salt. Set aside.

Spread the zucchini, eggplant, and bell pepper in single layers on 2 rimmed baking sheets. Brush the oil mixture on both sides of the vegetables. Place the pans in the oven and roast until the veggies are soft and golden, 25 to 35 minutes; switch the pans midway through to ensure even cooking. As some vegetables will cook faster than the rest, begin checking after 25 minutes and remove any that are done.

Meanwhile, make the hummus: Place the chickpeas, basil, garlic, lemon juice, and tahini in a mini food processor. Whizz or pulse until you have a smooth, thick spread. If the mixture is too dry, add a little of the reserved chickpea brine so it blends more easily. Season with the salt.

When the vegetables are ready, split the ciabatta rolls in half lengthwise. Brush each cut side with oil. Toast the bread in a hot frying pan or grill pan or under the broiler.

To make the first sandwich, spread some hummus on the cut sides of the top and bottom pieces of bread. Cut the roasted zucchini and eggplant slices as needed to fit the bread. Slice the burrata. Place one-quarter of the arugula on the bottom piece of bread, pile with half of the roasted bell pepper, eggplant, and zucchini, and top with half of the burrata and the same amount of arugula. Close the sandwich with the top piece of bread and cut in half.

Repeat the process to make the second sandwich.

plant swap:
Make it vegan by skipping the burrata or swapping it for a vegan mozzarella alternative.

spring soccas with minty pea pesto & watercress

serves

2

prep time:

10 minutes, plus
30 minutes to
rest batter

cook time:

12 minutes

If you ever find yourself in Nice on the French Riviera, you must try socca, a delicious gluten-free chickpea flatbread that originates across the border in Italy, where it is known as farinata or cecina. Nestled just behind the Port of Nice is the restaurant Chez Pipo, where you can enjoy socca prepared in a traditional oven—it is well worth a visit.

Traditionally, socca is served plain or simply seasoned as a snack or light meal. I have taken the liberty to make these spring soccas a more substantial and filling dish. The recipe yields two soccas. I love the freshness of the minty pea pesto paired with the heartiness of artichoke hearts and peppery bite of watercress.

SOCCAS:

2 cups (250g) chickpea flour

2 cups (475ml) water

¼ cup (60ml) olive oil, plus more for greasing the pans

1 teaspoon salt

PEA PESTO:

1 cup (125g) green peas, thawed if frozen

1¼ packed cups (30g) roughly chopped fresh basil

½ packed cup (10g) fresh mint leaves

½ cup (30g) grated Parmesan cheese

2 cloves garlic, roughly chopped

2 tablespoons fresh lemon juice

2 tablespoons extra-virgin olive oil

OTHER TOPPINGS:

1 cup (125g) jarred grilled artichoke hearts packed in oil, quartered

8 cherry or grape tomatoes, halved

4 radishes, sliced

2 tablespoons ricotta cheese

2 handfuls watercress

Prepare the socca batter: In a large bowl, whisk together the chickpea flour, water, ¼ cup (60ml) of the oil, and the salt until smooth. Cover and set aside to rest for at least 30 minutes.

Meanwhile, make the pesto: Place the peas in a mini food processor. Add the basil, mint, Parmesan, garlic, lemon juice, and oil. Pulse until well combined but still chunky; do not overprocess.

Preheat the oven to 475°F (250°C). Place two 10-inch (26cm) ovenproof frying pans in the oven. When the pans are hot, remove them from the oven and brush 1 tablespoon of oil in each pan (see note).

Pour half of the batter into each pan and bake for 10 to 12 minutes, until the soccas are browned and slightly blistered.

When done, ease the soccas out of the pans with a spatula and place on 2 serving plates. Serve warm, topped with the pesto, artichoke hearts, tomatoes, radishes, ricotta, and watercress.

note:

If you have only one ovenproof frying pan, simply bake the soccas one after the other. Keep the first socca warm, covered with foil, while you make the second one.

plant swap:

Swap the Parmesan for a vegetarian or vegan alternative. Substitute plant-based yogurt for the ricotta.

whipped ricotta toasts with figs & toasted pecans

serves
2

prep time:
10 minutes

cook time:
3 minutes

I am nursing our young and parsimonious fig tree in the hope that one day it will give us a bumper crop. Figs are one of my favorite fruits, and I would gladly eat them straight from the tree. I like using figs in both sweet and savory dishes. Here they are a perfect match for creamy whipped whole-milk ricotta flavored with lemon zest and thyme. A drizzle of honey and a sprinkle of crushed red pepper top everything off. So tasty! This toast can be served as a vegetarian option or with a sliver of prosciutto.

1 cup (250g) whole-milk ricotta cheese

Grated zest of 1 lemon

1 tablespoon fresh thyme leaves

Salt

¼ cup (30g) raw pecans

4 slices sourdough bread

4 fresh figs, quartered

2 slices prosciutto, cut in half (optional)

FOR GARNISH:

Light-colored honey

Crushed red pepper

2 fresh thyme sprigs, cut into small sections

Make the whipped ricotta: Place the ricotta, lemon zest, and thyme in a bowl and, using a hand mixer, whip on low speed until smooth and creamy, 2 to 3 minutes. Season with salt to taste. If using prosciutto, take into account the salty profile it will add to the toasts.

Dry-toast the pecans in a small frying pan over medium heat for about 3 minutes, until golden and fragrant. Stir often to prevent them from burning. Remove the nuts from the pan and set aside.

Toast the bread slices.

Spread one-quarter of the whipped ricotta on each slice of bread. Top each toast with 4 fig quarters, half a slice of prosciutto (if using), and one-quarter of the pecans. Finish each toast with a generous drizzle of honey, a sprinkle of crushed red pepper, and some pieces of thyme sprigs.

plant swap:
Make it vegan by replacing the ricotta with ½ cup (100g) of softened plain plant-based cream cheese, homemade (page 326) or store-bought. Omit the prosciutto and use light-colored, or golden, maple syrup instead of honey for drizzling.

soups

creamy cauliflower & carrot soup

serves
6

prep time:
10 minutes

cook time:
45 minutes

Cashews are the secret ingredient that makes this soup silky without dairy. They are cooked alongside the vegetables so they become extra soft and liquidize into a smooth cream that blends perfectly with the vegetables. For a similar texture, you can swap the cashews for blanched almonds. The crunchy dukkah and fresh cilantro toppings provide a nice textural contrast and a bright pop of flavor.

2 tablespoons vegetable oil

1 cup (125g) finely diced onions

2 cloves garlic, grated

2 tablespoons tomato paste

2 teaspoons ground coriander

1 teaspoon ground cumin

½ teaspoon ginger powder

½ teaspoon turmeric powder

1 small to medium head cauliflower (about 1 pound/450g), cored, florets cut into 1-inch (2.5cm) chunks

1 pound (450g) carrots, peeled and sliced into ½-inch (1.5cm)-thick rounds

½ cup (70g) raw cashews

6 cups (1.4L) vegetable stock

2 to 3 tablespoons fresh lemon juice, according to taste

Salt and pepper

FOR GARNISH:

Dukkah (page 310)

Fresh cilantro leaves

Heat the oil in a heavy-bottomed stockpot over medium heat. Add the onions and cook gently, stirring from time to time, until they start to soften, 6 to 8 minutes. Add the garlic, tomato paste, coriander, cumin, ginger, and turmeric and cook until aromatic, about 2 minutes.

Stir in the cauliflower, carrots, cashews, and stock. Bring to a boil over medium-high heat, then turn down the heat to medium, cover, and simmer until the vegetables are tender, 25 to 30 minutes.

Use an immersion blender to blend the soup until smooth. If needed, add a bit more water to adjust to your desired consistency. Season to taste with lemon juice, salt, and pepper.

Serve the soup topped with a sprinkle of dukkah and a few cilantro leaves.

gnocchi soup

Ready in 30 minutes, this is our go-to soup for cold, rainy evenings, and it's one of my daughter's favorites. To accommodate both vegetarians and meat-eaters, the chicken is added as an optional topping to individual servings rather than cooked with the rest of the ingredients. Leftover turkey or pulled pork works well too. This filling and comforting soup has a luscious creamy mouthfeel thanks to the half-and-half, milk, and Parmesan, but of course you can swap out the dairy for plant-based alternatives.

serves
4

prep time:
10 minutes

cook time:
20 minutes

1 small leek, white part only cut into ¼-inch (6mm)-thick semicircles (about ½ cup/50g)

3 tablespoons olive oil

½ cup (60g) finely diced onions

½ cup (50g) peeled and shredded carrots

½ cup (50g) thinly sliced celery

4 cloves garlic, grated

4 cups (950ml) vegetable stock

1 teaspoon dried thyme leaves

4 ounces (115g) broccoli florets, cut into bite-size pieces

1 (17.5-ounce/500g) package fresh gnocchi

1 cup (240ml) half-and-half

1 cup (240ml) 2% milk

1½ packed cups (50g) baby spinach

⅔ cup (40g) grated Parmesan cheese

Salt and pepper

FOR GARNISH (OPTIONAL):

Shredded cooked chicken

Fresh thyme sprigs

Place the leek semicircles in a bowl of fresh water and gently stir them with your fingers to dislodge any dirt; the dirt will sink to the bottom. Lift out the leek pieces with your hands or a slotted spoon to avoid disturbing the dirt at the bottom of the bowl, then drain.

Heat the oil in a heavy-bottomed stockpot over medium heat. Add the leek, onions, carrots, celery, and garlic and cook gently, stirring from time to time, until the vegetables start to soften, about 6 minutes.

Stir in the stock and thyme and bring to a boil. Lower the heat to maintain a lively simmer, then stir in the broccoli and cook until it starts to soften, about 2 minutes. Stir in the gnocchi and cook until the gnocchi is tender and soft and the broccoli is fork-tender, about 3 minutes more.

Stir the half-and-half, milk, spinach, and Parmesan and cook until the spinach has wilted, about 2 minutes. Season to taste with salt and pepper.

Serve the soup as is or topped with shredded cooked chicken and/or fresh thyme sprigs.

plant swap:
Make it vegan by omitting the chicken and swapping plant-based alternatives for the half-and-half, milk, and Parmesan. My Simple Cashew Cream (page 323) is a good plant-based substitute for half-and-half. For a vegetarian option, look for Parmesan-style cheese— sometimes labeled "Italian-style hard cheese"—that's suitable for vegetarians. (Traditional Parmesan is made with animal rennet, making it unsuitable for vegetarians.)

moroccan chickpea & lentil soup

serves
6

prep time:
10 minutes

cook time:
50 minutes

I first tried harira soup on a trip to Morocco and have loved it ever since. It is traditionally made with meat as well as pulses and takes at least a couple of hours to prepare, so I decided to make my own meat-free version that comes together in half the time. The lentils and chickpeas make it a hearty meal filled with the warming flavors of cinnamon and ginger. Zingy lemon juice enhances it beautifully.

Generous pinch of saffron threads

1 tablespoon hot water

2 tablespoons vegetable oil

1½ cups (190g) finely diced onions

2 medium celery stalks, thinly sliced

2 teaspoons ginger powder

1½ teaspoons ground cinnamon

½ teaspoon turmeric powder

1 teaspoon salt

1 (24-ounce/680g) jar tomato puree (aka passata or strained tomatoes)

6 cups (1.4L) vegetable stock

2 tablespoons tomato paste

1 cup (200g) French green lentils, picked over and rinsed (see note, page 144)

⅔ packed cup (25g) finely chopped fresh cilantro, divided

⅔ packed cup (25g) finely chopped fresh parsley, divided

1 (15-ounce/425g) can chickpeas, drained and rinsed

2 to 3 tablespoons fresh lemon juice, according to taste

Ground black pepper

FOR GARNISH (OPTIONAL):

Fresh parsley or cilantro sprigs

Lemon slices

Place the saffron in a small bowl and pour in the hot water. Set aside.

Heat the oil in a heavy-bottomed stockpot over medium heat. Add the onions and cook gently, stirring from time to time, until they start to soften, 6 to 8 minutes.

Add the celery, ginger, cinnamon, turmeric, and salt and cook gently, stirring occasionally, for a couple of minutes, until aromatic.

Stir in the tomato puree, stock, tomato paste, lentils, half of the herbs, and the saffron with its liquid. Bring to a boil over medium-high heat, then lower the heat to medium-low, cover, and simmer for 30 minutes, or until the lentils are cooked.

Stir in the chickpeas and the remaining herbs and simmer for a couple of minutes to heat through.

Season to taste with lemon juice, salt, and pepper before serving. Garnish each bowl with parsley or cilantro sprigs and/or lemon slices, if desired.

mushroom & wild rice soup

This delicious creamy soup, with lovely hints of thyme and lemon, is light yet satisfying thanks to the addition of wild rice. I like to sprinkle a little bit of crumbled blue cheese on top, but the cheese is entirely optional. You can swap dry sherry for the Marsala wine.

serves
6

prep time:
15 minutes

cook time:
45 minutes

3 tablespoons olive oil

1 cup (125g) finely diced onions

1 cup (125g) peeled and finely diced carrots

2 large celery stalks, finely diced

3 cloves garlic, grated

9 ounces (250g) baby bella mushrooms, sliced

½ cup (120ml) Marsala wine

3 sprigs fresh thyme, plus more for garnish

¾ cup (150g) wild rice blend

5 cups (1.2L) vegetable stock

Grated zest and juice of ½ lemon

½ cup (120ml) heavy cream

Salt and pepper

Crumbled blue cheese, for garnish (optional)

Heat the oil in a heavy-bottomed stockpot over medium heat, then add the onions, carrots, and celery and cook gently, stirring from time to time, until they start to soften, 6 to 8 minutes.

Stir in the garlic, mushrooms, Marsala wine, and thyme until well combined. Cook until the mushrooms start to soften, about 5 minutes.

Stir in the rice, stock, and lemon zest until well combined. Bring to a boil over medium-high heat, then turn down the heat to medium, cover, and simmer for 30 minutes, or until the rice is cooked.

Stir in the cream, then add the lemon juice and season with salt and pepper to taste.

Serve topped with thyme sprigs and crumbled blue cheese, if desired.

plant swap:
Make it vegan by swapping the heavy cream for Simple Cashew Cream (page 323).

soba noodle soup with mushrooms & bok choy

serves
4

prep time:
10 minutes

cook time:
15 minutes

This incredibly tasty and comforting noodle soup is the ultimate fast food. You can make it with pretty much any mix of fresh mushrooms you like. I always include some shiitakes, which add a deep and rich aroma that complements the noodles and vegetable stock. If you don't have hard-boiled eggs made ahead, I suggest you get those going first, then cook the soba noodles while the eggs are cooking. To make this soup vegan, simply omit the eggs.

6 ounces (170g) dried soba noodles (see notes)

1 tablespoon plus 2 teaspoons toasted sesame oil, divided

1 tablespoon vegetable oil

10 ounces (300g) mixed mushrooms (such as shiitake, baby bella, or button), sliced

2 cloves garlic, grated

2 tablespoons peeled and grated ginger

6 cups (1.4L) low-sodium vegetable stock (see notes)

¼ cup (70g) white miso

1 head baby bok choy, chopped

2 small to medium carrots, peeled and cut into strips

4 nori sheets, roughly torn

1 to 2 tablespoons tamari, according to taste

FOR GARNISH:

4 hard-boiled eggs, cut in half

4 medium scallions, sliced on the bias

¼ packed cup (5g) roughly chopped fresh cilantro

4 teaspoons sesame seeds

Crushed red pepper (optional)

Cook the noodles: Fill a large saucepan halfway with water and bring to a boil. Add the soba noodles and cook according to the package instructions until soft, generally 4 to 5 minutes. Drain and rinse under cold water. Drain well and transfer to a bowl. Toss the noodles in 2 teaspoons of the sesame oil to prevent them from sticking together. Set aside.

Meanwhile, heat the remaining tablespoon of sesame oil and the vegetable oil in a heavy-bottomed stockpot over medium-high heat. Add the mushrooms, garlic, and ginger and sauté until the mushrooms are starting to brown slightly, about 5 minutes.

Add the stock and miso to the pot and bring to a boil. Lower the heat to maintain a lively simmer and add the bok choy and carrots. Cook until the vegetables are just tender, about 3 minutes. Add the cooked soba noodles and simmer until heated through, about 2 minutes.

Stir in the nori and season with the tamari.

Divide the soup evenly among 4 serving bowls. Top each bowl with 2 egg halves and sprinkle evenly with the scallions, cilantro, sesame seeds, and crushed red pepper, if desired.

notes:

Dried soba noodles are often packaged in bundles, and most bundles are about 3 ounces each. For this recipe, you need 2 bundles.

It's best to use a low-sodium stock here because miso paste is already salty.

sweet potato chowder with tempeh bacon

serves
4

prep time:
15 minutes

cook time:
30 minutes

Hearty and satisfying, this chowder hits the spot every time. The sweet potatoes are cooked with red lentils and corn in creamy coconut milk. Fresh ginger and cayenne pepper bring just the right amount of spiciness to warm you from the inside out. I love soups, and I'm always on the lookout for interesting toppings. Here I have swapped the classic crispy bacon bits for a plant-based alternative: tempeh bacon. It is straightforward to prepare, and you can make it while the soup is simmering. Liquid smoke gives it a lovely BBQ flavor.

2 tablespoons vegetable oil

1½ cups (190g) finely diced onions

4 cloves garlic, grated

1 tablespoon peeled and grated ginger

½ teaspoon cayenne pepper, plus more if desired

1 teaspoon ground cumin

1½ pounds (750g) sweet potatoes, peeled and cubed

1½ cups (210g) corn kernels, fresh or frozen

½ cup (85g) split red lentils, picked over and rinsed

4 cups (950ml) vegetable stock

1 (13.5-ounce/400ml) can coconut milk

2 packed cups (70g) baby spinach

Juice of 1 to 2 limes, according to taste

Salt

Crushed red pepper, for garnish

Chopped fresh cilantro, for garnish

TEMPEH BACON BITS:

1 (8-ounce/225g) package tempeh

1 tablespoon vegetable oil

¼ cup (60ml) tamari

2 tablespoons pure maple syrup

1½ teaspoons hickory liquid smoke

1 teaspoon smoked paprika

½ teaspoon garlic powder

Heat the oil in heavy-bottomed stockpot over medium heat. Add the onions and cook gently, stirring from time to time, until they start to soften, 6 to 8 minutes. Add the garlic, ginger, cayenne pepper, and cumin and cook until aromatic, about 2 minutes.

Stir in the sweet potatoes, corn, lentils, stock, and coconut milk and bring to a boil over medium-high heat. Lower the heat to medium and cook, uncovered, until the potatoes and lentils are tender, about 15 minutes.

Meanwhile, make the tempeh bacon bits: Cut the tempeh into ⅓-inch (1cm) by ¾-inch (2cm) rectangles. Heat the oil in a medium frying pan over medium-high heat. Add the tempeh bits and cook until browned and crispy all over, about 10 minutes.

In a small bowl, stir the tamari, maple syrup, liquid smoke, smoked paprika, and garlic powder until well combined. Pour the mixture into the pan, stirring until the tempeh bits are well coated. Continue cooking, stirring often, until all of the liquid has been absorbed. Set aside.

Stir the spinach into the soup and cook until wilted, about 2 minutes. Stir in the juice of 1 lime and taste. The soup should have a bright citrus flavor; if needed, add the juice of the second lime to achieve the right balance. Season to taste with salt and add a little more cayenne pepper, if desired, keeping in mind that crushed red pepper is sprinkled on the top before serving.

Serve the soup topped with the tempeh bacon bits and a sprinkle of crushed red pepper and chopped cilantro.

tomato & zucchini soup
with mint almond pesto

serves
4 to 6

prep time:
10 minutes

cook time:
40 minutes

This fresh, vibrant, and aromatic recipe is one of my favorites during early fall when the temperature drops and I start craving a comforting bowl of soup. If you grow your own vegetables, it's perfect for using up a bumper crop of garden produce. You can make it ahead and freeze it or serve it straightaway. For extra flavor, I top the soup with a spoonful of fragrant almond pesto made with fresh basil and mint, a drizzle of cream, and some croutons.

2 tablespoons olive oil

1 cup (125g) finely diced red onions

1 pound (450g) zucchini, cubed

1 pound (450g) tomatoes, cut into 1-inch (2.5cm) chunks

2 medium red bell peppers, diced

2 cloves garlic, grated

2 teaspoons dried thyme leaves

1 tablespoon cornstarch

1 tablespoon tomato paste

4 cups (950ml) vegetable stock

2 packed cups (45g) roughly chopped fresh basil

1 tablespoon fresh lemon juice

Salt and pepper

Cream, for drizzling

Croutons, for garnish

ALMOND PESTO:

½ cup (70g) blanched almonds

¾ packed cup (15g) roughly chopped fresh basil

¾ packed cup (15g) roughly chopped fresh mint leaves

1 clove garlic, roughly chopped

½ cup (30g) grated Parmesan cheese

½ cup (120ml) extra-virgin olive oil

Salt

Heat the oil in a heavy-bottomed stockpot over medium heat. Add the onions and cook gently, stirring from time to time, until they start to soften, 6 to 8 minutes. Stir in the zucchini, tomatoes, bell peppers, garlic, thyme, cornstarch, tomato paste, and stock.

Bring to a boil over medium-high heat, then lower the heat to medium and cover. Simmer until the vegetables are soft, about 25 minutes.

Meanwhile, make the pesto: Place the almonds in a mini food processor with a drizzle basin or in a blender. Add the herbs, garlic, and Parmesan cheese. Whizz or pulse until everything is minced. With the food processor running on low speed, slowly pour in the oil and blend until the pesto is smooth.

Transfer the pesto to a serving bowl. Season to taste with salt.

Once the vegetables are cooked, use an immersion blender to blend the soup until smooth. Add the basil and blend again until everything is well combined. Stir in the lemon juice and season to taste with salt and pepper.

To serve, evenly top each bowl of soup with the pesto, then finish with a drizzle of cream and a few croutons.

plant swap:
Make it vegan by swapping the Parmesan cheese in the pesto for a plant-based alternative or replacing it with 2 tablespoons of nutritional yeast. Drizzle my Simple Cashew Cream (page 323) or another plant-based alternative on top at the end. For a vegetarian option, look for Parmesan-style cheese—sometimes labeled "Italian-style hard cheese"—that's suitable for vegetarians. (Traditional Parmesan is made with animal rennet, making it unsuitable for vegetarians.)

watercress & pea soup

serves
4

prep time:
10 minutes

cook time:
30 minutes

This healthy spring soup has a gorgeous color that simply glows. Just one look at it will make you feel invigorated! I love the sweetness of peas against the peppery notes of watercress, with mint and dill for a flavor boost. Complemented by a swirl of cream (dairy or plant-based) added just before serving, this is a quick and easy recipe that is truly satisfying. You can substitute spinach for the watercress.

2 tablespoons vegetable oil

1 cup (125g) finely diced onions

2 cloves garlic, grated

10 ounces (285g) all-purpose potatoes (such as Yukon Gold or Red Gold), peeled and cut into small chunks

4 cups (950ml) vegetable stock

1 (16-ounce/455g) bag frozen green peas, divided

3 ounces (85g) watercress, plus more for garnish if desired

½ packed cup (10g) roughly chopped fresh dill, plus more fronds for garnish if desired

¼ packed cup (5g) roughly chopped fresh mint leaves, plus more leaves for garnish if desired

2 to 3 tablespoons fresh lemon juice, according to taste

Salt and pepper

Cream, for drizzling

Heat the oil in heavy-bottomed stockpot over medium heat. Add the onions and cook gently, stirring from time to time, until they start to soften, 6 to 8 minutes.

Add the garlic and potatoes and cook until the garlic becomes aromatic, about 1 minute. Pour in the stock and bring to a boil over medium-high heat, then cover and simmer over medium heat until the potatoes are tender, about 15 minutes.

If desired, set aside a handful of peas for use as garnish; allow to thaw. Add 2 cups (275g) of the frozen peas and the watercress to the soup and return it to a simmer. Cook, uncovered, for 5 minutes, or until the peas and watercress are tender. Stir in the dill and mint.

Use an immersion blender to blend the soup until smooth. Stir in the lemon juice and season to taste with salt and pepper.

Add the remaining frozen peas and cook over medium heat for a couple of minutes, just until the peas are softened and heated through.

Serve topped with a drizzle of cream and, if desired, the reserved thawed peas, some watercress, and some dill fronds and/or mint leaves.

plant swap:
Make it vegan by swapping out the cream for my Simple Cashew Cream (page 323) or another plant-based alternative.

less meat, more plants mains

easy turkey pot pie

serves

4

prep time:

10 minutes

cook time:

40 minutes

Repurpose your turkey (or chicken) leftovers into this deliciously creamy pot pie. To give it a healthy twist, I use 2% milk rather than whole milk or cream and top the pie with a single crust. Because the meat goes in last, you can easily customize this recipe to be meat-free (see the Plant Swap below). If you are catering to different diets, you have the option to make individual pies in ramekins.

1 medium leek, cut into ½-inch (1cm) slices (about 1½ cups/130g)

2 tablespoons vegetable oil

3 tablespoons all-purpose flour

1½ cups (350ml) vegetable stock

½ cup (120ml) 2% milk, plus more for brushing

3 tablespoons chopped fresh parsley

2 cloves garlic, grated

1 teaspoon Dijon mustard

1 teaspoon Italian seasoning

2 cups (225g) frozen mixed vegetables

8 ounces (225g) shredded cooked turkey (white and/or dark meat)

1 (15.5-ounce/440g) can cannellini beans, drained and rinsed

Salt and pepper

1 sheet frozen puff pastry, thawed

plant swap:
Make it vegan by swapping the meat for 8 ounces (225g) of sliced baby bella mushrooms. Cook them with the leek. You can substitute unsweetened, unflavored soy, oat, or almond milk for the dairy milk. Check that the puff pastry you are using does not contain butter.

Place the sliced leek in a bowl of fresh water and gently stir with your hands to dislodge any dirt; the dirt will sink to the bottom. Lift out the leek pieces with your hands or a slotted spoon to avoid disturbing the dirt at the bottom of the bowl, then drain.

Heat the oil in a large frying pan over medium-high heat and cook the leek until it starts to soften, about 5 minutes.

Lower the heat to medium, add the flour, and cook for about 2 minutes, stirring continuously to keep the flour from browning. Add the stock, milk, parsley, garlic, mustard, and Italian seasoning. Simmer until the liquid thickens to a gravylike consistency, about 2 minutes.

Mix in the frozen vegetables, turkey, and beans until well combined. Season to taste with salt and pepper and remove the pan from the heat.

Preheat the oven to 400°F (200°C).

Transfer the filling to a 9-inch (23cm) pie dish.

Unfold the puff pastry and cut out a circle 10 inches (25cm) in diameter. Using a rolling pin, roll it out to an 11-inch (28cm) diameter circle. If desired, use the extra pastry to cut out decorative pieces.

Place the pastry on top of the filling. Roll and tuck the edges of the pastry under to create a border all around the pie. Brush milk all over the top of the pastry. If using, place the decorative off-cuts on top of the pastry and brush them with milk too.

Bake the pie until the pastry has a nice golden color, 25 to 30 minutes. Allow to cool for 5 minutes before serving.

thai salmon (or no-salmon) cakes

makes

16 small salmon cakes or 15 small no-salmon cakes (4 to 5 servings)

prep time:
15 minutes

cook time:
40 minutes

Crispy on the outside and soft on the inside, these fish (or no-fish) cakes are a popular midweek dinner in our house. Seasoned with Thai red curry paste, the cakes have a slightly spicy kick, making my Creamy Avocado Sauce the ideal accompaniment.

I have reduced the typical amount of salmon by half and bulked up the fish version with butter beans. If you are short on time, swap the fresh salmon fillets for drained canned salmon. Or, if you prefer to go without fish, you can make a plant-based version with jackfruit.

Salt

1 pound (450g) floury potatoes (such as russet or Maris Piper), peeled and cut into small chunks

8 ounces (225g) skinned salmon fillets, or 1 (14-ounce/400g) can young green jackfruit in brine, drained

1 (15.5-ounce/440g) can butter beans, drained and rinsed

1 to 1½ large nori sheets (depending on type of cake), finely chopped

⅓ packed cup (15g) finely chopped fresh cilantro

1 tablespoon Thai red curry paste (use vegan paste for no-salmon cakes)

4 medium scallions, finely chopped

Grated zest of ½ lime

1 tablespoon fresh lime juice

1 cup (125g) all-purpose flour

2 large eggs, beaten (for salmon cakes), or 1 cup (250g) plain dairy-free yogurt (for no-salmon cakes)

1 cup (60g) panko breadcrumbs

¼ cup (60ml) vegetable oil, plus more as needed

If making salmon cakes, preheat the oven to 400°F (200°C).

For both versions, fill a medium saucepan halfway with water and bring to a boil. Add ½ teaspoon of salt and the potatoes. Cook until soft, about 10 minutes.

Meanwhile, cook the salmon if making the fish cakes, or prepare the jackfruit if making the no-fish cakes.

To cook the salmon, wrap the fillets in foil and place on a rimmed baking sheet. Bake until just done, about 10 minutes. When you insert a fork in the thickest part of the fish, it should flake easily.

To prepare the jackfruit, put the drained jackfruit in a kitchen towel and squeeze to extract as much water as possible. Break up the chunks with your fingers. Slice any chunky bits.

When the potatoes are cooked, drain them well and transfer them to a large bowl. Add the beans and use a potato masher to mash everything to a chunky texture.

If making fish cakes, add 1 large sheet of finely chopped nori to the potato mixture; for no-fish cakes, use 1½ sheets. Stir in the cilantro, curry paste, scallions, lime zest, lime juice, and ¾ teaspoon of salt until everything is well combined.

Using your hands, gently combine the salmon (leaving some larger flakes) or jackfruit with the potato mixture.

Form the mixture into cakes: If making fish cakes, scoop up ¼ cup (60g) of the mixture; for no-fish cakes, scoop up ⅓ cup (75g). Using your hands, form into a patty a little less

FOR SERVING:

4 to 6 ounces (115 to 170g) mixed salad greens

1 batch Creamy Avocado Sauce (page 302)

¼ cup (60ml) sweet chili sauce

6 to 8 lime wedges

than ¾ inch (1.9cm) thick and set aside. Repeat until you have used up all of the mixture.

Place the flour, eggs or yogurt, and breadcrumbs in three separate shallow bowls. Dust each patty all over with flour, then dunk in the eggs or yogurt before coating with the breadcrumbs.

Heat the oil in a large frying pan over high heat. When the oil is shimmering, add 4 patties to the pan and fry for 2 to 3 minutes, then flip and fry for another 2 to 3 minutes, until golden all over. Set aside on a paper towel–lined plate and cover with foil to keep warm while you cook the remaining cakes. If needed, add more oil to the pan between batches.

Serve on a bed of mixed greens with the avocado sauce, chili sauce, and lime wedges.

fish tacos with sriracha mayo

makes

12 tacos

prep time:

15 minutes, plus
20 minutes to
marinate

cook time:

35 minutes

Whether you are eating with the family or entertaining friends, tacos are the perfect flexitarian dinner and can be customized to everyone's preferences. My kids love building their own tacos (and getting messy).

Served with a colorful and refreshing mango salsa, these fish tacos are super healthy. I add sweet potatoes so vegetarians and vegans can skip the fish (see the Plant Swap, opposite). Everyone else can enjoy the fish and sweet potatoes together. You can swap the salmon for any firm white-fleshed fish, such as tilapia, flounder, or cod. The Sriracha mayo is a delicious addition.

FISH & SWEET POTATOES:

2 teaspoons garlic powder

2 teaspoons ground coriander

2 teaspoons ground cumin

2 teaspoons smoked paprika

1 teaspoon sea salt

2 tablespoons fresh lime juice

14 ounces (400g) skin-on salmon fillets

14 ounces (400g) sweet potatoes

2 tablespoons olive oil

MANGO SALSA:

¾ cup (125g) canned black beans, drained and rinsed

¾ cup (115g) finely diced mangoes

1 medium avocado, diced

½ cup (75g) finely diced cucumbers

½ cup (75g) quartered cherry tomatoes

½ packed cup (20g) finely chopped fresh cilantro

¼ cup (30g) finely diced red onions

2 tablespoons fresh lime juice

½ teaspoon ground cumin

½ teaspoon salt

SRIRACHA MAYO:

½ cup (115g) mayonnaise

1 tablespoon fresh lime juice

2 teaspoons Sriracha sauce

1 small clove garlic, grated

FOR SERVING:

12 (6-inch/15cm) tortillas

2 to 3 tablespoons Pickled Red Onions (page 315)

Pickled sliced jalapeño peppers (optional)

Chopped fresh cilantro (optional)

In a small bowl, whisk together the spices and salt. Transfer 1 tablespoon of the seasoning blend to another small bowl and whisk in the lime juice to make a wet rub for the salmon; set the remainder aside for the sweet potatoes.

Place the salmon fillets skin side down in a shallow dish. Spread the wet rub over the salmon. Cover and leave to marinate in the fridge for 20 minutes or so while you prepare the sweet potatoes.

Have one oven rack in the middle position and a second rack in the bottom third of the oven. Preheat the oven to 400°F (200°C).

Peel the sweet potatoes and cut them into ¾-inch (1.9cm) dice. Toss in the oil and the reserved seasoning blend until they are coated all over. Spread the sweet potatoes on a rimmed baking sheet and roast on the middle rack until tender and browned, about 35 minutes.

After the sweet potatoes have been in the oven for 15 minutes, line another rimmed baking sheet with parchment paper. Place the salmon fillets, skin side down, on the pan and spread any marinade left in the dish on top of the fish. Place the fish on the bottom rack and bake for 20 minutes. Check that the salmon is cooked by inserting a fork in the thickest part of the fish. It should flake easily.

Meanwhile, make the salsa and the Sriracha mayo: For the salsa, place the beans, mangoes, avocado, cucumbers, tomatoes, cilantro, and onions in a large bowl. Toss everything in the lime juice, cumin, and salt. Set aside.

For the Sriracha mayo, whisk the mayonnaise, lime juice, Sriracha sauce, and grated garlic in a small bowl. Set aside.

To serve, pile some salsa on a tortilla. Top with some of the fish and sweet potatoes plus a drizzle of Sriracha mayo, some pickled red onions, and, if desired, some pickled jalapeños and chopped cilantro.

fish tacos
with sriracha
mayo

greek kebabs

greek kebabs

Served with homemade flatbreads, tzatziki, and Greek salad, these juicy and tender kebabs make an easy hybrid meal that caters to both meat eaters and non–meat eaters. I marinate the chicken and tofu separately in a rich and flavorful yogurt marinade. This is a fantastic make-ahead meal because the longer you leave the chicken and tofu to marinate (up to 4 hours), the better they taste. If you are using wooden skewers, don't forget to soak them in water for 20 to 30 minutes before building the kebabs to prevent them from burning when the kebabs are cooking.

makes
8 kebabs
(4 servings)

prep time:
30 minutes,
plus 1 hour
to marinate
chicken and tofu

cook time:
15 minutes

MARINADE:

¾ cup (180ml) plain Greek yogurt

3 tablespoons olive oil

3 tablespoons fresh lemon juice

1 tablespoon tomato paste

1 tablespoon red wine vinegar

1½ teaspoons dried oregano leaves

1½ teaspoons smoked paprika

1 teaspoon dried dill weed

1 teaspoon garlic powder

1 teaspoon salt

½ teaspoon dried thyme leaves

¼ teaspoon cayenne pepper

8 ounces (225g) boneless, skinless chicken breast, cut into 8 (1½-inch/4cm) cubes

7 ounces (200g) extra-firm tofu, pressed (see page 68) and cut into 8 (1½-inch/4cm) cubes

1 large red onion, cut into 1½-inch (4cm) cubes and layers separated

10 ounces (280g) zucchini, cut lengthwise into thin ribbons (see notes)

1 medium red bell pepper, cut into 1½-inch (4cm) pieces

1 medium yellow or orange bell pepper, cut into 1½-inch (4cm) pieces

Olive oil, for brushing

GREEK SALAD:

1 large tomato, cut into 8 wedges

½ medium cucumber, sliced

½ medium romaine lettuce heart

⅓ cup (45g) pitted Kalamata olives

½ small red onion, thinly sliced

2½ ounces (70g) feta cheese, diced

2 tablespoons extra-virgin olive oil

1 tablespoon red wine vinegar

Salt and pepper, to taste

FOR SERVING:

4 flatbreads, homemade (page 170) or store-bought

¾ cup (175g) tzatziki, homemade (page 141) or store-bought (see notes)

SPECIAL
EQUIPMENT:
8 (8-inch/20cm)
skewers

The zucchini ribbons should be thin enough to fold without breaking. The easiest way to cut them is to use a vegetable peeler, discarding the seedy core.

While I prefer traditional cucumber tzatziki with these kebabs, you can also use my beetroot tzatziki (page 141), if desired.

In a small bowl, mix all of the ingredients for the marinade.

Coat the chicken in half of the marinade. In a separate dish, coat the tofu in the other half of the marinade. Cover both dishes and leave to marinate in the fridge for at least 1 hour or up to 4 hours.

When you're nearly ready to build the kebabs, prepare the salad: Toss all of the ingredients in a large salad bowl. Set aside.

Assemble the kebabs: Thread a couple pieces of onion onto a skewer, followed by a piece of chicken. Next, fold a zucchini ribbon on the skewer, then a red bell pepper piece, another piece of chicken, a yellow bell pepper piece, and another zucchini ribbon. Finish with a couple pieces of onion. Repeat this pattern to make 3 additional chicken kebabs.

Make the tofu kebabs the same way, swapping the chicken for tofu pieces.

Preheat a large grill pan or grill to high heat. Brush some olive oil on the kebabs as well as the pan or grill grates. Cook the kebabs for 12 to 15 minutes, turning regularly, until the vegetables and tofu are charred and the chicken is cooked through and no longer pink in the middle.

Serve the kebabs hot with the flatbreads, tzatziki, and Greek salad on the side.

plant swap:
Make it vegan by omitting the chicken and using 14 ounces (400g) of tofu, and swapping the yogurt in the marinade and feta in the salad for plant-based alternatives.

roasted vegetable & meat platter with chimichurri sauce

serves
4 to 6

prep time:
15 minutes

cook time:
45 minutes

There's nothing like a big sharing platter to make a meal convivial. Here, vegetables take center stage and meat is the garnish (that you can skip if you prefer). Chimichurri is a delicious green sauce that originates from South America, where it is served with grilled meat but, in fact, goes with pretty much anything. My version has loads of parsley, oregano, and cilantro. It can be prepared a day ahead and kept in an airtight container in the fridge.

In summer, this is a great dish to cook on the grill. You can customize the recipe to suit whatever produce you have at hand. Corn on the cob, beetroots, tomatoes, carrots, and sweet potatoes would work; you just need to stagger their cooking times. The vegetables and pearl barley can be served warm or at room temperature.

1 medium orange bell pepper, quartered

1 medium red bell pepper, quartered

1 medium eggplant, cut crosswise into ½-inch (1.25cm)-thick rounds

2 large portabella mushrooms

1 medium zucchini, cut lengthwise into ½-inch (1.25cm)-thick planks

2 medium red onions, cut into ½-inch (1.25cm)-thick rounds

5 ounces (140g) thick asparagus

Olive oil, for brushing the vegetables

1 (12-ounce/340g) boneless sirloin or rib-eye steak (about 1¼ inches/3cm thick)

Salt

½ cup (95g) pearl barley

Ground black pepper

1 tablespoon vegetable oil, for the steak

CHIMICHURRI SAUCE:

1¼ packed cups (30g) roughly chopped fresh parsley

¼ packed cup (5g) roughly chopped fresh cilantro

¼ packed cup (5g) roughly chopped fresh oregano leaves

3 cloves garlic, roughly chopped

¼ cup (60ml) red wine vinegar

¾ cup (180ml) extra-virgin olive oil

1 teaspoon crushed red pepper

Salt

Have one oven rack in the middle position and a second rack in the bottom position. Preheat the oven to 400°F (200°C).

Brush all of the vegetables with olive oil. They are cooked together in the oven but require different roasting times. (See the note on page 214 for an overview of total cooking times.)

Spread the bell peppers on a rimmed baking sheet and place in the oven. After 5 minutes, add the eggplant to the pan. Then, 5 minutes later, add the mushrooms. Once the vegetables have been in the oven for 15 minutes, move the pan to the bottom rack.

(recipe continues on next page)

As a rough guide to total roasting times for the vegetables, bell peppers need about 40 minutes, eggplant 35 minutes, mushrooms 30 minutes, zucchini 20 minutes, and red onions and asparagus 15 minutes.

plant swap:

Swap the meat for a plant-based alternative, such as extra-firm tofu.

Spread the zucchini on another rimmed baking sheet and place on the middle rack in the oven. After 5 minutes, add the onions and asparagus to the pan with the zucchini.

Roast all of the vegetables for another 15 minutes. Keep an eye on them so they do not burn. If some are cooking quicker than others, remove them from the pan and keep them warm on the side. While the vegetables are in the oven, prepare the rest of the ingredients.

Remove the meat from the fridge and leave it at room temperature for 20 to 30 minutes.

Cook the pearl barley: Fill a medium saucepan halfway with water and bring to a boil. Add ½ teaspoon of salt and the barley. Cook until the grains are tender but still chewy, 25 to 30 minutes. Drain and set aside.

Make the chimichurri: Place the parsley, cilantro, oregano, garlic, and vinegar in a mini food processor or blender. Process until the herbs are finely minced. Transfer to a bowl and stir in the olive oil and crushed red pepper. Season to taste with salt.

Cook the meat just before you are ready to serve. Pat the steak dry and season lightly with salt and pepper.

Pour the vegetable oil into a medium heavy-bottomed frying pan over high heat. When the oil is shimmering, turn the heat down to medium-high and place the steak in the pan. Depending on how you like your meat cooked, it will take from 1 to 8 minutes. The steak needs about 30 seconds on each side for rare, 1 to 2 minutes for medium, or 3 to 4 minutes for well-done. Allow to rest for 5 minutes, then cut the meat into strips.

Place the cooked barley on a large serving platter and arrange the vegetables around it. Top with the meat strips. Drizzle with the chimichurri and serve immediately.

hoisin stir-fried noodles with pork or jackfruit

Stir-fry is our typical speedy midweek meal and my husband Graham's favorite dish to cook. This version is packed with veggies smothered in a delicious hoisin sauce and can be served as a meat, vegetarian, or hybrid option with two portions of each. Apologies in advance—the hybrid option requires more pans and therefore more washing up. I prefer using a wok for stir-frying, as it cooks food faster and its curved shape makes it easier to toss food around. If you do not have a wok, you can use a large frying pan.

serves
4

prep time:
15 minutes, plus
15 minutes to
marinate pork

cook time:
20 to 30 minutes,
depending on
version

MEAT OPTION:

7 ounces (200g) boneless pork loin, cut into 2½ by ¼-inch (6 by 0.6cm) strips

VEGETARIAN OPTION:

1 (14-ounce/400g) can young green jackfruit in brine, drained

2 tablespoons water

HYBRID OPTION:

4 ounces (115g) pork loin, cut into 2½ by ¼-inch (6 by 0.6cm) strips

7 ounces (200g) canned young green jackfruit in brine, drained

1 tablespoon water

½ to ¾ cup (120 to 180ml) hoisin sauce, divided

1 or 2 tablespoons vegetable oil (depending on version)

Salt

6 ounces (180g) stir-fry egg noodles, such as lo mein

1 tablespoon plus 1 teaspoon toasted sesame oil, divided

¾ cup (90g) finely diced red onions

1 medium red bell pepper, cut into ¼-inch (6mm) strips

5 ounces (150g) sugar snap peas or snow peas

1 cup (125g) peeled and thinly sliced carrots

1 cup (80g) thinly sliced mushrooms

2 cloves garlic, grated

1 (1½-inch/4cm) piece ginger, peeled and cut into strips

3 medium scallions, sliced on the bias

FOR GARNISH/SERVING:

¼ cup (30g) raw cashews, roughly chopped

¼ packed cup (12g) finely chopped fresh cilantro

Crushed red pepper, to taste

Soy sauce, to taste

meat & vegetarian options

If making the vegetarian option, skip ahead to the next step. *To make the meat option,* marinate the pork in 2 tablespoons of the hoisin sauce for 15 minutes, then skip ahead to prepare the noodles.

To make the vegetarian option, put the drained jackfruit in a kitchen towel and squeeze to extract as much water as possible. Break up the chunks with your fingers. Mix the jackfruit with 6 tablespoons (90ml) of the hoisin sauce and the water.

To cook the jackfruit, heat 1 tablespoon of vegetable oil in a wok over medium heat. Add the jackfruit and fry until slightly browned and tender, 10 to 15 minutes. As it cooks, gradually pull the jackfruit apart with 2 forks. When done, remove it from the wok and set aside.

Meanwhile, prepare the noodles: Fill a medium saucepan halfway with water and bring to a boil. Add ½ teaspoon of salt and the noodles. Cook according to the package instructions until soft, generally 4 to 5 minutes. Rinse the noodles under cold water, drain well, mix in 1 teaspoon of the sesame oil, and set aside.

When the meat is done marinating, heat 1 tablespoon of vegetable oil in a wok over high heat and stir-fry the meat until golden, about 4 minutes. Remove the meat from the wok and set aside.

Add the remaining tablespoon of sesame oil to the wok and stir-fry the onions, bell pepper, sugar snap peas, carrots, mushrooms, garlic, and ginger over medium-high heat for 3 to 4 minutes. Add the noodles, scallions, and pork or jackfruit plus 6 tablespoons (90ml) of the hoisin sauce and cook for 2 to 3 minutes more, until the vegetables are tender.

Serve topped with the cashews, cilantro, and crushed red pepper, with soy sauce on the side.

hybrid option

Marinate the pork in 1 tablespoon of the hoisin sauce for 15 minutes.

Put the drained jackfruit in a kitchen towel and squeeze to extract as much water as possible. Break up the chunks with your fingers. Mix the jackfruit with 3 tablespoons of hoisin sauce and 1 tablespoon of water.

Heat 1 tablespoon of the vegetable oil in a wok over medium heat. Add the jackfruit and fry for 10 to 15 minutes, until slightly browned and tender. As it cooks, gradually pull the jackfruit apart with 2 forks. When the jackfruit is done, remove it from the wok and set aside.

Meanwhile, cook the noodles: Fill a medium saucepan halfway with water and bring to a boil. Add ½ teaspoon of salt and the noodles. Cook according to the package instructions until soft, generally 4 to 5 minutes. Rinse the noodles under cold water, drain well, mix in 1 teaspoon of the sesame oil, and set aside.

Heat the remaining tablespoon of vegetable oil in a wok over high heat and stir-fry the meat until golden, about 4 minutes. Remove the meat from the wok and set aside. Wash the wok.

In the same wok, heat the remaining tablespoon of sesame oil over high heat and stir-fry the onions, bell pepper, sugar snap peas, carrots, mushrooms, garlic, and ginger for 3 to 4 minutes. Toss in the noodles and scallions until combined. Transfer half of the mixture to another wok or a large frying pan.

Add the cooked pork plus 3 tablespoons of hoisin sauce to one pan, and add the jackfruit plus 3 tablespoons of hoisin sauce to the other pan.

Cook the contents of both pans for 2 to 3 minutes more, until the vegetables are tender.

Serve topped with the cashews, cilantro, and crushed red pepper, with soy sauce on the side.

fish (or no-fish) koftas with broccoli rice & tahini dressing

Swap traditional meat koftas for this lighter fish version served on a bed of blended broccoli and brown rice and topped with my Herby Tahini Dressing. This is a quick and easy dinner, and once cooked, the koftas will keep in the fridge for a couple of days and can be reheated easily. For a light lunch, wrap them in flatbread with a crunchy green salad. If you prefer a plant-based option, I have included a vegan alternative made with tofu.

makes
24 fish koftas or
18 vegan koftas
(4 to 6 servings)

prep time:
15 minutes, plus
20 minutes to press
tofu for vegan version

cook time:
50 to 60 minutes,
depending on version

KOFTAS:

1 pound (450g) skinless white fish fillets, or 1 (14-ounce/400g) package extra-firm tofu

½ cup (90g) canned cannellini beans, drained and rinsed

½ cup (30g) panko breadcrumbs

2 cloves garlic, roughly chopped

2 tablespoons capers

1 tablespoon fresh lemon juice

1 large nori sheet, roughly torn (for vegan koftas)

1 teaspoon ground coriander

1 teaspoon ground cumin

½ teaspoon turmeric powder

½ teaspoon salt

½ packed cup (10g) roughly chopped fresh dill

½ packed cup (10g) roughly chopped fresh parsley

¼ cup (60ml) vegetable oil, for the baking pan

BROCCOLI RICE:

Salt

½ cup (100g) long-grain brown rice

10 ounces (275g) broccoli

2 tablespoons olive oil

1 clove garlic, grated

Ground black pepper

1 batch Herby Tahini Dressing (page 304), for serving

If making fish koftas, skip ahead to the next step. If making vegan koftas, press the tofu for 20 minutes (see page 68). Shred the pressed tofu on the coarse side of a box grater.

Get the broccoli rice underway, starting with the brown rice: Fill a medium saucepan halfway with water and bring to a boil. Add ½ teaspoon of salt and the rice. Cook according to the package instructions until tender, generally about 40 minutes. Drain and set aside.

Preheat the oven to 400°F (200°C).

Place all of the ingredients for the koftas (except the oil) in a food processor. Pulse to combine to a chunky texture.

Pour the oil onto a rimmed baking sheet, making sure it is coated all over.

Working with 1 heaping tablespoon at a time, shape the mixture into small balls about 1½ inches (4cm) in diameter. Place on the prepared baking sheet, not touching, and spray each kofta with oil. Bake the fish koftas until firm, about 15 minutes; bake the vegan koftas until firm and golden brown, 20 to 25 minutes.

Meanwhile, finish making the broccoli rice: Using the largest holes on a box grater, grate the broccoli florets and stalk to make broccoli rice. Alternatively, to make quick work of this task, place the florets and stalk in a food processor and pulse until the broccoli resembles rice. Set aside.

Heat the olive oil in a large frying pan over medium-high heat. Sauté the broccoli rice and garlic for 2 to 3 minutes. Mix in the cooked brown rice until well combined. Season to taste with salt and pepper.

Serve the koftas on a bed of rice, topped with tahini dressing.

less-meat lasagna

serves

6

prep time:

15 minutes

cook time:

85 minutes

A classic lasagna is often made with a rich beef and pork Bolognese sauce. This is a lighter alternative where half the meat is swapped for split red lentils. Layers of ricotta and mozzarella cheese add a creamy texture. The ultimate comfort food with a healthy twist.

BOLOGNESE SAUCE:

3 tablespoons olive oil, divided

1 pound (450g) 85% lean ground beef

1 cup (125g) finely diced onions

8 ounces (225g) baby bella mushrooms, finely chopped

2 cloves garlic, grated

¾ cup (130g) split red lentils, picked over and rinsed

3½ cups (800ml) smooth tomato sauce, homemade (page 312) or store-bought (see note)

1 cup (240ml) water

1¼ packed cups (30g) roughly chopped fresh basil

CHEESE MIXTURE:

1 large egg, beaten

2 cups (450g) ricotta cheese

¼ teaspoon freshly grated nutmeg

½ teaspoon salt

1 (9-ounce/255g) package oven-ready lasagna noodles

2⅓ cups (360g) shredded fresh mozzarella cheese, divided

Heat 1 tablespoon of the oil in a 5-quart (4.7L) Dutch oven over medium heat. Add the beef and cook until well browned, about 15 minutes, breaking up the meat with a wooden spoon as it cooks. Using a slotted spoon, transfer the meat to a bowl. Drain off any excess fat remaining in the pot.

Heat the remaining 2 tablespoons of oil in the same pot, still over medium heat, and cook the onions until softened and lightly browned, about 5 minutes.

Turn the heat up to medium-high and add the mushrooms to the pot. Cook until any moisture the mushrooms have released has evaporated and they are nicely browned, 6 to 8 minutes.

Lower the heat to medium and return the meat to the pot. Stir in the garlic, lentils, tomato sauce, water, and basil. Simmer, uncovered, until the sauce starts to thicken, 10 to 15 minutes.

Meanwhile, prepare the cheese mixture: In a medium bowl, mix together the egg, ricotta, nutmeg, and salt. Set aside.

Preheat the oven to 400°F (200°C).

To assemble the lasagna, spread 1 cup (240ml) of the Bolognese sauce in a 13 by 9-inch (33 by 23cm) baking dish. Add a single layer of lasagna noodles. Top with one-third of the remaining sauce followed by half of the cheese mixture and ⅔ cup (100g) of the mozzarella. Repeat the layers, ending with a layer of noodles and the remaining sauce. Scatter the remaining 1 cup (155g) of mozzarella on top.

Bake for 30 to 40 minutes, until the top has a nice golden brown color.

note:
If making my Easy Tomato Sauce, whizz it in a blender until smooth before using it for this lasagna.

plant swap:
Make it vegetarian by omitting the meat and tripling the amount of mushrooms, using 1½ pounds (775g).

less-meat (or no-meat) meatballs in red sauce

These tender and juicy meatballs are just as good as the real thing but have only half the meat. They are delicious with spaghetti or in a sub, and any leftovers are easy to reheat in the microwave. For extra flavor, I like to pan-fry them before simmering them in tomato sauce. If you prefer to bake them, simply place them on an oiled rimmed baking sheet and bake at 400°F (200°C) for 20 minutes.

You can easily make these meatballs vegan by swapping the meat for eggplant and the egg for chickpea flour and using vegan parmesan and Worcestershire sauce. The vegan meatballs are softer, so the mixture needs to rest before being formed into meatballs. I give both methods below.

makes
24 meatballs (4 to 6 servings)

prep time:
15 minutes, plus 15 minutes to rest vegan meatball mixture

cook time:
20 to 25 minutes, depending on version

VEGAN OPTION:

10 ounces (300g) eggplant, cubed

1 tablespoon olive oil

LESS-MEAT OPTION:

8 ounces (225g) 85% lean ground beef

1 (15-ounce/425g) can black beans, drained and rinsed

3 tablespoons roughly chopped onions

⅓ cup (45g) or ⅔ cup (90g) plain breadcrumbs (depending on version), plus more if needed

⅔ cup (40g) grated Parmesan cheese, plus more for garnish

1 large egg, beaten, or 2 tablespoons chickpea flour

2 tablespoons finely chopped fresh parsley leaves

1 tablespoon Worcestershire sauce

1 teaspoon Italian seasoning

½ teaspoon garlic powder

Salt

2 tablespoons olive oil, plus more as needed, for the pan

5 cups (1.2L) tomato sauce, homemade (page 312) or store-bought

8 ounces (225g) spaghetti or other pasta of choice, for serving

Fresh basil leaves, for garnish

If making the less-meat option, skip ahead. *To make the no-meat meatballs*, in a large frying pan, sauté the eggplant in the oil over medium-high heat until soft and golden, about 5 minutes.

Place the eggplant, beans, and onions in a food processor. Blend to combine into a thick mixture, then transfer the mixture to a medium bowl and add ⅔ cup (90g) breadcrumbs. Skip the next step.

To make the less-meat meatballs, place the beans and onions in a food processor. Blend to combine into a thick mixture. Transfer the mixture to a medium bowl and add the beef and ⅓ cup (45g) breadcrumbs.

To the bowl, add the Parmesan, egg or chickpea flour, parsley, Worcestershire sauce, Italian seasoning, garlic powder, and ½ teaspoon of salt. Using your hands, mix the ingredients until well combined. You may need to add a little more breadcrumbs to the vegan mixture if it is too wet. Allow the vegan mixture to rest for 15 minutes before forming into meatballs; the less-meat version can be formed right away.

To form the meatballs, roll 1 heaping tablespoon of the mixture between your palms to form a small ball (about ¾ inch/2cm). Repeat to make a total of 24 meatballs.

Heat the oil in a large frying pan over medium-high heat. Working with 6 meatballs at a time, cook the meatballs for 2 minutes, until browned all over. (You do not need to cook them completely.) Transfer them to a paper towel–lined plate while you cook the rest of the meatballs, adding more oil to the pan between batches as needed.

Meanwhile, bring the tomato sauce to a simmer in a large saucepan over medium heat.

Place the browned meatballs in the pan with the sauce and simmer, covered, for 8 to 10 minutes.

Cook the pasta: Fill a stockpot halfway with water and bring to a boil. Add ½ teaspoon of salt and the spaghetti. Cook according to the package instructions until al dente, generally 8 to 10 minutes. Drain well.

Serve the spaghetti topped with the meatballs and sauce, garnished with grated Parmesan and basil leaves.

turkey (or no-turkey) meatloaf

A popular midweek family dinner, this is a healthy twist on conventional meatloaf that I like to serve with mashed potatoes and green beans. Leftovers are delicious hot or cold and make a tasty add-on to lunch boxes.

The meat version uses turkey instead of beef, and I have replaced half of the meat with black beans and chickpeas. Hearty eggplant is the perfect meat substitute in the vegan version, and I use the chickpea brine (aquafaba) as an egg replacement.

A few tips for success:

- I prefer using a narrower 2-pound loaf pan. Mine measures 8½ by 4½ by 2¾ inches (21 by 11.5 by 7cm).

- To keep your meatloaf from being too dense, do not overmix the ingredients.

- Shape the meatloaf before transferring it to the loaf pan; the mixture will be wet.

- Once cooked, allow the meatloaf to rest for 15 to 20 minutes so it's easier to cut. This is key for the vegan version, which is softer than the meat version.

serves
6 to 8

prep time:
10 minutes

cook time:

1 hour 5 minutes (meat version) or 1 hour 35 minutes (vegan version)

LESS-MEAT OPTION:

⅓ cup (80ml) 2% milk

2 large eggs, beaten

1 pound (450g) ground turkey

VEGAN OPTION:

1½ pounds (675g) eggplant, cubed

3 tablespoons olive oil

⅓ cup (80ml) aquafaba (chickpea brine), reserved from can (below)

⅓ cup (80ml) oat or soy milk

Cooking oil spray

1 (15-ounce/425g) can black beans, drained and rinsed

¾ cup (90g) finely diced red onions

1 (15-ounce/425g) can chickpeas, drained and rinsed

1 cup (60g) panko breadcrumbs

½ packed cup (10g) roughly chopped fresh parsley

2 tablespoons tomato paste

1 tablespoon tamari

2 teaspoons Italian seasoning

1 teaspoon garlic powder

1 teaspoon smoked paprika

1 teaspoon salt

¾ teaspoon ground black pepper

Chopped fresh parsley, for garnish (optional)

GLAZE:

¾ cup (180ml) ketchup

2 tablespoons dark brown sugar

1 tablespoon apple cider vinegar

If making the meat version, skip ahead. *To make the vegan version*, preheat the oven to 450°F (230°C). Scatter the eggplant on a rimmed baking sheet and toss in the oil. Bake for 30 minutes, until golden brown.

Remove the eggplant from the oven and set it aside to cool.

Preheat the oven to 350°F (180°C). Line an 8½ by 4½ by 2¾-inch (21 by 11.5 by 7cm) loaf pan with foil, leaving some overhanging the sides, and spray the inside with cooking oil.

Place the beans and onions in a food processor and blend to a thick paste. Add the chickpeas and pulse to a slightly chunky texture.

Transfer the mixture to a large bowl. Stir in the rest of the ingredients, except the turkey or eggplant, until well combined. Add the turkey or eggplant and mix with your hands until everything just comes together. Do not overmix.

Shape the mixture into a loaf and transfer to the prepared loaf pan. Bake uncovered for 45 minutes.

Meanwhile, make the glaze: Mix together all of the glaze ingredients in a bowl.

Remove the meatloaf from the oven and brush half of the glaze on top. Return the meatloaf to the oven; bake the turkey version for another 10 minutes, the vegan version for another 20 minutes.

Brush the meatloaf with the remaining glaze and bake for 10 minutes more. To verify that the turkey version is fully cooked, check the internal temperature: when done, it should read 165°F (75°C). Remove the meatloaf from the oven and let stand for 10 minutes in the pan.

Transfer the meatloaf to a serving plate and carefully remove the foil. Before slicing and serving, let the turkey meatloaf stand for another 5 minutes, the vegan meatloaf for another 10 minutes. Garnish with chopped parsley, if desired.

linguine with pesto alla trapanese

Originally from Sicily, pesto alla Trapanese is a fresh and lively sauce made with ripe tomatoes, herbs, and almonds. Traditionally, all of the ingredients are pounded together using a mortar and pestle. However, you can whip it up in no time in a food processor and spoon it on top of your favorite pasta, grain, or even roasted vegetables. It is lighter than traditional Genovese pesto and lends so much flavor to this linguine recipe, which is simply the best summer pasta dish to enjoy al fresco. To accommodate different diets, you can make it with either fish or chickpeas—or both! The hybrid option makes two portions of each.

serves
4

prep time:
15 minutes

cook time:
12 minutes

PESTO:

1 cup (100g) sliced almonds

1 pound (450g) ripe tomatoes, quartered

3 cloves garlic, chopped

3 tablespoons fresh lemon juice

2 teaspoons granulated sugar

1 teaspoon crushed red pepper

2 packed cups (45g) roughly chopped fresh basil

½ packed cup (10g) roughly chopped fresh mint leaves

⅓ cup (80ml) extra-virgin olive oil

Salt and pepper

PASTA:

½ teaspoon salt

12 ounces (340g) linguine

1 tablespoon olive oil

SEAFOOD OPTION:

1 pound (450g) skinned white fish fillets

Salt and pepper

2 tablespoons olive oil

12 large shrimp, cooked and peeled

VEGAN OPTION:

1 (15-ounce/425g) can chickpeas, drained and rinsed

HYBRID OPTION:

8 ounces (225g) skinned white fish fillets

6 large shrimp, cooked and peeled

1 cup (150g) canned chickpeas, drained and rinsed

FOR GARNISH:

Fresh basil leaves

Shaved Parmesan cheese or plant-based alternative

Make the pesto: In a large frying pan, dry-toast the almonds over medium heat for about 2 minutes, until golden and fragrant. Stir often to prevent them from burning. Remove the almonds from the pan and set aside.

Place the tomatoes in a food processor. Add the garlic, lemon juice, sugar, and crushed red pepper. Blend until smooth. Add the toasted almonds, basil, and mint. Pulse until the almonds are roughly chopped. Transfer to a medium bowl and whisk in the oil. Season to taste with salt and pepper. Set aside.

Fill a stockpot halfway with water and bring to a boil. Add the salt and linguine. Cook the pasta according to the package instructions until al dente, generally 10 to 12 minutes. Drain and toss in 1 tablespoon of oil. Set aside and keep warm.

Meanwhile, cook the fish, if using: Pat the fillets dry with paper towels. Season both sides with salt and pepper. In a large nonstick frying pan, heat the oil over medium-high heat. When the oil is shimmering, add the fish and cook on one side until golden, about 2 minutes. Using a fish spatula, carefully flip the fillets over and continue cooking on the other side until the fish is cooked through and flakes easily at the thickest part, 1 to 2 minutes depending on thickness. Flip the fish only once; otherwise, you might damage the fillets.

When ready to serve, divide the pasta among 4 plates. Top with the fish and shrimp or the chickpeas, then the pesto. Garnish with basil leaves and shaved Parmesan.

loaded sloppy joe sweet potatoes

serves
4

prep time:
10 minutes

cook time:
50 minutes

A simple crowd-pleaser made healthier by swapping bread for tender baked sweet potatoes and replacing half of the meat with hearty lentils. I love the sweet smoky and tangy taste of BBQ sauce here. It is so addictive.

The sloppy joe mixture is prepared while the sweet potatoes are in the oven. If you are in a hurry, you can make the sloppy joe mixture a day ahead and bake the sweet potatoes in the microwave on the day of.

SWEET POTATOES:

4 medium to large or 6 small sweet potatoes (about 1⅓ pounds/600g), scrubbed

Olive oil

SLOPPY JOE MIXTURE:

2 tablespoons olive oil

8 ounces (225g) 85% lean ground beef

⅓ cup (40g) finely diced onions

½ medium green bell pepper, finely diced

2 cloves garlic, grated

¾ cup (180ml) tomato sauce, homemade (page 312) or store-bought

½ cup (120ml) ketchup

⅓ cup (80ml) BBQ sauce

1 tablespoon Worcestershire sauce

1 teaspoon Dijon mustard

1½ tablespoons dark brown sugar

1 (15-ounce/425g) can green or brown lentils, drained and rinsed

½ cup (120ml) water

FOR GARNISH:

Shredded cheese of choice

Sliced scallions

Preheat the oven to 425°F (220°C). Line a rimmed baking sheet or large baking pan with parchment paper.

Cut the sweet potatoes in half lengthwise and place cut side up on the prepared baking sheet. Drizzle some oil on top and bake for 45 to 50 minutes, until soft.

Meanwhile, start preparing the sloppy joe mixture: Heat the oil in a 5-quart (4.7L) Dutch oven over medium heat and cook the beef until browned, about 7 minutes. Use a wooden spoon to break up the meat as it cooks. Add the onions, bell pepper, and garlic and cook gently until soft, another 3 to 4 minutes.

Stir in the tomato sauce, ketchup, BBQ sauce, Worcestershire sauce, mustard, brown sugar, lentils, and water. Cook the mixture over medium heat, stirring from time to time, until the sauce has thickened, 10 to 15 minutes.

When the sweet potatoes are done, grate the flesh with a fork to create a small cavity in each one. Transfer to a serving platter or tray and spoon a generous amount of the sloppy Joe mixture on top of each sweet potato half.

Sprinkle with shredded cheese and scallions just before serving.

plant swap:
Make it vegan by omitting the meat and adding another 15-ounce (425g) can of lentils. Use vegan Worcestershire sauce and cheese.

sausage traybake

This traybake, with its fragrant basil and lemon green sauce, makes a straightforward and tasty dinner. You can use different vegetables than the ones I've suggested depending on what is in season, such as Brussels sprouts, butternut squash, eggplant, mushrooms, or sweet potatoes. To satisfy everyone, I make it with half vegetarian sausages and half meat sausages.

serves
4

prep time:
10 minutes

cook time:
40 minutes

Salt

1 pound (450g) baking potatoes (such as russet or King Edward), peeled and cut into 1½-inch (4cm) chunks

1 medium orange bell pepper, cut into ½-inch (1cm) strips

1 large red onion, cut into ¾-inch (2cm) wedges

8 ounces (225g) zucchini, cut crosswise into ½-inch (1cm) rounds

4 (3-ounce/85g) fresh sausages of choice

2 tablespoons olive oil

Ground black pepper

8 ounces (225g) cherry tomatoes

8 ounces (225g) green or savoy cabbage, thinly sliced

1 (15-ounce/425g) can pinto beans, drained and rinsed

GREEN SAUCE:

1¼ packed cups (30g) roughly chopped fresh basil

3 cloves garlic, roughly chopped

½ cup (50g) raw walnuts

Grated zest and juice of ½ lemon

¼ cup (60ml) extra-virgin olive oil

¼ teaspoon salt

Fill a large saucepan halfway with water and bring to a boil. Add ½ teaspoon of salt and the potatoes. Par-cook for 6 minutes, then drain and set aside.

Preheat the oven to 425°F (220°C).

Scatter the potatoes, bell pepper, onion, zucchini, and sausages on a rimmed baking sheet or other large baking pan. Toss the vegetables in the oil and season lightly with salt and pepper. Spread the vegetables in an even layer, place the sausages on top, and roast for 25 minutes.

Meanwhile, make the green sauce: Place all of the ingredients in a mini food processor and blend until the texture is similar to pesto (mostly smooth but with some small chunks remaining).

Remove the pan from the oven, add the tomatoes and cabbage, and give everything a good stir. Keep the sausages on top, flipping them around so they cook evenly. Bake for 10 minutes more. Stir in the beans and cook until the sausages are browned, about 5 minutes.

Remove from the oven and toss everything in the green sauce until well combined. Serve immediately.

plant swap:
Make it vegan by using plant-based sausages or replacing the sausages with another can of beans.

one-pan spanish-style chicken

Made with a fragrant, smoky marinade, this dish is a real crowd-pleaser. It also makes fantastic leftovers the next day. I do not eat meat, but the rest of my family does. Trying to please everyone can get complicated and time-consuming, and I often choose to make one dish that will feed everyone. I enjoy this dish without the meat while the rest of my family tucks in enthusiastically for the whole shebang.

serves

4 to 6

prep time:

20 minutes, plus
20 minutes to
marinate chicken

cook time:

65 minutes

MARINADE:

3 cloves garlic, minced

1 teaspoon salt

3 tablespoons finely chopped fresh rosemary, plus more sprigs for garnish if desired

2 tablespoons smoked paprika

2 tablespoons tomato paste

¼ cup plus 2 tablespoons (90ml) olive oil

¼ cup plus 2 tablespoons (90ml) fresh lemon juice

6 bone-in, skin-on chicken thighs or drumsticks (or a mix)

1 pound (450g) baby Dutch yellow potatoes, fingerling potatoes, or baby red potatoes, scrubbed

Salt

1 small eggplant (about 10 ounces/280g)

1 large yellow or orange bell pepper

1 large red bell pepper

1 medium red onion

10 ounces (280g) cherry tomatoes

1⅓ cups (185g) pitted green olives

1 (15.5-ounce/440g) can butter beans, drained

1 to 2 preserved lemons (according to taste), finely chopped (see note)

Ground black pepper

Using a large mortar and pestle, mash together the garlic, salt, and rosemary to form a paste. Mix in the smoked paprika, tomato paste, oil, and lemon juice. If you do not have a mortar and pestle, grate the garlic, chop the rosemary finely, and mix with the rest of the ingredients.

Place the chicken in a large bowl, pour in half of the marinade, and toss to coat. Set aside for 20 minutes. Reserve the remaining marinade for the vegetables.

Meanwhile, prepare the vegetables: Fill a large saucepan halfway with water and bring to a boil. Cut the potatoes in half lengthwise. When the water is boiling, salt the water and add the potatoes. Par-cook for 10 minutes, or until you can easily insert a knife in the potatoes but still feel a slight resistance. Drain the potatoes and set aside.

Preheat the oven to 400°F (200°C).

Cut the eggplant into ¾-inch (2cm) dice. Remove the seeds from the bell peppers and slice them. Cut the onion into ½-inch (1.25cm)-thick wedges.

Remove the chicken from the marinade and place in a large baking pan; discard any leftover marinade in the bowl.

Toss the prepped vegetables and par-cooked potatoes in the reserved marinade. Spread on top of the chicken in the pan.

Bake until the chicken is cooked through and the vegetables are tender, about 40 minutes.

Add the tomatoes and olives to the pan and cook until the tomatoes start to blister, about 10 minutes more.

Add the beans and cook for another 5 minutes to warm through.

Remove the pan from the oven. Spoon some of the pan juices over the vegetables and chicken.

Mix in the preserved lemons and season with salt and pepper to taste. Garnish with rosemary sprigs, if desired.

 note:

Preserved lemons have a unique pickled taste that lends a depth of flavor to dishes. You can find them in Middle Eastern or Asian grocery stores or specialty food stores. They are great flavor enhancers and will keep for a long time in the fridge. Alternatively, you can make your own. You could also substitute lemon juice (Meyer lemon juice would be particularly nice) for the preserved lemons, adding 1 to 2 teaspoons of lemon juice and a pinch of salt (preferably sea salt flakes), according to taste.

spiced herb chicken or tofu

Seasoned with aromatic herbs, cayenne pepper, and smoky paprika, this dish is packed with flavor and perfectly complemented by a fresh black-eyed pea salsa. It can be prepared with either chicken or tofu; the hybrid option makes two portions of each to accommodate different diets.

While the chicken or tofu is marinating, you prepare the salsa and start cooking the rice and zucchini. If I have time, I like to use frozen and thawed tofu because it has a heartier texture. Otherwise, pressed tofu also works well.

serves
6

prep time:
30 minutes,
plus 1 hour to
marinate chicken
and/or tofu

cook time:
45 minutes

MARINADE:

1 teaspoon salt

1 tablespoon smoked paprika

2 teaspoons dried oregano leaves

2 teaspoons dried parsley

2 teaspoons dried thyme leaves

1 teaspoon garlic powder

1 teaspoon onion powder

½ teaspoon cayenne pepper

½ cup (120ml) olive oil

CHICKEN OPTION:

1 pound (450g) boneless, skinless chicken breasts

VEGAN OPTION:

2 (14-ounce/400g) packages extra-firm tofu, thawed from frozen or pressed (see page 68) and cut into 16 slices

HYBRID OPTION:

8 ounces (225g) boneless, skinless chicken breast

1 (14-ounce/400g) package extra-firm tofu, thawed from frozen or pressed (see page 68) and cut into 8 slices

BLACK-EYED PEA SALSA:

4 medium tomatoes, finely diced

1 (15.5-ounce/440g) can black-eyed peas, drained and rinsed

1 clove garlic, grated

1 small jalapeño pepper, seeded and finely diced

½ packed cup (20g) roughly chopped fresh cilantro

2 tablespoons fresh lime juice

1 tablespoon extra-virgin olive oil

½ teaspoon salt

Salt

1½ cups (260g) long-grain brown rice

10 ounces (285g) zucchini, cut lengthwise into thin planks

2 tablespoons olive oil, plus more for the pan

Ground black pepper

Lime wedges, for serving

Make the marinade: In a small bowl, mix the salt with the spices and herbs. Whisk in the oil until everything is well combined. Set the marinade aside.

Lay the chicken breasts flat on a cutting board. Using a sharp knife, cut each breast in half horizontally to an even thickness. (See page 53 for a step-by-step tutorial.)

Put the chicken cutlets and/or tofu in a shallow dish(es) and coat all over with the marinade. Place in the fridge to marinate for 1 hour.

Make the salsa: Mix all of the ingredients in a small bowl until well combined.

After the chicken and/or tofu has marinated for 30 minutes, fill a large saucepan halfway with water and bring to a boil. Add ½ teaspoon of salt and the rice. Cook the rice following the package instructions until tender, generally 40 minutes. Drain and keep warm.

Meanwhile, toss the zucchini strips in the oil. Season with ½ teaspoon of salt and a good grind of pepper. Preheat a grill to medium-high heat or a grill pan or large frying pan over medium-high heat. Lightly grease the grill grate or pan with oil. Working in batches, grill or fry the zucchini for 2 minutes on each side, until browned all over and soft in the middle. Set aside and keep warm.

Place the chicken and/or tofu on the grill grate or in the pan and cook for 3 to 4 minutes on each side, until the chicken is cooked through and/or the tofu has a nice golden color all over.

Serve the chicken and/or tofu on a bed of rice with the zucchini, salsa, and lime wedges.

stuffed butternut squash with sage & walnut pesto—two ways

serves
4

prep time:
15 minutes

cook time:
1 hour
15 minutes

Topped with a tasty sage and walnut pesto, this colorful and satisfying squash dish makes a spectacular centerpiece. I designed this recipe to make two vegan portions and two meat portions, each cooked and served in its own squash boat. For one boat, the hearty filling—a combination of wild rice blend, mushrooms, spinach, cranberries, and walnuts—is bulked up with sausage, while the filling for the other boat is bulked up with green lentils.

This is a versatile recipe. If you wish to make all four servings with meat or all four servings vegan, simply double the quantity of sausage or lentils and skip the step of dividing the filling into two equal portions. For a less-meat option, add both the lentils and the sausage to the full amount of filling, skipping the step of dividing the filling base in half. Then evenly fill the two squash boats with the less-meat mixture.

ROASTED SQUASH:

1 medium butternut squash (about 3 pounds/1.4kg)

Olive oil

Salt

FILLING:

Salt

½ cup (90g) wild rice blend

Olive oil

1 cup (125g) finely diced onions

8 ounces (225g) baby bella mushrooms, thinly sliced

3 cloves garlic, grated

2 packed cups (70g) baby spinach

½ cup (70g) unsweetened dried cranberries

½ cup (50g) raw walnuts

2 tablespoons finely chopped fresh parsley

¼ teaspoon freshly grated nutmeg

Ground black pepper

8 ounces (225g) Italian sausage links

1 cup (160g) cooked French green lentils, drained and rinsed (see note, page 144)

PESTO:

1 packed cup (25g) roughly chopped fresh parsley

½ packed cup (10g) roughly chopped fresh sage leaves

½ cup (50g) raw walnuts

2 tablespoons fresh lemon juice, plus more if desired

3 cloves garlic, roughly chopped

½ teaspoon salt

¾ cup (180ml) extra-virgin olive oil

Ground black pepper, to taste

Preheat the oven to 400°F (200°C).

Halve the butternut squash lengthwise and remove the seeds. With a sharp knife, score the flesh in a diamond pattern. Place the squash cut side up on a rimmed baking sheet or other baking pan large enough to hold both halves. Brush with oil and season each half with a pinch or two of salt. Roast for 50 to 60 minutes, until soft.

Meanwhile, prepare the filling, starting with the rice: Fill a medium saucepan halfway with water and bring to a boil. Add ½ teaspoon of salt and the rice. Cook according to the package instructions until tender, generally 30 to 35 minutes. Do not overcook the rice or it will become mushy. Drain and set aside.

Prepare the rest of the filling ingredients: Heat 2 tablespoons of oil in a large frying pan over medium heat. Add the onions and cook gently, stirring from time to time, until they start to soften, 6 to 8 minutes. Turn the heat up to medium-high and add the mushrooms to the pan. Cook until any moisture the mushrooms have released has evaporated and they are nicely browned, 6 to 8 minutes.

Lower the heat to medium and stir in the garlic, spinach, cranberries, walnuts, parsley, and nutmeg. Cook until the spinach has wilted, 2 to 3 minutes. Season to taste with salt and pepper, then set the pan aside.

Remove the sausage from its casing and crumble it with a fork. Heat 1 tablespoon of oil in another large frying pan over medium heat and cook the sausage until browned all over and no pink is showing. Remove the meat with a slotted spoon and set aside.

Remove the squash from the oven. Using a spoon, carefully scoop out the flesh, leaving a ½-inch (1cm) border. Mix the squash flesh into the mushroom mixture. Gently stir in the rice.

Divide the filling into 2 equal portions, adding the lentils to one half and the sausage to the other. Season both mixtures to taste with salt and pepper. Spoon the mixture back into its respective squash half. Drizzle some oil on top and roast for 15 minutes more, until the filling starts to brown slightly.

Meanwhile, make the pesto: Place the parsley, sage, walnuts, lemon juice, garlic, and salt in a blender and blend to a slightly chunky paste. Transfer to a bowl, then slowly whisk in the oil. Add pepper along with more lemon juice and salt, if desired.

Serve the stuffed squash hot, drizzled with the pesto.

stuffed butternut
squash with sage
& walnut pesto

turkey enchilada skillet

turkey enchilada skillet

serves
4 to 6

prep time:
10 minutes

cook time:
45 minutes

This is my go-to Mexican recipe whenever I have leftover turkey (or chicken) to use. You won't need much meat, as the bulk of the dish is made up of a mix of vegetables, tortilla strips, and some cheese. But the meat-free version made with black beans (detailed in the Plant Swap, opposite) is just as delicious. I make my own enchilada sauce, but you can use a store-bought equivalent; you'll need 2½ cups (600ml). For a hybrid version yielding two to three less-meat servings and two to three vegetarian servings, turn the page.

ENCHILADA SAUCE:

3 tablespoons vegetable oil

3 tablespoons all-purpose flour

1½ teaspoons hot chili powder (see note, opposite)

1 teaspoon ground cumin

1 teaspoon dried oregano leaves

½ teaspoon smoked paprika

¼ teaspoon ground cinnamon

¼ teaspoon salt

3 tablespoons tomato paste

2½ cups (600ml) vegetable stock

2 to 3 teaspoons apple cider vinegar, according to taste

Ground black pepper

1 tablespoon vegetable oil

¾ cup (90g) finely diced onions

1 medium red bell pepper, diced

3 cloves garlic, grated

1 teaspoon ground cumin

1 teaspoon dried oregano leaves

3 packed cups (105g) baby spinach

1 cup (150g) frozen corn kernels

8 ounces (225g) shredded cooked turkey (white and/or dark meat)

8 (6-inch/15cm) corn tortillas, cut into strips

4 ounces (115g) shredded Mexican cheese blend or cheddar cheese

FOR SERVING:

Fresh cilantro leaves

1 large avocado, sliced

1 or 2 medium jalapeño peppers, sliced

Sour cream (optional)

Make the enchilada sauce: Heat the oil in a medium saucepan over medium-high heat until it is shimmering. Reduce the heat to medium and whisk in the flour. Whisking constantly, cook until browned, 30 seconds to 1 minute, then stir in the spices and salt and cook for another 30 seconds to 1 minute.

Whisk in the tomato paste, stock, and vinegar. Bring to a boil, then cook the sauce, stirring continuously, until it is thick enough to coat the back of a spoon, about 8 minutes. Remove from the heat and season to taste with pepper and more salt, if needed. The sauce should have a smoky and spicy flavor; depending on the acidity of your tomato paste, you may wish to add up to 1 more teaspoon vinegar to give it slightly more tang. Set the sauce aside.

Preheat the oven to 350°F (180°C).

Heat the oil in a large ovenproof frying pan over medium heat. Add the onions and cook gently, stirring from time to time, until they start to soften, 6 to 8 minutes. Add the bell pepper and garlic and cook until aromatic, about 2 minutes.

Add the cumin, oregano, spinach, corn, and enchilada sauce and mix well. Stir in the turkey. Cook until the spinach has wilted, about 2 minutes. Stir in the tortilla strips until well combined.

Sprinkle the cheese on top and bake until it is melted and golden brown, 20 to 25 minutes.

Serve immediately topped with cilantro, avocado, jalapeños, and sour cream, if desired.

hybrid option:

Use 4 ounces (115g) of cooked turkey and ⅔ cup (120g) of cooked black beans, drained and rinsed.

Complete the first 4 steps as written, except hold off on adding the turkey. After mixing in the tortilla strips, divide the enchilada mixture between 2 small ovenproof frying pans or pie dishes 6½ or 7 inches (16.5 or 17.75cm) in diameter, or 2 baking dishes about 7½ by 6½ by 2 inches (19 by 16.5 by 5cm). Mix the turkey into the enchilada mixture in one frying pan or dish and the beans into the other.

Divide the cheese evenly between the pans or dishes, then bake for 15 to 20 minutes.

note:

If you do not have hot chili powder, you can use regular chili powder and add ⅛ to ¼ teaspoon of cayenne pepper.

meat-free mains

butternut & leek casserole with herby dumplings | 244

creamy stuffed shells in red sauce | 246

eggplant & potato curry | 248

pan-fried eggplant with green lentil & tomato stew | 250

golden rice & cabbage | 252

vegan mushroom alfredo pasta | 254

one-pot orzo primavera | 256

pan-fried gnocchi with eggplant puttanesca | 258

red lentil dahl with crunchy kale & coconut | 260

roasted cabbage with beluga lentils & salsa verde | 262

roasted cauliflower with pearl couscous salad | 264

root vegetable tagine | 268

smoky sweet potato stew | 270

sweet & sour tofu with cauliflower rice | 272

grilled tofu satay skewers with rice noodle salad | 276

teriyaki tempeh bowls | 278

three-bean chili with jalapeño cornbread topping | 280

butternut & leek casserole with herby dumplings

This warming and hearty vegetarian casserole is served with scrumptious herby dumplings. Cooked in a creamy cheesy sauce, it is the perfect meal for a cold evening. I use a mixture of white and whole-grain spelt flours for the dumplings. Spelt is an ancient grain that is high in protein and has a delicious nutty flavor. It is one of my favorite nutrient-rich flours and works well in a wide range of recipes. If needed, you can substitute half all-purpose flour and half whole-wheat flour.

serves
6

prep time:
20 minutes

cook time:
40 minutes

CASEROLE:

1 pound (450g) leeks, cut into ¼-inch (6mm)-thick semicircles

2 tablespoons olive oil

4 cloves garlic, grated

1 small to medium butternut squash (about 2 pounds/900g), peeled, seeded, and cubed

1 teaspoon dried parsley

1 teaspoon dried thyme leaves

3 cups (750ml) vegetable stock

2 tablespoons cornstarch

2 tablespoons water

1 (15.5-ounce/440g) can cannellini beans, drained and rinsed

1 cup (240ml) half-and-half

1⅓ cups (100g) shredded sharp cheddar cheese

Salt and pepper

Chopped fresh parsley, for garnish

DUMPLINGS:

1 cup (125g) white spelt flour

1 cup (125g) whole-grain spelt flour

2 teaspoons baking powder

½ teaspoon salt

½ cup (120g) unsalted cold butter, diced

2 tablespoons chopped fresh parsley

2 tablespoons chopped fresh thyme

¼ cup (60ml) cold water, plus more if needed

Place the leek semicircles in a bowl of fresh water and gently stir with your hands to dislodge any dirt; the dirt will sink to the bottom. Lift out the leek pieces with your hands or a slotted spoon to avoid disturbing the dirt at the bottom of the bowl, then drain and set aside.

Make the dumplings: Put the flours, baking powder, and salt in a large bowl and whisk to combine. Using your fingertips, rub the butter into the flour mixture until it begins to resemble breadcrumbs, then add the fresh herbs. Continue to mix with your fingertips, adding the cold water 1 tablespoon at a time, until the dough sticks together to form a large ball. (If it is too dry and won't come together, add up to 1 tablespoon more water.) Divide the dough into 12 even pieces, then roll each piece into a small ball. Set the dough balls aside.

Heat the oil in a 5-quart (5L) Dutch oven over medium heat and cook the leeks until they start to soften, about 5 minutes. Add the garlic and cook for another 2 minutes, until aromatic.

Stir in the butternut squash, dried herbs, and stock. Whisk the cornstarch with the water to form a slurry, then add the slurry to the pot and stir. Bring to a boil, then reduce the heat to a lively simmer and cook, covered, until the squash starts to soften, 8 to 10 minutes.

Preheat the oven to 400°F (200°C).

Using a wooden spoon, carefully stir the beans, cream, and cheese into the squash mixture until well combined. Season to taste with salt and pepper.

Arrange the dumplings on top of the vegetable mixture. Bake the casserole, uncovered, until the dumplings have doubled in size and are light golden brown, about 20 minutes.

Serve with chopped parsley on top.

plant swap:
Make it vegan by swapping the butter, cream, and cheese for plant-based alternatives.

creamy stuffed shells in red sauce

Quick and easy, this fun twist on a pasta bake is another of our family favorites. The shells are filled with creamy zucchini and cooked in a tasty tomato sauce. You might get lucky and get some extra help, as kids often enjoy stuffing the shells. If you are short on time, you can prepare everything in the morning and simply pop the casserole in the oven for dinner. It's not traditional in Italian cooking, but I like the sharpness of cheddar cheese here; you can use shredded mozzarella if you prefer.

serves
4

prep time:
10 minutes

cook time:
40 minutes

½ teaspoon salt

8 ounces (225g) jumbo pasta shells (see notes)

4 cups (950ml) smooth tomato sauce, homemade (page 312) or store-bought (see notes)

FILLING:

1 tablespoon olive oil

¾ cup (90g) diced onions

1 pound (450g) zucchini, shredded

2 cloves garlic, grated

1 teaspoon Italian seasoning

¾ cup (200g) whole-milk ricotta cheese

1½ cups (115g) shredded sharp cheddar cheese, divided

Salt and pepper

notes:
Allow 6 shells per person plus a few extra in case some break while boiling.

My Easy Tomato Sauce works really well here, but because it has a slightly chunky texture, it does need to be whizzed smooth in a blender.

Fill a stockpot halfway with water and bring to a boil. Add the salt and pasta. Cook according to the package instructions until al dente, generally about 15 minutes.

Meanwhile, prepare the filling: Heat the oil in a large frying pan over medium heat. Add the onions and cook gently, stirring from time to time, until they start to soften, 6 to 8 minutes.

Increase the heat to medium-high, add the zucchini, garlic, and Italian seasoning, and cook until the zucchini starts to soften, 2 to 3 minutes.

Stir in the ricotta and half of the cheddar cheese. Season to taste with salt and pepper.

Spoon the tomato sauce into a 13 by 9-inch (33 by 23cm) baking dish or a 12-inch (30cm) round baking pan. (I like to use my braiser here for a pretty presentation at the table.)

Preheat the oven to 425°F (220°C).

Stuff each shell with 1 heaping tablespoon of the zucchini filling and place on top of the tomato sauce. Nestle the shells tightly in the dish and push them down into the sauce so they are almost submerged. Scatter the remaining cheddar cheese on top of the shells.

Bake for 20 to 25 minutes, until the cheese has melted and the top is golden brown.

plant swap:
Make it vegan by swapping the ricotta for plain vegan cream cheese, store-bought or homemade (page 326), and the cheddar cheese for a plant-based alternative.

eggplant & potato curry

serves
4 to 6

prep time:
15 minutes

cook time:
45 minutes

This is my take on aloo baingan, a hearty North Indian curry. It makes an easy and comforting midweek meal and delicious leftovers for packed lunches the next day. Though rarely used in this particular curry, I add a little coconut milk to make the sauce extra creamy. It is a mild curry, so feel free to play around with the heat by adding cayenne pepper or crushed red pepper when you add the spices.

¼ cup (60ml) plus 1 tablespoon vegetable oil, divided

1¼ pounds (600g) eggplant, cubed

Salt

1 cup (125g) finely diced onions

5 cloves garlic, grated

1 green chili pepper (such as Indian, Thai, serrano, or jalapeño), seeded and finely chopped

1 tablespoon peeled and grated ginger

1 tablespoon plus ¼ teaspoon garam masala, divided

1 teaspoon cumin seeds

½ teaspoon turmeric powder

1¼ pounds (600g) baking potatoes (such as russet or King Edward), peeled and cubed

1 (14.5-ounce/410g) can diced tomatoes

1½ cups (350ml) water

1 cup (240ml) canned coconut milk

1 (15-ounce/425g) can chickpeas, drained and rinsed

Juice of 1 lemon

1 to 2 teaspoons granulated sugar, according to taste (optional)

1¼ packed cups (30g) roughly chopped fresh cilantro, plus extra sprigs for garnish if desired

FOR GARNISH/SERVING:

Plain yogurt

Crushed red pepper

Naan or other flatbread, homemade (page 170) or store-bought

Lemon wedges

Heat ¼ cup (60ml) of the oil in a large frying pan over medium-high heat and cook the eggplant until softened and browned, 12 to 15 minutes. Stir often so the eggplant does not burn. When done, season with ¾ teaspoon of salt and set aside.

Meanwhile, heat the remaining tablespoon of oil in a 5-quart (5L) Dutch oven over medium heat. Add the onions and cook gently, stirring from time to time, until they start to soften, 6 to 8 minutes.

Add the garlic, chili pepper, and ginger and cook for a minute. Stir in 1 tablespoon of the garam masala, the cumin seeds, and turmeric, then add the potatoes, tomatoes, and water.

Bring to a boil, then cook, covered, over medium-high heat at a lively simmer until the potatoes are par-cooked, about 15 minutes. Stir from time to time so the potatoes do not stick to the pan.

Mix in the cooked eggplant and coconut milk. Reduce the heat to medium and simmer, uncovered, until the potatoes are tender, 12 to 15 minutes. Stir in the chickpeas.

Add the remaining ¼ teaspoon of garam masala, the lemon juice, and salt to taste. If you find the curry too acidic, add 1 to 2 teaspoons of sugar to balance the flavor. Stir in the cilantro.

Serve topped with a drizzle of yogurt, a sprinkle of crushed red pepper, and some cilantro sprigs, if desired, with naan and lemon wedges on the side.

pan-fried eggplant with green lentil & tomato stew

This is such a flavorsome recipe, loosely inspired by one of my favorite veggie dishes, caponata. Pan-fried eggplant slices are topped with a sweet and sour chunky tomato stew infused with capers, olives, and herbs. I added lentils to the mix for a healthy plant-based protein boost. I like to serve this dish with couscous, but it is also delicious with quinoa, rice, or any other grain of your choosing.

I prefer this dish slightly spicy, so I use my Easy Tomato Sauce, which has a little bit of heat. You can substitute any chunky tomato sauce of your liking and add some crushed red pepper to build up fieriness.

serves

4

prep time:

15 minutes, plus
15 minutes to
drain eggplant

cook time:

45 minutes

1 pound (450g) eggplant

Salt

Olive oil, for the pan

STEW:

Salt

⅓ cup (70g) French green lentils, picked over and rinsed (see note, page 144)

2 tablespoons olive oil

¾ cup (90g) finely diced onions

1 large celery stalk, finely diced

1 medium red bell pepper, diced

2 cups (475ml) chunky tomato sauce, homemade (page 312) or store-bought

1 clove garlic, grated

3 tablespoons capers

⅓ cup (45g) pitted black olives, halved

¼ cup (35g) raisins

1 tablespoon red wine vinegar, plus more if desired

2 teaspoons granulated sugar, plus more if desired

1 to 2 teaspoons crushed red pepper, according to taste (optional; see note)

2 tablespoons finely chopped fresh parsley

2 tablespoons finely chopped fresh mint

Ground black pepper

FOR SERVING/GARNISH:

1 cup (175g) couscous

1 cup (240ml) boiling hot water

Salt

Fresh basil leaves

Cut the eggplant into ¼-inch (0.5cm) rounds. Salt each slice generously and place in a colander. Set in the sink or over a shallow dish for about 15 minutes, then wipe each slice with a paper towel to remove the salt and moisture.

Meanwhile, make the stew: Fill a medium saucepan halfway with water and bring to a boil. Add ½ teaspoon of salt and the lentils. Cook over medium-high heat until soft, 12 to 15 minutes (do not overcook or the lentils will become mushy). When done, drain and set aside.

Heat the oil in a stockpot over medium heat. Gently cook the onions, celery, and bell pepper until soft, 5 to 8 minutes.

Add the tomato sauce, garlic, capers, olives, raisins, vinegar, sugar, and crushed red pepper, if using, to the stockpot. Cover with a lid and simmer gently for 10 to 15 minutes, until thickened. Stir in the herbs and cooked lentils until well combined. Season with salt and pepper to taste. The flavor should be sweet and savory. If necessary, add more vinegar and/or sugar. Set aside and keep warm.

Meanwhile, cook the eggplant: Heat 2 tablespoons of oil in a large frying pan over medium-high heat. Working in batches, cook the eggplant slices until golden, 2 to 3 minutes on each side. Remove to a paper towel–lined plate to absorb the excess oil. Keep warm while you cook the rest of the slices, adding more oil to the pan as needed between batches.

Make the couscous: Place the couscous in a heatproof bowl and cover with the boiling hot water. Cover and leave until the couscous is soft, 5 to 8 minutes. Fluff with a fork and season with a little salt.

To serve, divide the couscous among 4 plates and top evenly with the eggplant slices and tomato stew. Garnish with basil leaves.

note:

If you are using my Easy Tomato Sauce, you can omit the crushed red pepper.

golden rice & cabbage

serves

6

prep time:

15 minutes

cook time:

50 minutes

Minimum fuss, minimum washing up . . . this is the way I like it, especially on busy weekdays. This one-pot rice casserole makes a warming and satisfying meal. The ginger and crushed red pepper add a nice spicy kick, while turmeric gives the dish a comforting yellow glow. Any leftovers reheat brilliantly and will be even more fragrant as the flavors will have had more time to develop.

2 tablespoons vegetable oil

1 cup (125g) finely diced onions

1 cup (175g) long-grain rice of choice (see note)

2 cloves garlic, grated

1 tablespoon peeled and grated ginger

2 teaspoons mild curry powder

1 teaspoon crushed red pepper

1 teaspoon turmeric powder

1 teaspoon yellow mustard seeds

1 cup (240ml) vegetable stock

1 (13.5-ounce/400ml) can coconut milk

1 pound (450g) savoy or green cabbage, thinly sliced

8 ounces (225g) tomatoes, cut into 1-inch (2.5cm) chunks

7 ounces (200g) carrots, peeled and diced

1 (15.5-ounce/440g) can red kidney beans, drained and rinsed

Juice of 1 lemon

Salt

1¼ packed cups (30g) roughly chopped fresh cilantro

½ cup (50g) sliced almonds

Heat the oil in a 3½-quart (3.3L) braiser or Dutch oven over medium heat. Add the onions and cook gently, stirring from time to time, until they start to soften, 6 to 8 minutes. Stir in the rice, garlic, ginger, curry powder, crushed red pepper, turmeric, and mustard seeds and cook for 2 minutes, stirring from time to time.

Stir in the stock and coconut milk, then add the cabbage, carrots, and tomatoes. Bring to a boil and cook, covered, over medium heat for 30 to 35 minutes, stirring from time to time, until the vegetables and rice are cooked.

Mix in the beans and cook for 2 to 3 minutes more to warm through. Stir in the lemon juice and season to taste with salt.

Dry-toast the almonds in a small frying pan over medium heat for about 2 minutes, until golden and fragrant. Stir often to prevent them from burning.

Stir in the cilantro and almonds just before serving.

note:

You can use any kind of rice for this dish. Just double-check the package instructions to make sure it cooks in 30 to 35 minutes.

vegan mushroom alfredo pasta

serves

4

prep time:

10 minutes

cook time:

15 minutes

There is nothing more comforting than a creamy pasta dish. In this recipe, pasta is smothered in my silky cashew cream and tossed with mushrooms and spinach for a quick and easy dinner filled with plant-based indulgence. Feel free to swap in dairy alternatives for the cream and vegan parmesan.

2 tablespoons olive oil

12 ounces (340g) baby bella mushrooms, sliced

4 packed cups (140g) baby spinach

2 cloves garlic, grated

½ cup (120ml) dry white wine

½ teaspoon freshly grated nutmeg

1 cup (240ml) Simple Cashew Cream (page 323) (see note)

2 to 3 tablespoons fresh lemon juice, according to taste

Salt and pepper

10 ounces (280g) fettuccine or tagliatelle

¼ packed cup (12g) finely chopped fresh parsley

Grated vegan parmesan, for serving

Cook the pasta: Fill a stockpot halfway with water and bring to a boil. Add ½ teaspoon of salt and the pasta. Cook until al dente, 10 to 12 minutes. Drain, reserving 1 cup (240ml) of the cooking liquid.

Meanwhile, make the mushroom sauce: Heat the oil in a large frying pan over medium-high to high heat. Add the mushrooms and sauté until they have released their moisture and are soft and browned, 8 to 10 minutes.

Add the spinach, garlic, wine, and nutmeg. Cook until the spinach has wilted, about 5 minutes. Stir in the cashew cream and lemon juice. Season to taste with salt and pepper.

Toss the pasta in the frying pan with the mushroom sauce. If needed, thin the sauce with some of the reserved cooking liquid. Stir in the parsley and divide among 4 shallow bowls. Sprinkle with vegan parmesan and serve.

note:

You can swap my homemade cashew cream for a store-bought dairy-free cream alternative or, if you prefer a vegetarian option, heavy cream.

one-pot orzo primavera

serves

4 to 6

prep time:

10 minutes

cook time:

20 minutes

This quick and easy one-pot dish encapsulates the freshness of spring. You can customize it by swapping some of the vegetables for what you have in your fridge or freezer. Anything that once cut into small pieces can cook in ten minutes is ideal. Zucchini, green beans, or fennel as well as bell pepper, tomatoes, or carrots would make delicious substitutions.

3 tablespoons olive oil

½ cup (60g) finely diced onions

3 cloves garlic, grated

12 ounces (340g) orzo

5 ounces (140g) broccoli florets, cut into small chunks

4 ounces (115g) medium-thick asparagus, tough ends removed

4 cups (950ml) vegetable stock, plus more if needed

1 cup (150g) frozen fava beans (aka broad beans) or lima beans

1 cup (140g) frozen green peas

¾ cup (180ml) cream (see note), plus more if needed

Grated zest and juice of 1 lemon

Salt and pepper

FOR GARNISH:

A few sprigs of fresh thyme, cut into sections

Grated Parmesan cheese

Heat the oil in a large frying pan over medium heat. Add the onions and cook gently, stirring from time to time, until they start to soften, 6 to 8 minutes.

Stir in the garlic and orzo and cook for 1 minute, stirring occasionally. Add the broccoli, asparagus, and stock. Bring to a boil, then reduce the heat to medium and cook at a lively simmer for 5 minutes.

Mix in the beans, peas, cream, and lemon zest until well combined. Cook for 5 minutes more, until the orzo and vegetables are tender and most of the liquid has been absorbed. Add a little more stock or cream if the orzo is too dry.

Stir in the lemon juice and season to taste with salt and pepper. Serve topped with thyme sprigs and a generous amount of Parmesan.

note:
I use my Simple Cashew Cream (page 323) to make this dish extra creamy, but you can use a variety of creams here. Vegan whipping cream or soy cream works well, as do conventional dairy options such as half-and-half and heavy cream.

plant swap:
Make it vegan by using dairy-free cream and vegan parmesan.

pan-fried gnocchi with eggplant puttanesca

Crispy on the outside and soft on the inside, pan-fried gnocchi are simply amazing. Here they are served on top of a hearty plant-based eggplant puttanesca sauce. I have swapped the anchovies used in a traditional puttanesca sauce for nori and a dash of soy sauce. Like the original, this version packs a lot of umami, so there is no need to top with grated cheese.

serves

4

prep time:
10 minutes, plus 20 minutes to drain eggplant

cook time:
30 minutes

1 pound (450g) eggplant, cubed

1 teaspoon salt

½ cup (120ml) olive oil, divided

½ cup (60g) finely diced red onions

1 (28-ounce/800g) can diced tomatoes

¾ cup (105g) pitted Kalamata olives

3 cloves garlic, grated

2 tablespoons capers

1 tablespoon tomato paste

1 nori sheet, thinly sliced

¼ teaspoon crushed red pepper

1 (17.5-ounce/500g) package fresh gnocchi

1 to 2 teaspoons granulated sugar

Dash of low-sodium soy sauce

½ packed cup (10g) roughly chopped fresh basil

Place the eggplant in a colander and sprinkle with the salt. Set in the sink or over a shallow dish and allow to drain for 20 minutes. Use a paper towel to brush off the salt and absorb the excess liquid.

In a large frying pan, heat ¼ cup (60ml) of the oil over medium-high heat. Cook the eggplant, stirring often, until browned, 12 to 15 minutes. Using a slotted spoon, remove the eggplant from the pan and set aside.

Lower the heat to medium. Add 2 tablespoons of the oil to the same frying pan. Add the onions and cook gently, stirring from time to time, until they start to soften, 6 to 8 minutes.

Stir in the tomatoes, olives, garlic, capers, tomato paste, nori, crushed red pepper, and cooked eggplant until well combined. Turn the heat to medium-low heat and simmer, uncovered, for 10 minutes to allow the flavors to deepen.

Meanwhile, cook the gnocchi: Pour the remaining 2 tablespoons of oil into another large frying pan over medium-high heat. Add the gnocchi straight from the package (no need to precook them) and pan-fry for 8 to 10 minutes, until crisp and golden.

Once the sauce has simmered for 10 minutes, stir in 1 teaspoon of sugar and the soy sauce. Taste and add up to 1 teaspoon more sugar, if desired. Stir in the basil.

Top the sauce with the pan-fried gnocchi and serve.

red lentil dahl with crunchy kale & coconut

serves
4

prep time:
10 minutes

cook time:
35 minutes

Hearty, comforting, and nourishing, this tasty dahl is filled with goodness. I jazz it up with a crunchy topping of baked chopped kale and shredded coconut tossed in garam masala. Serve it with naan or another flatbread for a quick and easy lunch or dinner that will leave you satisfied.

1¼ cups (250g) split red lentils, picked over and rinsed

2 tablespoons vegetable oil

1 cup (125g) finely diced onions

3 cloves garlic, grated

1 tablespoon peeled and grated ginger

1 teaspoon crushed red pepper

1 teaspoon ground coriander

1 teaspoon ground cumin

1 teaspoon garam masala

1 teaspoon turmeric powder

1 teaspoon yellow mustard seeds

1 (14.5-ounce/410g) can diced tomatoes

1 (13.5-ounce/400ml) can coconut milk

3 cups (700ml) vegetable stock

2 to 3 tablespoons fresh lemon juice, according to taste

Salt

CRUNCHY KALE:

7 ounces (200g) kale, stemmed and roughly chopped

½ cup (35g) unsweetened shredded coconut

2 tablespoons vegetable oil

½ teaspoon garam masala

Salt

FOR SERVING:

Dairy or dairy-free plain yogurt

Naan or other flatbread, homemade (page 170) or store-bought

Place the lentils in a fine-mesh sieve and rinse thoroughly under cold water for a couple of minutes, or until the water runs clear. Set aside.

Heat the oil in a 5-quart (5L) Dutch oven over medium heat. Add the onions and cook gently, stirring from time to time, until they start to soften, 6 to 8 minutes. Add the garlic, ginger, and spices and cook for 2 minutes more, until the spices release their aromas and the mustard seeds have popped.

Add the lentils, tomatoes, coconut milk, and stock to the pot. Cook, stirring from time to time, for 20 to 25 minutes, until the lentils are tender and the liquid has thickened. Add the lemon juice and season with salt to taste.

Meanwhile, prepare the kale: Preheat the oven to 300°F (150°C). Spread the kale leaves and coconut on a rimmed baking sheet. Toss in the oil and garam masala. Bake for 10 to 15 minutes, until the kale is crispy and browned and the coconut is nicely toasted. Season lightly with salt.

Serve the dahl topped with a drizzle of yogurt and the toasted kale and coconut, with naan on the side.

roasted cabbage with beluga lentils & salsa verde

serves
4

prep time:
10 minutes

cook time:
30 minutes

I think cabbage is highly underrated. Although it's often considered bland and boring, it is in fact a very versatile ingredient. Roasted cabbage has a wonderful nutty and sweet taste, and the contrast of the crunchy caramelized outer leaves with the soft inner side of the wedges is truly delicious. Here the cabbage wedges are served on a bed of beluga lentils and topped with a punchy salsa verde.

Mild and earthy, beluga lentils are tiny black lentils that resemble caviar. They are not as common as other varieties but are a worthwhile addition to your pantry. If you don't find them at your local grocery store, you can order them online.

¼ cup (60ml) olive oil

1½ teaspoons garlic powder

Salt

1 (2¼-pound/1kg) head green cabbage

Ground black pepper

1 cup (200g) beluga lentils (aka black lentils), picked over and rinsed

1 lemon, halved or quartered, for serving

SALSA VERDE:

¾ cup (180ml) extra-virgin olive oil

2 tablespoons fresh lemon juice

1 tablespoon red wine vinegar

¾ packed cup (35g) finely chopped fresh parsley

¼ packed cup (12g) finely chopped fresh mint leaves

¼ packed cup (12g) finely chopped fresh dill

3 tablespoons fresh tarragon leaves, finely chopped

3 tablespoons capers, finely chopped

2 teaspoons Dijon mustard

1 clove garlic, grated

¼ teaspoon salt

Preheat the oven to 400°F (200°C).

In a small bowl, mix together the oil, garlic powder, and ½ teaspoon of salt. Set aside.

Slicing through the core so the leaves hold together, cut the cabbage into 8 wedges. Brush each wedge generously on all sides with the oil mixture. Sprinkle generously with pepper. Arrange the wedges on a rimmed baking sheet. Roast until soft and browned, about 30 minutes, carefully flipping the wedges over with a spatula after 15 minutes so they cook evenly.

Meanwhile, cook the lentils and prepare the salsa. To cook the lentils, fill a medium saucepan halfway with water and bring to a boil. Add ½ teaspoon of salt and the lentils. Cook over medium-high heat just until soft, 15 to 20 minutes. Do not overcook or the lentils will become mushy. Drain and set aside.

Make the salsa verde: In a small bowl, whisk together the oil, lemon juice, and vinegar. Stir in the herbs, capers, mustard, garlic, and salt until well combined. Set aside.

Spread the lentils on a serving dish. Place the cabbage wedges on top. Top with the salsa verde. Serve with lemon halves or quarters on the side.

roasted cauliflower with pearl couscous salad

Cauliflower is another vegetable that deserves much more attention than it gets. It is so versatile and delicious. A whole roasted head of cauliflower makes an impressive and hearty plant-based centerpiece. In this Moroccan-inspired version, it is coated with a fragrant spice blend and served on a bed of pearl couscous salad with a zesty yogurt drizzle for a tantalizing contrast.

serves
4 to 6

prep time:
20 minutes

cook time:
35 minutes

1 medium head cauliflower (about 1¼ pounds/600g), trimmed

¼ cup (60ml) olive oil

1 teaspoon ground cinnamon

1 teaspoon ground cumin

1 teaspoon garlic powder

1 teaspoon smoked paprika

1 teaspoon salt

PEARL COUSCOUS SALAD:

½ teaspoon salt

1 cup (175g) pearl couscous

1 (15-ounce/425g) can chickpeas, drained and rinsed

1¼ cups (190g) cherry tomatoes, quartered

10 pitted dates, roughly chopped

6 tablespoons chopped fresh mint, divided

3 tablespoons chopped fresh cilantro

3 tablespoons chopped fresh parsley

⅔ cup (75g) crumbled feta cheese

DRESSING:

¼ cup (60ml) extra-virgin olive oil

3 tablespoons fresh lemon juice

1 teaspoon ground cumin

1 teaspoon pure maple syrup or honey

1 clove garlic, grated

¼ teaspoon salt

YOGURT DRIZZLE:

1 cup (250g) plain yogurt

1 clove garlic, grated

½ teaspoon ground cumin

2 tablespoons fresh lemon juice

2 teaspoons pure maple syrup or honey

plant swap:
Make it vegan by swapping the feta and yogurt for plant-based alternatives.

Fill a large pot (big enough to submerge the whole cauliflower head) halfway with water and bring to a boil.

Carefully slide in the cauliflower head. Cook over medium-high heat for 6 to 8 minutes, just until you can insert a paring knife into the cauliflower. Do not overcook.

Preheat the oven to 400°F (200°C).

Mix together the oil, cinnamon, cumin, garlic powder, smoked paprika, and salt.

When the cauliflower is par-cooked, remove it from the water and leave to stand for 5 minutes to cool and drain. Pat dry to remove any excess water.

Place the cauliflower on a rimmed baking sheet. Brush all over with the spiced oil. Roast for 20 to 25 minutes, until soft enough that a skewer goes into the center easily. Meanwhile, prepare the rest of the components.

Cook the couscous: Fill a medium saucepan halfway with water and bring to a boil. Add the salt and couscous. Cook, uncovered, over medium-high heat for 6 to 8 minutes, until the couscous is just tender. Drain and rinse well under cold water. Drain well and place in a large salad bowl.

Make the dressing: Whisk together all of the ingredients in a small bowl.

Make the yogurt drizzle: Whisk together all of the ingredients in another small bowl.

To the bowl with the couscous, add the chickpeas, tomatoes, dates, 4 tablespoons of the mint, the cilantro, parsley, feta, and dressing. Give it a good mix. Set aside.

Spread the couscous salad on a large serving dish. Set the roasted cauliflower head on top of the salad. Top with the yogurt drizzle and the remaining 2 tablespoons of chopped mint. Serve straightaway.

roasted cauliflower
with pearl couscous
salad

*root vegetable
tagine*

root vegetable tagine

serves

6

prep time:
20 minutes

cook time:
35 minutes

This vegetarian tagine is packed with warming Moroccan spices that make it the perfect comfort food. The hearty root vegetables are cooked in a rich tomato sauce sweetened with honey and prunes. For a contrasting salty note, I add olives and serve a fragrant herby chermoula on the side. I prefer the nuttiness of whole-wheat couscous, but ordinary couscous works well too. The sweet potatoes will cook faster than the turnips and carrots and therefore need to be cut into slightly larger chunks than the other vegetables.

2 tablespoons olive oil

8 ounces (225g) medium shallots, peeled (see note)

4 cloves garlic, grated

1½ teaspoons ginger powder

1 teaspoon ground coriander

1 teaspoon paprika

1 cinnamon stick

¼ teaspoon saffron threads

10 ounces (300g) sweet potatoes, peeled and cut into 1-inch (2.5cm) cubes

10 ounces (300g) turnips or rutabaga, peeled and cut into ¾-inch (2cm) cubes

10 ounces (300g) large carrots, peeled and cut into ½-inch (1cm)-thick semicircles

1 (14.5-ounce/410g) can diced tomatoes

8 ounces (225g) soft prunes (aka dried plums)

2 cups (475ml) vegetable stock

1 (15-ounce/425g) can chickpeas, drained and rinsed

½ cup (70g) pitted green olives

2 to 3 tablespoons honey

2 to 3 tablespoons fresh lemon juice, according to taste

Salt

CHERMOULA:

1¼ packed cups (30g) roughly chopped fresh cilantro

1 packed cup (25g) roughly chopped fresh parsley

4 cloves garlic, roughly chopped

Grated zest of ½ lemon

2 tablespoons fresh lemon juice

2 teaspoons ground cumin

1 teaspoon ginger powder

1 teaspoon paprika

¼ teaspoon salt

⅓ to ½ cup (80 to 120ml) extra-virgin olive oil

Pinch of crushed red pepper

COUSCOUS:

1¾ cups (300g) whole-wheat couscous

1 teaspoon turmeric powder

¼ teaspoon salt

2 cups (475ml) boiling hot water

FOR GARNISH:

½ cup (50g) sliced almonds

Leaves from 1 small bunch fresh cilantro, chopped

plant swap:

Make it vegan by replacing the honey with pure light-colored, or golden, maple syrup or agave nectar.

Heat the oil in a 5-quart (5L) Dutch oven over medium-high heat and cook the shallots until slightly golden, about 2 minutes.

Lower the heat to medium, stir in the garlic and spices, and cook until the spices start to release their aromas, about 1 minute.

Add the sweet potatoes, turnips, carrots, tomatoes, prunes, and stock. Stir well and bring to a boil over high heat, then lower the heat to medium. Simmer, covered, until the vegetables are tender, 25 to 30 minutes; do not overcook.

Meanwhile, make the chermoula: Place all of the ingredients in a blender, starting with ⅓ cup (80ml) of oil, and blend to a thick textured sauce (it should not be smooth). Blend in the rest of the oil if the sauce is too thick. Set aside.

Dry-toast the almonds in a small frying pan over medium heat for about 2 minutes, until golden and fragrant. Stir often to prevent them from burning. Set aside.

When the vegetables are tender, stir the chickpeas, olives, and honey into the tagine. Add the lemon juice and season to taste with salt. Gently simmer, uncovered, while you prepare the couscous.

Make the couscous: In a heatproof bowl, mix the couscous with the turmeric and salt. Pour in the boiling hot water and cover. Leave the couscous to absorb the water, 3 to 5 minutes. Fluff with a fork.

Serve the tagine on a bed of couscous, with the toasted almonds and cilantro on top and the chermoula on the side.

smoky sweet potato stew

serves
6

prep time:
15 minutes

cook time:
40 minutes

This hearty stew is a delicious combination of plant-based goodness: sweet potatoes, quinoa, and black beans cooked in a smoky and spicy tomato sauce. It has just the right amount of heat to warm you from the inside out.

I like to serve this dish with homemade tortilla chips. They are easy to make and healthier than the store-bought variety. One word of caution, though: they burn easily, so make sure to keep an eye out while they are in the oven.

2 tablespoons olive oil

1 cup (125g) finely diced onions

3 cloves garlic, grated

1 tablespoon tomato puree

2 teaspoons smoked paprika

1½ teaspoons ground coriander

1½ teaspoons ground cumin

¼ teaspoon cayenne pepper

3 cups (750ml) vegetable stock

⅔ cup (120g) tri-color quinoa

1 pound (450g) sweet potatoes, peeled and cubed

1 medium red bell pepper, diced

1 (14.5-ounce/410g) can diced tomatoes

2 teaspoons dried oregano leaves

1 (15-ounce/425g) can black beans, drained and rinsed

⅔ cup (100g) canned corn kernels, drained and rinsed

2 tablespoons fresh lime juice

Salt

TORTILLA CHIPS:

8 (6-inch/15cm) corn tortillas

3 tablespoons vegetable oil

Salt

FOR SERVING:

Fresh cilantro sprigs

Sliced avocado

Shredded cheddar cheese

Lime halves or quarters

plant swap:
Make it vegan by using dairy-free cheese.

Heat the olive oil in a large saucepan over medium heat. Add the onions and cook gently, stirring from time to time, until they start to soften, 6 to 8 minutes.

Add the garlic, tomato puree, smoked paprika, coriander, cumin, and cayenne pepper and cook for another minute.

Stir in the stock, quinoa, sweet potatoes, bell pepper, tomatoes, and oregano. Bring to a boil, then reduce the heat and simmer, covered, for 20 minutes, stirring occasionally so the mixture does not stick to the pan.

Meanwhile, make the tortilla chips: Preheat the oven to 400°F (200°C). Brush the tortillas on both sides with the vegetable oil, then use scissors to cut each one into 8 triangles. Arrange them in a single layer, not touching, on 2 or 3 rimmed baking sheets. Bake 2 pans at a time until golden, 7 to 8 minutes, flipping the chips midway through so they are evenly colored on both sides. Sprinkle with salt and set aside.

Once the stew has cooked for 20 minutes, mix in the beans and corn and cook for 5 to 10 minutes more, until the sweet potatoes and quinoa are tender. Season with the lime juice and salt to taste.

Serve topped with the tortilla chips, cilantro, avocado slices, shredded cheese, and lime halves or quarters.

sweet & sour tofu with cauliflower rice

Looking for a tasty and healthy alternative to the classic sweet and sour takeout? Try this plant-based version, with pan-fried tofu smothered in a delicious homemade sauce and topped with sesame seeds and scallions. I like to serve this dish with cauliflower rice, a satisfying low-carb alternative to white rice.

serves

4

prep time:
10 minutes, plus 20 minutes to press tofu

cook time:
40 minutes

1 (14-ounce/400g) package extra-firm tofu

¼ cup (35g) cornstarch

3 tablespoons toasted sesame oil

SAUCE:

2 tablespoons vegetable oil

1 small onion, finely diced

1 medium red bell pepper, cut into 1-inch (2.5cm) pieces

1 medium orange bell pepper, cut into 1-inch (2.5cm) pieces

8 ounces (225g) sugar snap peas or snow peas, halved

⅔ cup (160ml) ketchup

5 tablespoons light brown sugar

3 tablespoons unseasoned rice vinegar or apple cider vinegar

2 tablespoons low-sodium soy sauce

2 cloves garlic, grated

1 teaspoon peeled and grated ginger

½ teaspoon crushed red pepper

1½ cups (435g) canned pineapple chunks packed in juice

1 cup (240ml) pineapple juice from the can

1 tablespoon cornstarch

CAULIFLOWER RICE:

1 large head cauliflower (about 1¾ pounds/800g), trimmed

3 tablespoons vegetable oil

2 cloves garlic, grated

½ teaspoon salt

FOR GARNISH:

Sesame seeds

Sliced scallions

Press the tofu for 20 minutes (see page 68), discarding as much liquid as possible. Cut the pressed tofu into cubes.

Meanwhile, start making the sweet and sour sauce: Heat the vegetable oil in a large saucepan over medium heat and cook the onion until it starts to soften, 6 to 8 minutes. Add the bell peppers and sugar snap peas and cook for 2 minutes more. Stir in the ketchup, brown sugar, vinegar, soy sauce, garlic, ginger, crushed red pepper, and pineapple chunks.

Whisk together the pineapple juice and cornstarch until the cornstarch has dissolved, then add the mixture to the saucepan. Bring to a boil, then reduce the heat to medium-low and let the sauce simmer until thickened, about 30 minutes, stirring often so the sauce does not stick to the pan.

While the sauce is simmering, prepare the tofu: Place the cubed tofu in a bowl and gently toss with the cornstarch until evenly coated all over.

Heat a large frying pan over medium-high heat, then add the sesame oil and tofu. Fry the tofu, turning occasionally with a slotted spatula, until crispy and browned all over, about 15 minutes.

Transfer the tofu to the pan with the sauce and let it simmer over low heat while you prepare the cauliflower rice.

Make the cauliflower rice: Cut the head of cauliflower, including the core, into chunks. Using the largest holes on a box grater, grate the cauliflower; alternatively, you can use a food processor for this task (see note). Heat the vegetable oil over medium heat in the same pan you used to fry the tofu. Add the grated cauliflower, garlic, and salt. Cook until the cauliflower starts to soften, 3 to 4 minutes.

Serve the cauliflower rice topped with the sweet and sour tofu. Sprinkle with sesame seeds and scallions.

sweet & sour tofu
with cauliflower rice

grilled tofu
satay skewers
with rice noodle
salad

grilled tofu satay skewers with rice noodle salad

These skewers are served on a bed of rice noodle salad and topped with a rich and creamy peanut sauce—a mouthwatering combination for a thoroughly satisfying meal. To save time, you can press the tofu in the fridge up to one day ahead.

serves

4

prep time:
20 minutes,
plus 35 minutes
to press and
marinate tofu

cook time:
12 minutes

SPECIAL
EQUIPMENT:
*4 (8-inch/20cm)
skewers*

1 (14-ounce/400g) package extra-firm tofu

Vegetable oil, for the grill/pan and skewers

1 teaspoon white sesame seeds, for garnish

1 teaspoon black sesame seeds, for garnish

MARINADE:

2 tablespoons tamari

1 tablespoon pure maple syrup

1 tablespoon unseasoned rice vinegar

1 teaspoon garlic powder

SATAY SAUCE:

¼ cup (65g) smooth natural peanut butter

2 tablespoons tamari

2 tablespoons fresh lime juice

1 tablespoon unseasoned rice vinegar

1 tablespoon pure maple syrup

2 teaspoons toasted sesame oil

1 teaspoon peeled and grated ginger

1 teaspoon Sriracha sauce

½ teaspoon garlic powder

NOODLE SALAD:

5½ ounces (155g) vermicelli rice noodles

1 tablespoon toasted sesame oil

½ teaspoon salt

1 cup (140g) frozen shelled edamame

2 cups (110g) shredded green cabbage

1 cup (100g) peeled and shredded carrots

¼ cup (35g) roasted and salted peanuts, roughly chopped

3 tablespoons chopped fresh cilantro

4 medium scallions, sliced on the bias

⅔ cup (160ml) Asian-Style Dressing (page 309)

If using wooden skewers, soak them in water for 20 to 30 minutes.

Press the tofu for 20 minutes (see page 68), discarding as much liquid as possible. Cut the pressed tofu into 16 cubes.

Make the marinade: Whisk together all of the ingredients until well combined.

Toss the tofu cubes in the marinade and set aside for 15 minutes. Meanwhile, prepare the rest of the ingredients.

Make the satay sauce: Whisk together all of the ingredients until well combined, then set aside.

Prepare the salad: Place the rice noodles in a heatproof bowl and cover with boiling hot water; set aside for 5 minutes, until tender. Drain and rinse under cold water. Transfer the noodles to a large salad bowl and toss with the sesame oil.

Preheat a grill to high heat and lightly oil the grate. Alternatively, you can cook the skewers on the stovetop in a hot oiled grill pan or frying pan over medium-high heat.

Finish making the salad while the grill or pan heats up: Fill a medium saucepan halfway with water and bring to a boil. Add the salt and edamame. Blanch for 2 minutes, then drain.

Mix the edamame, cabbage, carrots, peanuts, cilantro, and scallions into the noodles. Set aside.

When the tofu is ready, thread 4 cubes onto each skewer. Brush all over with 2 tablespoons of vegetable oil and grill until golden, 8 to 10 minutes, turning them from time to time.

Pour the dressing over the noodle salad and toss to coat. Transfer the dressed salad to a serving platter.

Serve the skewers on top of the noodle salad. Top with a drizzle of the satay sauce and sprinkle with the sesame seeds. Serve the remaining satay sauce on the side.

teriyaki tempeh bowls

Tempeh has a hearty texture and a slightly nutty taste that I like to combine with strong flavors. Here it is coated in a delicious homemade teriyaki sauce and stir-fried with vegetables and cashews. Served on a bed of brown rice, this is a nourishing and satisfying dish to enjoy for lunch or dinner.

serves
2

prep time:
10 minutes

cook time:
40 minutes

¾ cup (150g) long-grain brown rice

½ teaspoon salt

TERIYAKI SAUCE:

¼ cup (60ml) tamari, plus more for serving

¼ cup (60ml) water

¼ packed cup (45g) light brown sugar

1 tablespoon honey, pure maple syrup, or agave nectar

1 teaspoon peeled and grated ginger

1 clove garlic, grated

1 tablespoon unseasoned rice vinegar

2 teaspoons cornstarch mixed with 1 teaspoon water

1 tablespoon toasted sesame oil

1 tablespoon vegetable oil

1 clove garlic, grated

1 (8-ounce/225g) package tempeh, diced

1 medium carrot, peeled and cut into 2 by ¼-inch (5 by 0.5cm) strips

½ medium red bell pepper, seeded and diced

1 heaping cup (85g) broccoli florets, cut into bite-size pieces

⅔ cup (90g) shelled edamame, thawed if frozen

⅓ cup (50g) raw cashews

FOR GARNISH:

2 medium scallions, sliced on the bias

2 teaspoons sesame seeds

Cook the rice: Fill a medium saucepan halfway with water and bring to a boil. Add the salt and rice. Lower the heat to maintain a lively simmer and cook the rice according to the package instructions until tender (do not overcook or the rice will become mushy), generally about 40 minutes. Drain.

Meanwhile, make the teriyaki sauce: In another medium saucepan, heat the tamari, water, brown sugar, honey, ginger, and garlic over medium-high heat. Whisk until slightly thickened, about 5 minutes. Whisk in the vinegar and cornstarch slurry until well combined. Carry on cooking until the sauce has thickened a bit more, about 2 minutes. Set aside.

About 10 minutes before the rice is done, start the stir-fry: Heat the sesame and vegetable oils in a wok or large frying pan over high heat. Add the garlic, tempeh, vegetables, and cashews. Stir-fry until the vegetables start to soften, about 5 minutes. Stir in the teriyaki sauce, reduce the heat to medium-high, and cook for another 3 minutes, until the vegetables are just tender.

Divide the rice between 2 serving bowls. Top with the vegetable and tempeh mixture, scallions, and sesame seeds. Serve with extra tamari on the side.

three-bean chili with jalapeño cornbread topping

serves
6

prep time:
15 minutes

cook time:
50 minutes

On a cold and rainy day, there's nothing more comforting than a bowl of chili. This one is a delicious combination of hearty beans cooked in a smoky and spicy tomato sauce. The cheesy cornbread topping adds a crunchy contrast that pairs perfectly with the chili.

CHILI:

2 tablespoons olive oil

1 cup (140g) peeled and finely diced carrots

1 cup (125g) finely diced onions

2 medium celery stalks, finely diced

1 medium red bell pepper, diced

3 cloves garlic, grated

2 teaspoons ground coriander

2 teaspoons ground cumin

2 teaspoons smoked paprika

2 teaspoons crushed red pepper

1 teaspoon dried oregano leaves

½ teaspoon ground cinnamon

¼ teaspoon cayenne pepper

1 (28-ounce/800g) can diced tomatoes

4 cups (950ml) vegetable stock

1 tablespoon tomato paste

1 (15.5-ounce/440g) can red kidney beans, drained and rinsed

1 (15-ounce/425g) can black beans, drained and rinsed

1 (15-ounce/425g) can pinto beans, drained and rinsed

1 tablespoon unsweetened cocoa powder

2 to 3 tablespoons fresh lime juice, according to taste

Salt

plant swap:
Make it vegan by swapping the egg for a flax egg (see page 63) and the milk, cheese, and butter for plant-based alternatives.

CORNBREAD TOPPING:

1 cup (140g) yellow cornmeal or polenta

1 cup (125g) all-purpose flour

1 teaspoon baking powder

½ teaspoon salt

1 cup (240ml) whole milk

½ cup (120g) unsalted butter, melted

¼ packed cup (45g) light brown sugar

1 large egg, beaten

1 cup (75g) shredded cheddar cheese

2 medium scallions, thinly sliced

1 medium jalapeño pepper, seeded and finely diced

SUGGESTED TOPPINGS:

Shredded cheddar cheese

Diced or mashed avocado

Chopped fresh cilantro

Make the chili: Heat the oil in a 5-quart (5L) Dutch oven over medium-high heat. Add the carrots, onions, celery, and bell pepper and cook until the vegetables start to soften, about 10 minutes. Add the garlic, coriander, cumin, smoked paprika, crushed red pepper, oregano, cinnamon, and cayenne pepper and cook for another 2 minutes.

Add the tomatoes, stock, tomato paste, beans, and cocoa powder. Bring to a boil, then reduce the heat to medium and simmer gently for 20 minutes. Stir in the lime juice and season to taste with salt.

Preheat the oven to 400°F (200°C).

Make the cornbread topping: In a large bowl, whisk together the cornmeal, flour, baking powder, and salt. Add the rest of the ingredients and stir until combined.

Spread the cornbread batter on top of the chili as evenly as you can. Don't worry if it is a little patchy. Bake for 20 to 25 minutes, until the cornbread is golden.

Serve topped with shredded cheese, avocado, and/or cilantro.

sweet treats

apple & blackberry galette

This deliciously fruity galette is an impressive dessert but is really straightforward to make. The sweet and flaky crust is made with white spelt flour, coconut sugar (which you can swap for light brown sugar), and coconut oil. The quintessential late-summer combination of apples and blackberries is easily adapted to seasonal fruits. In early summer, I like to mix strawberries and rhubarb (with vanilla and ginger). Stone fruits also work well. Serve the galette on its own or with ice cream or a drizzle of "Salted" Caramel Sauce with Miso (page 316).

serves

6 to 8

prep time:

10 minutes, plus 1 hour to chill dough

cook time:

30 minutes

CRUST:

2 cups (250g) white spelt flour

¼ cup (40g) coconut sugar

¼ teaspoon salt

⅔ cup (110g) virgin coconut oil, room temperature (see note)

4 tablespoons ice-cold water

1 pound (450g) tart cooking apples, such as Granny Smith, Rome Beauty, or Bramley

¼ cup (40g) plus 1 tablespoon coconut sugar, divided

1 tablespoon cornstarch

1 tablespoon fresh lemon juice

1 teaspoon ground cinnamon

½ teaspoon ginger powder

⅔ cup (90g) blackberries

1 tablespoon almond milk

2 tablespoons sliced almonds

Fresh mint leaves, for garnish

GLAZE:

1 tablespoon apricot jam

2 teaspoons warm water, plus more if needed

note:

The ideal consistency of the coconut oil for this recipe is solid but soft. If your oil has hardened, soften it slightly in the microwave or a pan of hot water.

Make the crust: In a large bowl, stir together the flour, sugar, and salt. Using your fingertips, rub the coconut oil into the flour until the mixture resembles sand.

Adding 1 tablespoon of the cold water at a time, use your fingertips to work the mixture until it comes together, then knead the dough briefly until smooth (you might need to add more flour or water). Wrap the dough in plastic wrap and place in the fridge to chill for 1 hour.

Preheat the oven to 400°F (200°C).

Lightly dust a rolling pin with flour. Place the dough in the middle of a large piece of parchment paper. Roll it out to a circle 11 to 12 inches (28 to 30cm) in diameter and ¼ inch (6mm) thick. If the dough breaks, simply patch it up; don't worry if there are small lumps of coconut oil. Carefully slide the parchment paper with the crust onto a rimmed baking sheet.

Peel and core the apples and cut them into ¼-inch (6mm)-thick slices. Toss in a bowl with ¼ cup (40g) of the sugar, the cornstarch, lemon juice, cinnamon, and ginger until well combined. Carefully fold in the blackberries.

Arrange the fruits and their juices on top of the pastry, leaving a 2- to 3-inch (5 to 8cm) border all the way around.

Fold the edge of the dough inward over the fruit, pleating the dough as needed to maintain a round shape. Brush the border with the almond milk and sprinkle the remaining tablespoon of sugar all around the edge.

Bake until the fruits are soft and the crust is golden, about 30 minutes.

Meanwhile, dry-toast the almonds in a small frying pan over medium heat for about 2 minutes, until golden and fragrant. Stir often to prevent them from burning.

Make the glaze: Mix the jam with the warm water to make a glaze that's thin enough to be brushed; if needed, thin it with a little more water.

When the galette is baked, brush it all over with the apricot glaze and scatter the toasted almonds on top. Let cool completely on the pan before slicing. Decorate with mint leaves before serving.

apricot & mango energy balls

Whenever I feel midmorning or midafternoon sluggishness, I try to avoid caffeine and chocolate and reach for a healthy snack instead. These little energy balls are ideal to get me back on track. They are bursting with fruity flavors that are perfectly balanced with the warming aromas of fresh ginger, cinnamon, and cardamom.

makes
about 20 energy balls

prep time:
15 minutes, plus 1 hour to set

1 cup (175g) dried apricots

½ cup (40g) dried mango strips

6 dates, pitted, plus 1 or 2 more according to taste

1 cup (140g) raw almonds

1 tablespoon peeled and grated ginger

½ teaspoon ground cinnamon

Seeds from 3 cardamom pods, crushed

Pinch of salt

⅓ cup (30g) unsweetened shredded coconut

Place all of the ingredients except the coconut in a food processor. Pulse until everything is finely chopped and has become a sticky dough that holds together. Taste for sweetness; if desired, add 1 or 2 more dates and pulse to combine.

Scatter the coconut on a plate. Roll 1 tablespoon of the fruit mixture into a ball between your palms. Roll the ball in the coconut to coat it. Repeat with the rest of the fruit mixture to form about 20 energy balls.

Place the energy balls in the fridge to set for 1 hour before eating them.

Store leftover energy balls in an airtight container in the fridge for up to 3 days. They can also be frozen for up to 3 months.

chocolate mousse
with passion fruit curd

Light and airy, these chocolate mousse pots are topped with a layer of tangy
passion fruit curd and some fresh passion fruit pulp—a perfect combination for
a truly scrumptious dessert. The mousse is made without eggs. Aquafaba, the
liquid from a can of chickpeas, is high in protein and, like egg whites, expands to
form soft or stiff peaks when whisked at high speed. It works really well for plant-
based mousses, meringues, and other baked goods. So, the next time a recipe
calls for canned chickpeas, save the aquafaba to make a yummy dessert.

serves
6

prep time:
20 minutes, plus
overnight to set
and 2 hours to
chill

cook time:
20 minutes

CHOCOLATE MOUSSE:

¾ cup (180ml) aquafaba (chickpea brine) (see notes)

½ teaspoon cream of tartar

3 tablespoons superfine sugar

7 ounces (200g) dark chocolate, broken into chunks

1½ teaspoons ginger powder

PASSION FRUIT CURD:

½ cup (120ml) seedless passion fruit puree (see notes)

1¼ cups (300ml) almond milk

⅓ cup (75g) granulated sugar

2 tablespoons cornstarch

3 tablespoons vegan buttery spread

FOR GARNISH:

3 large passion fruits

Chocolate shavings

notes:

Check the label to confirm that the chickpeas do not contain salt; otherwise, the mousse will be salty.

One (15-ounce/425g) can of chickpeas should give you about ¾ cup (180ml) of brine. If the can you're using yields more, reserve the extra for another recipe; if it yields less, open a second can.

You can use fresh passion fruits for the curd; you will need about 8 fruits to get ½ cup (120ml) of puree. The easiest way to remove the seeds is to gently heat the pulp in a pan to help detach the seeds from the flesh, then press the pulp through a fine-mesh sieve. Or you can buy passion fruit puree, which is most often used to make cocktails and already has the seeds removed.

Using a stand mixer fitted with the whisk attachment, or a large mixing bowl and a hand mixer, whip the aquafaba on high speed until stiff peaks form (as you would do with egg whites), about 5 minutes. Add the cream of tartar and sugar and whip for another 10 seconds to combine.

Place the chocolate in a heatproof bowl that fits snugly over a saucepan. Bring about 1 inch (2.5cm) of water to a simmer in the saucepan and set the bowl of chocolate over the simmering water. Melt the chocolate, stirring often.

Once the chocolate has melted, stir in the ginger. Remove the bowl from the pan and allow the chocolate to cool until it's no longer hot but is still warm and in liquid form. If you let it cool too long, it will harden and will not mix well for the next step.

With a silicone spatula, carefully fold half of the melted chocolate into the whipped aquafaba. Once it is well mixed, carefully fold in the remaining half.

Divide the mousse evenly among six 8-ounce (225ml) glass ramekins, filling each about halfway. Once cool, transfer the ramekins to the fridge and leave the mousse to set overnight.

The next day, make the passion fruit curd: Place all of the ingredients except the buttery spread in a medium saucepan over medium heat, whisking until the mixture is thick enough to coat the back of a wooden spoon and reduced to about 1½ cups (350ml), 8 to 10 minutes. Remove from the heat and whisk in the buttery spread until well combined. Let cool for 5 minutes.

Spoon the curd over the mousse, using about ¼ cup (60ml) per ramekin, and place in the fridge to chill for a couple of hours.

Just before serving, cut the passion fruits in half and evenly scoop the pulp onto the layer of passion fruit curd. Finish with chocolate shavings.

mango & raspberry mini pavlovas with banana sorbet

These crispy mini pavlovas are topped with a guilt-free banana sorbet and fresh fruits. This is an indulgent yet healthy dessert that you can customize with any kind of seasonal fruit topping.

The meringue nests are made with aquafaba, which expands as egg whites do when whipped at high speed. Do not skip the cornstarch and white wine vinegar because they help stabilize the meringue. I like crunchy meringues, but if you prefer them chewy inside, simply reduce the cooking time to 1 hour.

makes

6 mini pavlovas

prep time:

25 minutes, plus 2 hours to freeze bananas and dry meringues

cook time:

1 hour 25 minutes

BANANA SORBET:

3 large ripe bananas, cut into chunks

MERINGUES:

¾ cup (180ml) aquafaba (chickpea brine (see notes)

½ teaspoon cornstarch

½ teaspoon white wine vinegar

½ cup (100g) superfine sugar (see notes)

FOR GARNISH:

3 tablespoons unsweetened coconut flakes

1 large mango, very thinly sliced

1 cup (125g) raspberries

2 fresh mint sprigs, snipped into sections

notes:

Check the label to confirm that the chickpeas do not contain salt; otherwise, the meringues will be salty.

One (15-ounce/425g) can of chickpeas should give you about ¾ cup (180ml) of brine. If the can you're using yields more, reserve the extra for another recipe; if it yields less, open a second can.

Superfine sugar will dissolve better in the meringue mixture. If you do not have superfine sugar, simply pulse some granulated sugar 3 or 4 times in a mini food processor or blender.

Place the banana chunks in a resealable freezer bag and put them in the freezer.

Preheat the oven to 275°F (140°C). Line a cookie sheet with parchment paper.

Heat the aquafaba in a small saucepan over medium heat and simmer to reduce by half, or to about ⅓ cup (80ml), about 8 minutes.

In a small bowl, mix together the cornstarch and vinegar. Set aside.

Transfer the reduced aquafaba to a stand mixer fitted with the whisk attachment, or use a large mixing bowl and a hand mixer. Whip on high speed until soft peaks form and the aquafaba has doubled in volume, 5 to 6 minutes. Add the cornstarch and vinegar mixture. Still whipping on high speed, beat in the sugar 1 tablespoon at a time and continue beating until glossy stiff peaks form, 8 to 10 minutes.

Spoon the mixture into a piping bag fitted with an open star tip and pipe onto the prepared cookie sheet into 3-inch (8cm)-diameter circles. Create a cavity in the middle of each meringue by piping more meringue around the edge.

Bake for 75 minutes, or until the meringue nests are crisp. Turn off the oven and leave the nests to cool completely inside the oven with the door closed for about 2 hours.

Meanwhile, dry-toast the coconut flakes in a small frying pan over medium heat, stirring often to prevent them from burning, until golden and fragrant, about 2 minutes. Transfer to a bowl and set aside.

When the meringues have cooled, make the sorbet: Place the frozen banana chunks in a mini food processor. Blend until smooth and creamy, about 2 minutes.

Place a scoop of sorbet in each meringue nest. Top with the mango slices, raspberries, and toasted coconut. Decorate with mint sprigs.

muesli cookies

These super simple cookies—naturally sweetened with raisins, banana, and orange juice—are a delicious healthy treat that you can enjoy as a snack or even for breakfast. Ready in about 30 minutes, they can be eaten warm or cold.

makes
12 to 14 cookies

prep time:
15 minutes

cook time:
20 minutes

½ cup (65g) white spelt flour

½ cup (65g) whole-meal spelt flour

½ cup (70g) raisins

½ cup (50g) rolled oats

⅓ cup (40g) chopped raw hazelnuts

¼ cup (30g) flax meal

2 tablespoons raw pumpkin seeds (pepitas)

2 tablespoons raw sunflower seeds

1 teaspoon baking powder

1 teaspoon ground cinnamon

½ teaspoon salt

½ cup (110g) mashed overripe banana (about 1 medium banana)

⅓ cup (80ml) pure maple syrup

¼ cup (60ml) virgin coconut oil, melted

1 teaspoon pure vanilla extract

Grated zest of 1 orange

3 tablespoons fresh orange juice

Have one oven rack in the middle of the oven and a second rack in the bottom half. Preheat the oven to 350°F (180°C). Line 2 cookie sheets with parchment paper.

In a large bowl, mix together the flours, raisins, oats, hazelnuts, flax meal, pumpkin seeds, sunflower seeds, baking powder, cinnamon, and salt.

In another bowl, mix together the banana, maple syrup, coconut oil, vanilla, orange zest, and orange juice.

Stir the wet ingredients into the dry ingredients until well combined.

Place 2 heaping tablespoons of dough on a cookie sheet. Flatten the dough to a circle about 2½ inches (6cm) in diameter. Repeat with the rest of the dough, placing 6 or 7 cookies on each sheet. Make sure they all are similar in size and thickness so they bake evenly.

Bake the cookies for 15 to 20 minutes, until slightly golden, switching the pans midway through baking. Remove from the oven and let cool on the pans for 5 minutes.

Enjoy while still warm, or transfer the cookies to a wire rack to finish cooling. Store the cooled cookies in an airtight container on the counter; they'll keep for up to 3 days.

poached pears with caramel sauce

serves
4

prep time:
10 minutes, plus
1 or 2 hours
to soak pears
(optional)

cook time:
30 minutes

Simple yet impressive, this melt-in-your-mouth dessert is the perfect finish to a dinner party. The pears are poached in a lightly spiced syrup and served with a one-of-a-kind "salted" caramel sauce that gets its salty profile from a touch of umami-rich miso. Giving the pears time to soak in the syrup is not imperative, but it does improve their flavor. If you can plan ahead, let them sit in the pan for an hour or two.

4 cups (950ml) water

1½ cups (300g) granulated sugar

3 whole cloves

2 cinnamon sticks

1 star anise pod

1 vanilla bean, cut in half lengthwise

1 (2-inch/5cm) piece ginger, peeled and roughly chopped

Grated zest of 1 orange

4 ripe but firm pears, such as Anjou, Bosc, or Bartlett, peeled

FOR SERVING:

½ cup (50g) sliced almonds

¾ to 1 cup (180 to 240ml) "Salted" Caramel Sauce with Miso (page 316), thinned with almond milk if needed

1 medium orange, cut into semicircles

Stir together the water, sugar, cloves, cinnamon sticks, star anise pod, vanilla, ginger, and orange zest in a medium saucepan. Bring to a boil over medium-high heat. Reduce the heat to a simmer, then place the pears in the pan and cook gently until they are soft (you should be able to easily pierce them with a knife), 20 to 25 minutes. Remove the pan from the heat.

For the best flavor, leave the pears to soak in the syrup for another hour or two before removing them from the pan.

Dry-toast the almonds in a medium frying pan over medium heat for about 2 minutes, until golden and fragrant. Stir often to prevent them from burning.

If the caramel sauce is too thick to pour, thin it with a splash of almond milk.

Using a slotted spoon, transfer the cooked pears to a serving dish. If they do not stand up straight, cut off a bit of the bottom of each pear to create a flat edge. Serve the pears drizzled with the caramel sauce and sprinkled with the toasted almonds, with orange slices on the side.

puffed quinoa chocolate chip bars

These no-bake bars double as a delicious high-protein snack. I make them with puffed quinoa, peanut butter, raisins, nuts, seeds, and dark chocolate chips. Warning: They are addictive! To maintain their shape and pleasingly chewy texture, the bars are best kept in the fridge.

Puffed quinoa is similar to puffed rice in texture but has a higher protein content. I have not had much luck making puffed quinoa at home, so I buy it from the supermarket or a health food store. It has a satisfying crunch and can be added to both sweet and savory dishes.

makes
sixteen 2-inch (4cm) square bars

prep time:
10 minutes, plus overnight to set

cook time:
6 minutes

¼ cup (35g) sesame seeds

1½ cups (50g) puffed quinoa

½ cup (70g) raw almonds, roughly chopped

½ cup (70g) raisins

¼ cup (35g) raw pumpkin seeds (pepitas)

¼ cup (35g) raw sunflower seeds

1 teaspoon ground cinnamon

½ teaspoon ginger powder

¼ teaspoon salt

1 cup (250g) smooth natural peanut butter

⅓ cup (80ml) pure maple syrup

2 tablespoons virgin coconut oil

¾ teaspoon pure vanilla extract

½ cup (80g) dark chocolate chips

Line an 8-inch (20cm) square baking pan with parchment paper.

Dry-toast the sesame seeds in a small frying pan over medium heat for about 2 minutes, until golden and fragrant. Stir often to prevent them from burning. Transfer the sesame seeds to a medium bowl.

To the bowl with the toasted sesame seeds, add the puffed quinoa, almonds, raisins, pumpkin seeds, sunflower seeds, cinnamon, ginger, and salt.

Gently warm the peanut butter, maple syrup, coconut oil, and vanilla in a large saucepan, whisking continuously for 3 to 4 minutes, until smooth. Remove the pan from the heat.

Add the seed mixture to the saucepan and mix with a wooden spoon until well combined. Fold in the chocolate chips.

Firmly pack the mixture into the prepared baking pan, making sure the top is level. Place in the fridge to set overnight.

Cut into 16 squares. Store the bars in an airtight container in the fridge for up 5 days.

strawberry labneh ice pops

makes
10 ice pops

prep time:
5 minutes, plus
overnight to
freeze

These homemade ice pops make a healthy summer treat and can be customized with other fruits, such as blueberries, blackberries, raspberries, or mango. You can have fun by layering different flavors too. Labneh has a lovely dense and creamy texture that is ideal for frozen desserts. You can buy it in Middle Eastern grocery stores and increasingly in supermarkets, or easily make it at home. Or simply use plain whole-milk Greek yogurt (adding a pinch of salt), though it's not as dense and tangy as labneh.

2 cups (425g) labneh, homemade (page 131) or store-bought

1 teaspoon pure vanilla extract

5 to 6 tablespoons (75 to 90ml) pure maple syrup, divided

1 pound (450g) fresh strawberries, hulled

SPECIAL EQUIPMENT:

Ice pop mold with 10 (3-ounce/90ml) wells

10 wooden ice pop sticks

In a medium bowl, stir together the labneh, vanilla, and 3 tablespoons (45ml) of the maple syrup. Set aside.

Place the strawberries in a food processor and blend to a thick puree. Sweeten with 2 to 3 tablespoons (30 to 45ml) of maple syrup, according to taste; how much syrup is needed will depend on the sweetness of the berries.

Swirl the strawberry puree into the labneh.

Pour the mixture into a 10-well ice pop mold. Insert the sticks and freeze overnight (see note).

note:
If your ice pop mold does not have a lid to hold the sticks in place, freeze the pops for 1 hour, then insert the sticks and freeze overnight.

plant swap:
Make it vegan by using plant-based plain Greek yogurt with an added pinch of salt instead of the labneh.

dressings, sauces & other basics

creamy avocado sauce

makes
1 cup (240ml)

prep time:
10 minutes

This go-to green condiment has a tantalizing fresh taste and an extra-smooth and creamy texture. So versatile, it is delicious with roasted vegetables, fritters, chicken, and fish and doubles as a spread for sandwiches and wraps.

1 large ripe avocado

½ packed cup (10g) roughly chopped fresh cilantro

½ packed cup (10g) roughly chopped fresh mint leaves

½ packed cup (10g) roughly chopped fresh parsley

3 cloves garlic, roughly chopped

¼ cup (60ml) water

3 tablespoons fresh lime juice, plus more if needed

½ teaspoon ground cumin

½ teaspoon salt

Place all of the ingredients in a blender or mini food processor and blend or pulse until combined and smooth. Taste and season with more salt and/or lime juice if needed.

Use right away or transfer to an airtight container and refrigerate. This sauce will keep for up to 2 days.

creamy tahini dressing—three ways

Tahini is a smooth paste made from ground sesame seeds that has an earthy, slightly bitter taste. When whisked with lemon juice and water, it makes a delicious dressing that you can enjoy on salads, bowls, and falafel. Because the taste varies quite a bit from one brand to another—some being more bitter than others—it is important that you sweeten these dressings teaspoon by teaspoon until you get your desired sweetness. Tahini can also vary in consistency, some being more pastelike, others more liquid-y. You may need to thin the dressing with a bit more water or lemon juice if your tahini is on the thicker side.

Following are three variations: a simple tahini dressing, a slightly silkier version with yogurt that has a lovely tang, and one with an herby twist that you can make using either of the first two dressings as a base.

simple tahini dressing

This basic dressing can be added to pretty much anything. Creamy and rich, it makes a nice change from vinaigrette.

makes
⅔ cup (160ml)

prep time:
3 minutes

¼ cup (60g) tahini

3 tablespoons fresh lemon juice

3 tablespoons water, plus more if needed

1 clove garlic, grated

¼ teaspoon ground cumin

¼ teaspoon salt

3 to 4 teaspoons honey or pure maple syrup, according to taste

In a small bowl, whisk together the tahini, lemon juice, and water until well combined. Stir in the garlic, cumin, and salt. Sweeten with the honey or maple syrup; how much sweetener is needed will depend on the flavor of the tahini and how acidic the lemon juice is.

If needed, add a little more water to adjust the consistency until creamy and smooth.

Use straightaway or store in a sealed jar in the fridge. This dressing will keep for up to 5 days.

plant swap:
Make it vegan by using maple syrup rather than honey.

yogurt tahini dressing

makes
¾ cup (180ml)

prep time:
3 minutes

I love the fresh and tangy flavor of this yogurt-based dressing. It is super versatile and delicious.

½ cup (120ml) plain yogurt

2 tablespoons tahini

2 tablespoons fresh lemon juice

1 clove garlic, grated

¼ to ½ teaspoon salt, according to taste

2 to 3 teaspoons honey or pure maple syrup, according to taste

Water, if needed

In a small bowl, whisk together the yogurt, tahini, and lemon juice until well combined. Stir in the garlic and salt. Sweeten with the honey or maple syrup. How much sweetener is needed will depend on how acidic the lemon juice is and the flavor of the tahini.

If needed, add a little water to adjust the consistency until creamy and smooth.

Use straightaway or store in a sealed jar in the fridge. This dressing will keep for up to 5 days.

plant swap:
Make it vegan by using dairy-free yogurt and maple syrup.

herby tahini dressing

makes
⅔ cup to ¾ cup (160 to 180ml)

prep time:
7 minutes

This dressing can be made with pretty much any fresh herb. I like equal amounts of dill, cilantro, and mint, but you can also use chives, parsley, chervil, and basil. For the base, use either Simple Tahini Dressing or Yogurt Tahini Dressing.

1 batch Simple Tahini Dressing (page 303) or Yogurt Tahini Dressing (above)

⅓ packed cup (15g) finely chopped fresh herbs

Place the dressing in a small bowl. Whisk in the herbs.

Use straightaway or store in a sealed jar in the fridge. This dressing will keep for up to 5 days.

simple tahini
dressing

yogurt tahini
dressing

herby tahini
dressing

french vinaigrette

zingy citrus dressing

carrot ginger dressing

asian-style dressing

herby vinaigrette

five easy salad dressings

Growing up, I was in awe of my godmother, who always made the best vinaigrette. Whisked to perfection every single time she made it, it was smooth, thick, and so delectable I used to sponge up every drop with a piece of bread.

The secrets of a good vinaigrette? For a good texture, whisking is key. Otherwise, the ingredients will not combine well. For taste, the quality of ingredients is paramount. The usual ratio is 3 parts oil to 1 part vinegar. However, depending on the strength and acidity of the vinegar I use, I find 4 parts oil to 1 part vinegar often gives better results because the oil (alongside the sugar) balances out the acidity of the vinegar. Salt enhances the overall flavor.

If the dressing has been stored in the fridge, the oil may congeal; simply set it on the counter to warm up a bit before using it.

Here are the five core dressings that I use in my kitchen.

french vinaigrette

makes
¾ cup (180ml)

prep time:
3 minutes

This basic French vinaigrette goes with pretty much any salad. Make a batch ahead and store it in a lidded jar to use over a few days. The oil and vinegar will separate over time, so give it a good shake before using it. The choice of vinegar will influence the taste of your dressing and dictate the quantity used. Red wine vinegar is more punchy than white wine vinegar, while apple cider vinegar tends to be milder yet. If using a mild vinegar, you may find that 3 tablespoons gives the perfect balance, while as little as 2 tablespoons of a sharper vinegar may be sufficient. For something a bit different, try sherry vinegar. It has a rich and nutty aroma that is absolutely delicious. For maximum flavor, make sure to pick a high-quality vinegar made without added sugars, colorings, or preservatives. The list of ingredients should be short and concise.

1 tablespoon Dijon or whole-grain mustard

2 to 3 tablespoons high-quality vinegar of choice, according to taste

½ cup (120ml) extra-virgin olive oil

1 teaspoon grated garlic, or 3 tablespoons minced shallots

¼ teaspoon salt

Good grind of black pepper

1 to 2 teaspoons granulated sugar, honey, or pure maple syrup, according to taste

In a small bowl, whisk together the mustard and vinegar until well combined. Carry on whisking while slowly pouring in the oil until the ingredients emulsify into a silky and creamy liquid.

Add the garlic, salt, and pepper. Sweeten with the sugar, honey, or maple syrup. How much sweetener is needed for balance will depend on how vinegary you like your dressing, and on the type of vinegar used.

Use straightaway or store in a sealed jar in the fridge. This vinaigrette will keep for up to 5 days.

zingy citrus dressing

makes
⅔ cup (160ml)

prep time:
3 minutes

This dressing can be made with lemon or orange juice. It is ideal with a crunchy green salad or a grain salad. Make a big batch ahead and remember to give it a good shake before using it.

1 teaspoon Dijon mustard

3 tablespoons fresh lemon or orange juice

⅓ cup (80ml) extra-virgin olive oil

2 cloves garlic, grated

¼ teaspoon salt

Good grind of black pepper

1 to 2 teaspoons granulated sugar, honey, or pure maple syrup, according to taste

In a small bowl, whisk together the mustard and citrus juice until well combined. Keep whisking while slowly pouring in the oil until the ingredients emulsify into a silky and creamy liquid.

Add the garlic, salt, and pepper. Sweeten with the sugar, honey, or maple syrup. How much sweetener is needed for balance will depend on whether you used lemon juice or orange juice.

Use straightaway or store in a sealed jar in the fridge. This dressing will keep for up to 5 days.

herby vinaigrette

makes
⅔ to ¾ cup
(160 to 180ml)

prep time:
3 minutes

This vinaigrette can be made with pretty much any fresh herb. I like parsley, chives, and tarragon, but you can experiment with basil, dill, cilantro, chervil, thyme, mint, or oregano. For the base, you can either use the French Vinaigrette or the Zingy Citrus Dressing.

1 batch French Vinaigrette (page 307) or Zingy Citrus Dressing (above)

1 tablespoon finely chopped fresh chives

1 tablespoon finely chopped fresh parsley leaves

1 tablespoon finely chopped fresh tarragon leaves

Put the vinaigrette or dressing in a small bowl and whisk in the herbs.

Use straightaway or store in a sealed jar in the fridge. This vinaigrette will keep for up to 3 days.

asian-style dressing

makes
⅔ cup (160ml)

prep time:
2 minutes

This is my go-to dressing when making a salad that has Asian flavors. The ginger gives it a bold aroma, and it is perfect with cabbage, carrots, broccoli, zucchini, or rice.

3 tablespoons fresh lime juice

2 tablespoons extra-virgin olive oil

2 tablespoons toasted sesame oil

1 tablespoon unseasoned rice vinegar

2 tablespoons dark brown sugar

1 tablespoon peeled and grated ginger

2 cloves garlic, grated

2 teaspoons soy sauce

Whisk together all of the ingredients in a small bowl.

Use straightaway or store in a sealed jar in the fridge. This dressing will keep for up to 5 days.

carrot ginger dressing

makes
1¼ cups (295ml)

prep time:
5 minutes

I first tried this dressing in a Japanese restaurant and fell in love with it instantly. I have adapted it so it can easily be made with pantry ingredients. If you do not have any rice vinegar, you can use apple cider vinegar instead. Delightfully fresh, this dressing has a vibrant orange glow that will liven up any salad or bowl.

1 cup (125g) peeled and sliced carrots

½ cup (60g) chopped onions

2 tablespoons peeled and grated ginger

½ cup (120ml) vegetable oil

¼ cup (60ml) unseasoned rice vinegar

2 tablespoons fresh lime juice

1 tablespoon plus 1 teaspoon honey, pure maple syrup, or agave nectar

1 teaspoon tamari

1 teaspoon toasted sesame oil

Pinch of salt

Place all of the ingredients in a blender. Blend until everything is well combined and smooth.

Use straightaway or store in a sealed jar in the fridge. This dressing will keep for up to 3 days.

dukkah

makes

1½ cups (190g)

prep time:

3 minutes

cook time:

5 minutes

I wish I could say that I discovered dukkah during a holiday in Egypt. Alas, no. Instead, I first tried it in a countryside British pub where it was served alongside bread and olive oil for dunking. Since then, dukkah has become my go-to topping for flatbread, dips, salads, and soups. I continue to enjoy it as a dry "dip" for olive oil–soaked breads. You can also use it to crust meat, fish, or tofu. It is absolutely delicious and so versatile that it will soon become an essential ingredient in your kitchen.

½ cup (70g) raw almonds

½ cup (65g) blanched hazelnuts

3 tablespoons sesame seeds

2 tablespoons coriander seeds

2 teaspoons cumin seeds

1 teaspoon fennel seeds

1 teaspoon paprika

¾ teaspoon salt

½ teaspoon ground black pepper

In a large frying pan, dry-toast the almonds and hazelnuts over medium heat for about 3 minutes, until fragrant. Stir often to prevent them from burning. Transfer to a food processor.

In the same pan, dry-toast the sesame, coriander, cumin, and fennel seeds for about 2 minutes, until fragrant. Stir often to prevent them from burning. Add to the food processor.

Pulse until the nuts are roughly chopped; be careful not to pulse too much or you'll end up with nut butter.

Season with the paprika, salt, and pepper.

Transfer to an airtight container. This dukkah will keep at room temperature for up to 3 weeks.

easy tomato sauce

makes
6 cups (1.4L)

prep time:
8 minutes

cook time:
45 minutes

I like to prepare a batch of this sauce to use throughout the week. It is so easy to make and much tastier (and cheaper) than store-bought alternatives. It's superb for pasta, lasagna, or anything else that requires tomato sauce or marinara sauce. It has a slightly chunky texture but, once cooked, can be whizzed in a blender if you'd like something smoother. Sugar balances out the acidity of the tomatoes, which can vary quite a lot, so I usually start with 1 tablespoon of sugar and adjust the sweetness near the end of the cooking. Two teaspoons of crushed red pepper give this sauce a delicious spicy kick. If you prefer less heat, use just 1 teaspoon.

3 tablespoons olive oil

1¼ cups (150g) finely diced onions

2 (28-ounce/800g) cans diced tomatoes

4 cloves garlic, grated

1 tablespoon tomato paste

1 teaspoon dried basil

1 teaspoon dried oregano leaves

1 teaspoon dried parsley

1 teaspoon dried thyme leaves

1 to 2 teaspoons crushed red pepper, according to taste

1 to 2 tablespoons granulated sugar, according to taste

1 packed cup (25g) roughly chopped fresh basil

Salt

Heat the oil in a 5-quart (5L) Dutch oven over medium heat. Add the onions and cook gently, stirring from time to time, until they start to soften, 6 to 8 minutes.

Add the diced tomatoes, garlic, tomato paste, dried herbs, crushed red pepper, and 1 tablespoon of sugar. Bring to a boil, then reduce the heat to medium and cover. Simmer for 25 to 35 minutes, stirring occasionally, until the sauce is reduced by about one-third.

Add the fresh basil and simmer for another 5 minutes. Season to taste with salt and up to 1 tablespoon of additional sugar if needed.

Let cool before transferring to an airtight container. The sauce will keep in the fridge for up to a week.

sweet chili dipping sauce

makes
½ cup (120ml)

prep time:
5 minutes

This is a versatile dipping sauce that I use over and over again. Zingy and sharp, it is perfect with my Summer Rolls (page 114), Crispy Baked Egg Rolls (page 120), or Kimchi Fritters (page 124).

2 tablespoons sweet chili sauce

2 tablespoons unseasoned rice vinegar

2 tablespoons toasted sesame oil

2 tablespoons fresh lime juice

2 teaspoons dark brown sugar

1 teaspoon tamari

1 tablespoon chopped fresh mint leaves

Whisk together all of the ingredients in a small bowl.

Transfer to an airtight container and keep refrigerated for up to 4 days.

pickled red onions

Sweet and tangy and flavored with garlic and peppercorns, these pickled onions are the perfect topping for burgers, salads, sandwiches, etc. They're quick and easy to make and are ready to eat the next day, although they improve in texture and taste over time.

makes

one 12-ounce (340ml) jar

prep time:

5 minutes, plus 1 day to pickle

cook time:

1 minute

1 medium red onion, peeled

2 cloves garlic, peeled

1 teaspoon black peppercorns

½ cup (120ml) white wine vinegar

½ cup (120ml) water

1½ tablespoons granulated sugar

1½ teaspoons finely ground sea salt

Using a very sharp knife or a mandoline, cut the onion into thin slices. Place the slices in a heatproof 12-ounce (350ml) lidded jar with the garlic and peppercorns.

Combine the vinegar, water, sugar, and salt in a medium saucepan, stirring to dissolve the sugar and salt. Bring to a boil, then pour the mixture over the onions.

Leave at room temperature for 1 hour. Seal the jar and transfer to the fridge.

The onions can be eaten the next day, once they are bright pink and soft. They will keep in the fridge for up to 2 weeks.

"salted" caramel sauce with miso

makes
1 cup (240ml)

prep time:
2 minutes

cook time:
7 minutes

Salted caramel is one of my guilty pleasures. I like to add it to pretty much anything sweet. Its origins can be traced to Brittany, a region in the northwest of France that is famous for, among other things, salted butter.

This dairy-free version contains no salt; instead, it gets its salty profile from fermented miso, which also gives it plenty of umami. Quick and easy to make, this is a truly versatile sauce that you can serve with fruit, pancakes, waffles, or ice cream.

1 cup (240ml) store-bought dairy-free cream (see note) or Simple Cashew Cream (page 323)

¼ cup (60g) dairy-free buttery spread

¾ packed cup (135g) coconut sugar or light brown sugar

1 teaspoon pure vanilla extract

1 to 2 teaspoons white miso, according to taste

Splash of dairy-free milk, if needed

note:

For this sauce, I prefer a dairy-free cream that does not have a pronounced coconut flavor. Both store-bought nondairy whipping cream and single soy cream work well. Alternatively, you can use my Simple Cashew Cream thinned to half-and-half consistency. If you do, the caramel sauce will have a thicker consistency (that you can adjust with a splash of dairy-free milk) and will need to simmer for only 3 minutes.

If using homemade cashew cream, thin it with water until it has the consistency of half-and-half. Whisk the cream and buttery spread in a medium saucepan over medium-high heat until the spread has melted.

Stir in the sugar and vanilla. Bring to a boil, then reduce the heat to a lively simmer and cook, stirring occasionally, until thickened and silky. If using store-bought cream, this should take about 5 minutes; if using cashew cream, 3 minutes should do it.

Whisk in 1 teaspoon of miso until well combined. Taste and add up to 1 teaspoon more, until the sauce has a pleasant hit of saltiness that balances the sweetness; how much miso is needed will depend on how salty your miso is. Set the sauce aside to cool.

The sauce should be creamy and pourable. If it becomes too thick once it has cooled, thin it with a splash or two of dairy-free milk as needed.

Once cool, store the sauce in an airtight container in the fridge for up to 3 days. Just before serving, if desired you can rewarm it in the microwave or in a saucepan over gentle heat.

five-minute date "caramel" spread

makes
1 cup (265g)

prep time:
5 minutes

Sweetened with dates, this is a healthy yet addictively tasty alternative to traditional caramel with the added benefit of containing no refined sugar. Dates (especially Medjool dates) are wonderfully rich, with flavors reminiscent of caramel. Though not as creamy and pourable as my "Salted" Caramel Sauce with Miso (page 316), this recipe makes an ideal spread or dip for serving with fruit, pancakes, waffles, etc.

1 cup (175g) pitted and roughly chopped soft, moist dates (see notes)

½ cup (120ml) dairy-free milk, plus more if needed (see notes)

½ teaspoon pure vanilla extract

½ teaspoon salt

Put the dates in a blender or mini food processor. Add the milk, vanilla, and salt and whizz until smooth. Add a splash of additional milk if needed to adjust to your desired consistency.

notes:

Medjool dates are best for this recipe. Other types are suitable as long as they are moist and soft. If the dates you're using are a bit too dry, soak them in warm water for 15 minutes, then drain before using.

I prefer almond milk for this recipe as its nutty flavor complements the dates, but you can use any other dairy-free milk alternative.

vegan mayonnaise—four ways

makes
1 to 1¼ cups
(240 to 300ml)

prep time:
5 minutes

This vegan mayonnaise recipe is foolproof and can be made using either aquafaba or soy milk. Do not be tempted to substitute another dairy-free milk for the soy milk or the resulting mayonnaise will have a thinner, runnier consistency instead of being nice and thick. When made with soy milk, this recipe yields 1⅓ cups (320ml) of mayonnaise; when made with aquafaba, it yields 1 cup (240ml). I use both ingredients alternatively, depending on what I have on hand. I never open a new can of chickpeas for the brine, using instead the leftover brine from making hummus or other dishes. (One 15-ounce [425g] can of chickpeas yields about ½ cup [120ml] of aquafaba.)

This is an easy recipe. Just remember to add the oil very slowly so you get a thick and creamy emulsion. I have included some of my favorite flavors: classic, Sriracha, herby, and miso sesame.

classic mayonnaise

This is my go-to classic mayonnaise. It has a neutral flavor, with just a touch of garlic for added depth, and is really versatile. You can use it as a dip, condiment, or spread.

¼ cup (60ml) aquafaba (chickpea brine), or ½ cup (120ml) soy milk

1 small clove garlic, grated

2 teaspoons apple cider vinegar

1 teaspoon Dijon mustard

½ teaspoon salt (see note)

Pinch of turmeric powder (optional, for color)

1 cup (240ml) sunflower oil

Place the aquafaba, garlic, vinegar, mustard, salt, and turmeric powder, if using, in a blending jar. Mix using an immersion blender until well blended.

Keep mixing while very slowly pouring in the oil. If you add it too fast, the mayonnaise will not thicken well. Keep on blending, moving the blade up and down until you have a thick and creamy texture.

This mayonnaise will keep in an airtight container in the fridge for up to a week. You can use it as is or as the base for one of the flavored variations that follow.

note:
Omit the salt if you intend to use this as a base for the miso sesame mayonnaise on page 322.

classic

herby

sriracha

miso sesame

sriracha mayonnaise

Sriracha sauce gives mayonnaise a delicious spicy kick and will liven up roasted vegetables, sandwiches, and wraps.

2 to 3 tablespoons Sriracha sauce, according to taste

1 cup (240ml) Classic Mayonnaise (page 320)

Whisk the Sriracha into the mayonnaise. This mayonnaise will keep in an airtight container in the fridge for up to a week.

herby mayonnaise

This fresh herby mayonnaise makes a delicious potato salad or dip for steamed spring vegetables. I think tarragon is a must-have, but you can vary the herbs to include basil or oregano.

2 tablespoons chopped fresh chives

2 tablespoons chopped fresh dill

2 tablespoons chopped fresh parsley

2 tablespoons chopped fresh tarragon

1 cup (240ml) Classic Mayonnaise (page 320)

Whisk the herbs into the mayonnaise. This mayonnaise will keep in an airtight container in the fridge for up to 3 days.

miso sesame mayonnaise

For the ultimate umami experience, try this miso sesame mayonnaise with fries or roasted vegetables.

1 to 2 tablespoons white miso, according to taste

1 cup (240ml) Classic Mayonnaise (page 320)

Drizzle of toasted sesame oil, plus more if desired

Whisk 1 tablespoon of the miso into the mayonnaise. Taste and add up to 1 tablespoon more; miso varies in flavor and saltiness, so you may or may not need the full 2 tablespoons. Whisk in the sesame oil, then taste and add more if desired. This mayonnaise will keep in an airtight container in the fridge for up to a week.

simple cashew cream

makes

1¼ cups (300ml)

prep time:

10 minutes, plus
20 minutes to
soak cashews

Whether you are vegan or simply looking to cut down on dairy, this simple vegan cashew cream is a staple you will keep coming back to. It has the consistency of heavy cream, but you can thin it with more water if you want something lighter, similar to half-and-half, or use less water for a creamy dip or scoopable cream that can be folded into recipes (see the note below). You can vary the flavor from plain to cheesy (adding nutritional yeast and grated garlic), spicy (adding Sriracha or hot sauce and grated garlic), or sweet (adding maple syrup).

1 cup (140g) raw cashews

1 cup (240ml) water (see note)

Pinch of salt

note:

For a cream with the consistency of half-and-half, increase the amount of water to 1¼ cups (300ml). For a scoopable cream or dip, decrease it to ¾ cup (180ml).

Place the cashews in a heatproof bowl and cover with boiling water. Leave to soak for 20 minutes.

Drain the cashews and place them in a high-powered blender with the water. Blend until smooth and silky. Season with the salt.

Transfer the cashew cream to an airtight container and refrigerate. It will keep for up to 3 days.

raspberry chia jam

makes
1 cup (300g)

prep time:
5 minutes, plus
time to cool and
set

cook time:
5 minutes

Growing up, my mom would preserve seasonal fruits and vegetables so we could enjoy them throughout the year. An entire storage room in the basement was dedicated to her mouthwatering creations. To this day, I love making my own jams using less sugar and more fruit than commercial brands do. I also find it a savvy way to make use of produce that is past its prime.

This raspberry chia jam is made with only 2 tablespoons of honey and contains no refined sugar. It is runnier than traditional jam and does not keep as long, so I tend to prepare small batches, which is ideal when our homegrown berries are in short supply. You can use other berries (either fresh or frozen), such as blueberries, blackberries, or strawberries.

This jam is delicious spread on toast or in PB&J sandwiches (see my recipe for this classic on page 102). It is also the perfect yogurt, waffle, or pancake topping.

2 cups (240g) raspberries, thawed if frozen

2 tablespoons chia seeds

2 tablespoons honey

1 tablespoon fresh lemon juice

½ teaspoon pure vanilla extract

Heat the raspberries in a medium saucepan over medium heat until the berries are soft and their juice is bubbling, about 5 minutes.

Break down the berries into a chunky paste with a fork.

Remove the pan from the heat. Stir in the chia seeds, honey, lemon juice, and vanilla. Leave to cool completely and thicken.

This jam will keep in an airtight container in the fridge for up to 2 weeks.

plant swap:
Make it vegan by using light-colored, or golden, maple syrup instead of honey.

"cream cheese"—three ways

makes

1 to 1½ cups (200 to 300g), depending on flavor

prep time:

10 minutes, plus 20 minutes or overnight to soak cashews

The mere scent of fresh bagels conjures up great memories for me. After graduating from college, I secured my first job in Manhattan. Our office had a prestigious location on Fifth Avenue, and every morning I grabbed a cream cheese–smeared bagel and a coffee from the street cart just around the corner. Whenever I could, I would run down to the bagel shop to enjoy a bagel with cream cheese for lunch too! Around the same time, I started developing a slight lactose intolerance, and sadly cream cheese became off-limits for a while. I wish I had known then that you can turn nuts into "cheese" by soaking them in water.

Here are three versions: plain, herby, and fruity. Dairy-free and high in plant-based protein, each spread is a real treat. The fruity version can be made with other types of berries and is delicious as a smooth and creamy dip; just drop the hulled strawberries—no need to mash them—into the blender when you add the vanilla and blend until smooth.

BASE:

1 cup (140g) raw cashews

1 tablespoon fresh lemon juice

1 tablespoon water, plus more if needed

PLAIN:

½ teaspoon salt

HERBY:

½ teaspoon salt

1 teaspoon garlic powder

2 tablespoons finely chopped fresh chives

1 tablespoon finely chopped fresh basil

1 tablespoon finely chopped fresh parsley

FRUITY:

½ teaspoon pure vanilla extract

1 cup (240g) fresh strawberries, hulled and mashed with a fork

Granulated sugar, if needed

Make the base: Submerge the cashews in a bowl of water and leave to soak overnight on the counter. If you live in a hot climate, place the nuts in the fridge to soak. Alternatively, for a shortcut that works equally well, soak the nuts for 20 minutes in boiling hot water.

Drain the cashews and place in a blender. Add the rest of the base ingredients.

To make the plain version, add the salt and blend until smooth.

To make the herby version, add the salt and garlic powder and blend until smooth. Transfer the mixture to a bowl and combine with the finely chopped herbs.

To make the fruity version, add the vanilla and blend until smooth. Transfer the mixture to a bowl and add the strawberries. Stir to combine, then taste and sweeten with a little sugar if necessary.

For all versions, if the texture is too thick, add up to another tablespoon of water and blend until smooth.

Transfer the spread to an airtight container. These spreads can be eaten straightaway or will keep in the fridge for up to 4 days.

plain

fruity

herby

homemade roasted nut, seed, or peanut butter

makes
1 cup (240ml)

prep time:
15 minutes

cook time:
6 to 10 minutes, depending on type of nuts or seeds used

When making your own nut, seed, or peanut butter, you have lots more options than you can find at a typical grocery store. Feel free to use any nut or seed you like—almonds, cashews, hazelnuts, pecans, walnuts, and sunflower or pumpkin seeds (pepitas) are all good choices. (Seeds are a great option if you're allergic to nuts.) If you have a variety of leftover nuts and/or seeds on hand, try blending them together. You can also use this recipe to make peanut butter. Be as creative as you like, tweaking the recipe by adding spices, herbs, cocoa powder, coconut (flakes or shredded), matcha powder, vanilla extract or seeds, fruit powder, and so on.

The process of making the butter is pretty straightforward. Roasting the nuts, seeds, or peanuts first not only improves the flavor but also gives the butter a better texture. For a smooth and creamy butter, you need a good food processor. Even when using a powerful appliance, make sure to switch it on and off often while blending to relieve the strain on the motor.

2 cups (300g) raw nuts or seeds of choice or blanched peanuts

Pinch of salt (or more to taste)

note:

Hazelnut skins are bitter, so it's best to remove them before grinding the nuts into butter. To do so, place the roasted nuts on a clean tea towel and rub them around to break off the skins. You won't be able to remove 100 percent of the skins; just do the best you can.

Preheat the oven to 300°F (150°C). Spread the nuts, seeds, or peanuts on a rimmed baking sheet and roast until lightly browned, about 10 minutes for nuts or peanuts or 6 minutes for seeds. (If using hazelnuts, remove the skins after roasting them; see note.)

Place the roasted nuts, seeds, or peanuts in a food processor and start whizzing. If you prefer a crunchy butter, remove a couple of tablespoons of nut fragments from the processor and set aside.

From time to time, turn off the food processor and scrape down the sides of the bowl.

After about 3 minutes, a paste will begin to form.

After about 5 minutes, you should see a ball forming. Don't forget to turn off the motor occasionally to give your food processor a rest!

After 10 to 15 minutes, you should have a smooth and creamy butter. If desired, stir in the reserved nut fragments and salt.

Transfer the butter to an airtight glass container and store in the fridge for up to 2 months.

simple nut milk

makes

2 cups (475ml)

prep time:

10 minutes,
plus 20 minutes
or overnight to
soak nuts

Here is a simple method for making plain nut milk. Feel free to use almonds, cashews, hazelnuts, pecans, walnuts, or another nut of your choosing. Although plain milk is best for savory preparations, you can easily make sweetened or flavored milk by following the variations below. However, you need not feel limited to these options. Why not experiment with matcha powder, cinnamon, nutmeg, turmeric, or ginger? The possibilities are endless.

1 cup (150g) raw nuts of choice

2 cups (475ml) water, plus extra to thin if needed

note:

The leftover nut meal can be used to make cookies, crackers, and other baked goods and can also double as a gluten-free crusty topping for fish, meat, casseroles, and fruit crumbles.

Soak the nuts in a bowl of water overnight; if you live in a warm climate, place the bowl in the fridge. Alternatively, for a shortcut method that works equally well, soak the nuts in a bowl of boiling hot water for 20 minutes.

Drain the nuts and place in a high-powered blender along with 2 cups (475ml) of fresh water. Blend until completely smooth.

Line a fine-mesh sieve with cheesecloth and place it over a 1-quart (1L)-sized pitcher. Pour the milk through the lined sieve into the pitcher. Gather up the edges of the cheesecloth and squeeze to extract as much liquid as possible. (See note for ways to use the leftover nut meal.)

Thin the milk to your liking by adding 1 to 2 cups (240 to 475ml) more water. Store in an airtight container in the fridge for up to 4 days.

variations:

Pour 2 cups (475ml) of plain nut milk into a blender, then add the ingredients for the flavor of your choice and blend until smooth.

sweetened milk

2 to 3 pitted dates, or 1 to 2 teaspoons pure maple syrup

½ teaspoon vanilla extract

strawberry milk

½ cup to 1 cup (70 to 140g) hulled fresh strawberries

1 or 2 pitted dates, or 1 teaspoon pure maple syrup

½ teaspoon vanilla extract

chocolate milk

2 tablespoons unsweetened cocoa powder

5 to 6 pitted dates, or 1 to 1½ tablespoons pure maple syrup

plain

strawberry

chocolate

sweetened

thank you

To Graham, you have been there every step of the way. Thank you for your unwavering support, belief in me, patience, and hand-modeling skills. You always challenge me for the better, and I could not imagine my life without you.

Maman et Papa, votre amour et soutient comptent énormement pour moi. Merci de répondre toujours présents. Maman, merci, de m'avoir donné l'amour de la cuisine.

To Zac and Maya, you two make my world complete. Thank you for eating your way through these recipes. I am so proud to be your mom.

To the amazing team at Victory Belt Publishing, for bringing this book to life. Lance Freimuth, for giving me this incredible opportunity. Holly Jennings, for your outstanding work editing and helping make these recipes coherent. Pam Mourouzis, for your top-class editing, support, and help structuring the first part of this book. Susan Lloyd, for your enthusiasm and support in marketing this cookbook. Elita San Juan and Justin-Aaron Velasco, for your work on the cover. Yordan Terziev and Boryana Yordanova, for all the great graphics and work on the design and layout.

To my father-in-law Brian, I am always grateful for your support and encouragement.

To my friends, Sabrina Beaubay, Caroline De St Quentin, Valérie Hartland, Laëtitia Lord, Lydie Plancke, Anna Pollard, and Clémence Routaboul, for your input, especially on choosing a cover, and for your support throughout. Rob Lord, for inspiring me to dig deep when deadlines loomed. Suzanne Clare, David Slemmer, Dörte Wren, and Sharon Willoughby, for your enthusiasm and support.

To Tina Seskis and Kate Mills, for your help and insight into the publishing world.

Last but not least, my thanks to every single one of you who has read this cookbook, cooked from it, and followed my blog. I am so grateful and would love to hear from you and see pictures of your creations. #lessmeatmoreplants

appendix A:
american to british cooking terms

US	UK
All-purpose flour	Plain flour
Arugula	Rocket
Baby bella mushrooms (aka cremini)	Chestnut mushrooms
Baking soda	Bicarbonate of soda
Bok choy	Pak choi
Canned tomatoes	Tinned tomatoes
Cilantro	Fresh coriander
Coconut flakes	Coconut shavings
Crushed red pepper (aka red pepper flakes)	Crushed chili flakes
Eggplant	Aubergine
Half-and-half	Single cream
Heavy cream	Double cream
Shredded	Grated on the coarse side of a box grater
Stovetop	Hob
2% milk	Semi-skimmed milk
Whole-wheat flour	Wholemeal flour
Zucchini	Courgette

appendix B: conversions

VOLUME

US QUANTITY	METRIC EQUIVALENT
1 teaspoon	5 milliliters
1 tablespoon	15 milliliters
2 tablespoons	30 milliliters
¼ cup or 2 fluid ounces	60 milliliters
⅓ cup	80 milliliters
½ cup or 4 fluid ounces	120 milliliters
⅔ cup	160 milliliters
¾ cup or 6 fluid ounces	180 milliliters
1 cup or 8 fluid ounces or ½ pint	240 milliliters
1½ cups or 12 fluid ounces	350 milliliters
2 cups or 1 pint or 16 fluid ounces	475 milliliters
3 cups or 1½ pints	700 milliliters
4 cups or 2 pints or 1 quart	1 liter

note:
These numbers are rounded for convenience.

WEIGHT

US QUANTITY	METRIC EQUIVALENT
1 ounce	28 grams
4 ounces or ¼ pound	115 grams
⅓ pound	150 grams
8 ounces or ½ pound	225 grams
⅔ pound	300 grams
12 ounces or ¾ pound	340 grams
16 ounces or 1 pound	450 grams
32 ounces or 2 pounds	900 grams

OVEN TEMPERATURE

FAHRENHEIT	CELSIUS	FAN CELSIUS	GAS MARK
275°F	140°C	120°C	1
300°F	150°C	130°C	2
325°F	170°C	150°C	3
350°F	180°C	160°C	4
375°F	190°C	170°C	5
400°F	200°C	180°C	6
425°F	220°C	200°C	7
450°F	230°C	210°C	8
475°F	240°C	220°C	9

appendix C:
further resources

When it comes to food (and other things in life, for that matter!), making a perfect choice is not always possible.

Every one of us will approach a plant-forward diet for different reasons. My main motivation was the environment. Yours might be health, animal welfare, or a mix of several reasons. At times, you might find it difficult to come to clear-cut decisions. Is it better to drink local organic milk or a dairy-free alternative that has been flown in from miles away? Should you eat a grass-fed meat burger or go for a plant-based patty? Depending on your personal situation and viewpoint, your answers to these questions may differ from the next person's.

As I mentioned in the introduction to this book, the necessity to change my diet was not apparent to me at first. Yet, once I started to educate myself, it quickly became obvious that I needed to make a change, and why. A better understanding of the issues at stake was key in shaping my plant-forward journey. There is a lot of information out there, and wading through it will help you make educated decisions that make sense for you and your particular needs. Here are some of the sources that helped me along the way.

	US	UK
CAMPAIGNS	Meatless Monday www.mondaycampaigns.org/meatless-monday	Meat Free Monday meatfreemondays.com
	Veganuary veganuary.com/en-us/	
FOOD ASSOCIATIONS	American Vegan Society americanvegan.org	Slow Food in the UK www.slowfood.org.uk
	Feedback feedbackglobal.org	The Vegan Society www.vegansociety.com
	North American Vegetarian Society (NAVS) navs-online.org	The Vegetarian Society vegsoc.org
	ProVeg International proveg.com/us/	
	Slow Food USA slowfoodusa.org	
ANIMAL RIGHTS GROUPS	Compassion in World Farming USA www.ciwf.com	Compassion in World Farming www.ciwf.org.uk
	The Humane League thehumaneleague.org	The Humane League United Kingdom thehumaneleague.org.uk
	Animal Welfare Institute awionline.org	
	WWF www.worldwildlife.org	

	US	UK
CONSUMER INFORMATION	Eat Wild www.eatwild.com	Pasture for Life www.pastureforlife.org
	Environmental Working Group www.ewg.org	
	Marine Stewardship Council (MSC) www.msc.org/en-us	
	Seafood Watch www.seafoodwatch.org	
ENVIRONMENTAL ORGANIZATIONS	Friends of the Earth www.foe.org	Sustain www.sustainweb.org
	Greenpeace www.greenpeace.org/usa/	Sustainable Food Trust www.sustainablefoodtrust.org

books

Animal Liberation, by Peter Singer

The China Study, by T. Colin Campbell, PhD, and Thomas M. Campbell II, MD

Dead Zone: Where the Wild Things Were, by Philip Lymbery

Eating Animals, by Jonathan Safran Foer

Farmageddon: The True Cost of Cheap Meat, by Philip Lymbery with Isabel Oakeshot

Grass-Fed Nation, by Graham Harvey

Plucked! The Truth About Chicken, by Maryn McKenna

Whole: Rethinking the Science of Nutrition, by T. Colin Campbell, PhD, with Howard Jacobson, PhD

Why We Love Dogs, Eat Pigs, and Wear Cows: An Introduction to Carnism, by Melanie Joy, PhD

magazines

Forks Over Knives Magazine

Vegan Food & Living (UK)
www.veganfoodandliving.com

Vegetarian Times
www.vegetariantimes.com

VegNews
vegnews.com

documentaries

Before the Flood (2016)

Cowspiracy (2014)

Eating Our Way to Extinction (2021)

Food Inc. (2008)

Forks Over Knives (2011)

The Game Changers (2018)

Seaspiracy (2021)

What the Health (2017)

recipe index

breakfast

chocolate cherry
smoothie bowl

overnight porridge

apple & cranberry
bircher muesli

spiced oatmeal
with caramelized
bananas & pecans

blueberry & peach
baked oatmeal

tofu scramble
on toast

healthier carrot
muffins

zucchini chocolate
pancakes

peanut butter &
banana sandwich
with homemade
raspberry chia jam

veggie breakfast
bowls

butter bean & feta
shakshuka

fruity nut & seed
loaf

very berry granola

small bites

summer rolls

loaded polenta fries

crispy baked
egg rolls

tomato & tapenade
tart

kimchi fritters

carrot & cilantro
quinoa fritters

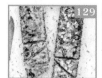
quinoa crust
quiches—two ways

labneh

three
mediterranean dips

mushroom & lentil
pâté

quick muhammara

spiced
butter bean dip

tzatziki—two ways

hearty salads & bowls

beetroot & orange
salad

crunchy broccoli
salad with roasted
sriracha chickpeas

kale & grilled corn
salad

mediterranean
orzo salad

quinoa & edamame
salad with lime
ginger dressing

roasted butternut
squash & cabbage
salad with pearl barley

spinach falafel bowl

"sushi" bowls with
carrot ginger
dressing

watermelon
panzanella

zucchini noodle
salad with
baked feta

sandwiches & flatbreads

banh mi with
smoky tempeh

curried chickpea
sandwich

quick flatbreads

spiced mushroom
flatbreads

spinach & artichoke
flatbread pockets

roasted vegetable
sandwich with
basil hummus

spring soccas with
minty pea pesto &
watercress

whipped ricotta
toasts with figs &
toasted pecans

soups

creamy cauliflower
& carrot soup

gnocchi soup

moroccan chickpea
& lentil soup

mushroom &
wild rice soup

soba noodle soup
with mushrooms
& bok choy

sweet potato
chowder with
tempeh bacon

tomato & zucchini
soup with mint
almond pesto

watercress & pea
soup

less meat, more plants mains

easy turkey pot pie

thai salmon (or no-salmon) cakes

fish tacos with sriracha mayo

greek kebabs

roasted vegetable & meat platter with chimichurri sauce

hoisin stir-fried noodles with pork or jackfruit

fish (or no-fish) koftas with broccoli rice & tahini dressing

less-meat lasagna

less-meat (or no-meat) meatballs in red sauce

turkey (or no-turkey) meatloaf

linguine with pesto alla trapanese

loaded sloppy joe sweet potatoes

sausage traybake

one-pan spanish-style chicken

spiced herb chicken or tofu

stuffed butternut squash with sage & walnut pesto— two ways

turkey enchilada skillet

meat-free mains

butternut & leek casserole with herby dumplings

creamy stuffed shells in red sauce

eggplant & potato curry

pan-fried eggplant with green lentil & tomato stew

golden rice & cabbage

vegan mushroom alfredo pasta

one-pot orzo primavera

pan-fried gnocchi with eggplant puttanesca

red lentil dahl with crunchy kale & coconut

roasted cabbage with beluga lentils & salsa verde

roasted cauliflower with pearl couscous salad

root vegetable tagine

smoky sweet potato stew

sweet & sour tofu with cauliflower rice

grilled tofu satay skewers with rice noodle salad

teriyaki tempeh bowls

three-bean chili with jalapeño cornbread topping

sweet treats

apple & blackberry galette

apricot & mango energy balls

chocolate mousse with passion fruit curd

mango & raspberry mini pavlovas with banana sorbet

muesli cookies

poached pears with caramel sauce

puffed quinoa chocolate chip bars

strawberry labneh ice pops

dressings, sauces & other basics

creamy avocado sauce

creamy tahini dressing— three ways

five easy salad dressings

dukkah

easy tomato sauce

sweet chili dipping sauce

pickled red onions

"salted" caramel sauce with miso

five-minute date "caramel" spread

vegan mayonnaise— four ways

simple cashew cream

raspberry chia jam

"cream cheese"— three ways

homemade roasted nut, seed, or peanut butter

simple nut milk

general index

Printed in the United States
by Baker & Taylor Publisher Services